Playing for High Stakes

The Men, Money, and Power
of Corporate Wives

Also by Elaine Denholtz

PLAYS
Frozen
The Dungmen Are Coming
Hey Out There, Is There Anyone Out There?
Some Men Are Good at That
The Highchairs
Love Games

FILMS
Summerhill
Waiting . . . The Life Styles of the Elderly
The Dental Auxiliary
What's Inside
Is That What You Want for Yourself?
Another Mother (Eugene O'Neill adaptation for television)

BOOKS
Education, Where It's Been, Where It's At, Where It's Going
(contributor)
The Highchairs
How to Save Your Teeth and Your Money (co-author)
The Dental Facelift (co-author)
Having It Both Ways: A Report on Married Women with Lovers

PLAYING FOR HIGH STAKES

The Men, Money, and Power
of Corporate Wives

ELAINE DENHOLTZ

AN AUTHORS GUILD BACKINPRINT.COM EDITION

AN AUTHORS GUILD BACKINPRINT.COM EDITION

Published by iUniverse.com, Inc.

For information address:
iUniverse.com, Inc.
620 North 48th Street, Suite 201
Lincoln, NE 68504-3467
www.iuniverse.com

Originally published by Freundlich Books

ISBN: 0-595-09236-5

Printed in the United States of America

For Mel and Peeps
Constant, loving boosters

Over a period of three years, I interviewed hundreds of people for this book and I promised them anonymity. To honor this commitment, I have deliberately disguised their true identities. To protect their privacy, I have not used their real names or the real identities of their corporations, and I have changed other specific points of identification. However, their stories and the events of their lives are real, and the words they spoke are the ones I honestly recorded.

ELAINE DENHOLTZ

Preface

Within a few years, I lost three of my closest, oldest friends. We didn't quarrel. They didn't die. They simply pulled up stakes and moved, leaving me to ponder the wretched holes they left in my life.

Why?

We were friends for over twenty years. Kindred souls who had tasted each other's pain and savored each other's triumphs.

Joan and I spoke almost daily. The nitty-gritty of our days embroidered together like threads via anecdotes about our husbands, our kids, and our work.

Carla and I went to college together and each wound up teaching at universities. We read the same books, saw the same movies and argued over the same dumb issues.

Allison lived across the street. My children played with hers. Our husbands exchanged tools and played tennis on sunny Sunday mornings. She believed strongly in being a full-time mother and she filled her days with art courses, volunteer work, and gardening.

What would it be like for them to tear up roots and start all over again in California and Washington and Florida? It had to be traumatic for all of us.

"It'll never be the same," I wailed for weeks to anyone who would listen.

"C'mon. You'll make new friends," was the common, comforting reply.

But *I* knew, and *they* knew, that you don't replace old friends like pieces of worn out furniture. We had shared a history and now they were gone.

I stumbled around for months feeling their loss.

Why? Why did they do it?

Why did they agree to move when their husband's corporation demanded it?

Would *I* have relocated for a corporation?

How would they weather the change?

These questions gave rise to other questions. What is it really like for the corporate wife? We know a great deal about the Fortune 500 companies, their CEO's, their mergers and tender offers. We have only to read *The Wall Street Journal* or study *Barron's* to keep track of their inner workings. But what about the wives? *Did anyone ever ask corporate wives what it was like for them?*

Of course over the years, I'd heard the grumblings when a husband was traveling or away for a birthday party. But basically, my friends had made peace with their lots. They had learned early in the marriage to give in for the sake of their husband's corporate image. To be fair, the trappings helped to smooth irritations. Big cars, European vacations, jewelry, the best summer camps, lovely homes—these were not bad tradeoffs for the inconveniences.

Still, when asked to tear up roots, they reacted with anger, grief, fear, and not a little bit of self-pity.

Carla resisted her husband's relocation almost to the end. She had put in twelve years teaching and only recently had been appointed chairperson of the Political Science Department of a major university. She would have to give up tenure, prestige, and a network of academicians who supported her work.

"No! I won't go!" she told her husband.

So they constructed a commuter marriage for about six months. While he set up the company's new international division in California, Carla continued her life on the East Coast. Until the marriage started to rock. In the end, Carla moved. She took a part-time teaching position in a second rate college as an adjunct-lecturer. For a long time, she felt resentful. But in the end, her position as a corporate wife won out.

"It's either my marriage or my job," she told me.

Joan wimpered and welped like a hurt puppy when her husband announced the move to Washington. But we all knew she would go. She had a stoical nature. Perhaps because she had no work to leave, it was easier. Perhaps, she was more flexible.

"Maybe we'll be back in a few years."

She kissed me goodbye and we clung together, my jaw clenched, her teeth biting her lips.

Allison, a psychiatric nurse, like Joan, gave it a good fight. Her nursing career could be transferred to Florida, she explained to everyone. However, leaving her elderly parents hurt most. Still, when the time came, she packed up the kids, the grand piano, the dogs, and the skis.

"What the devil am I going to do with skis in Florida?"

In each case, all three friends "relocated" for the sake of their husband's position. In each case, they behaved like obedient corporate wives. In each case, their first priority was to be good corporate wives to their husbands. It struck me that women married to high powered executives rarely take the path of mutiny.

Was I right?

For months, I thought about the subject. What is it like for corporate wives? Do they ever resist the corporate pressures? Do their husbands blame them if they do? What are the joys of being married to a corporate chief? Do the marriages falter or thrive after the sacrifice to "relocate" is made?

And that's how this book began.

Like most authors, I became obsessed with the subject. The questions tumbled around in my brain for almost a year. I began reading intensively about corporations and the family life they support. Apparently a lot of things were changing. How could I find out? Would the wives of high powered executives talk to me about life at the top? Would they report that it was heaven or hell?

The subject had not been explored, and this intrigued me.

For the next three years, I interviewed women across the country: corporate wives just starting out; those in the middle of the ladder; and wives of high powered CEO's.

What they had to say is the spine of this book. I am deeply grateful to every corporate wife who talked with me. I promised them anonymity, so I cannot name them. But I hope they will feel I told their story justly. Every single one of them—like my own three friends—knew they were PLAYING FOR HIGH STAKES.

ELAINE DENHOLTZ

Contents

xiii

The Players

(in order of appearance)

STAGE ONE
Jane
Patty
Mary

STAGE TWO
Anne
Bonnie Sue
Risa
Kim
Tracy
Carol

STAGE THREE
Darlene
Georgia
Dolly

xvi   *The Players*

Arlene
Susan
Lorraine
Margaret
Buffy
Joan
Melinda
Ariel

THE WORLD IS TOO MUCH
WITH US; LATE AND SOON

The world is too much with us; late and soon,
Getting and spending, we lay waste our powers;
Little we see in Nature that is ours;
We have given our hearts away, a sordid boon!
The sea that bares her bosom to the moon;
The winds that will be howling at all hours,
And are upgather'd now like sleeping flowers;
For this, for everything, we are out of tune;
It moves us not.—Great God! I'd rather be
A Pagan suckled in a creed outworn;
So might I, standing on this pleasant lea,
Have glimpses that would make me less forlorn;
Have sight of Proteus rising from the sea;
Or hear old Triton blow his wreathèd horn.

WILLIAM WORDSWORTH
1806

1

The Stages of Corporate Life: The Fish. The Reptile. The Bird.

I have known corporate wives all my life. Wives of men in finance, real estate, banking. I have watched many of them grow from insecure young women, eager to please their husbands and his corporation, into attorneys, boutique owners, professors.

Some made the change with seemingly little effort. Some tried and failed. Some changed only mildly along the way. And a few changed not at all.

Some marriages were shot wide open. Some wives were divorced and dumped. Some divorced their husbands. Other couples became tighter and more loving along the way.

Almost every one of these corporate wives, plus more than two hundred women I interviewed for three years, started out with husbands at the bottom rung of the ladder. Their dreams were his. They began as devoted helpmates whose satisfactions were clearly defined and they felt their goals would be achieved through wifedom—that delicious state that promised to confer a queenly bounty of riches. If only their husbands could move up in corporate life. They were women for whom affiliation to husband and corporation, rather than personal achievement, was the way to the top. These women were playing for high stakes. And they were convinced they were going to love the ride.

I call this *Stage One*.

Some of them did! Twenty years later, I watched them beam. Their husbands are executives, vice presidents, chief executive officers. Their closets bulge with designer fashions. In their driveways, Jags and Mercedes sparkle in the sunshine. They feel content. Their dreams never faded. The payoff they worked so hard for came through.

But others, *a substantially larger proportion*, began to examine the dream. At some point, they found it wanting. They needed more. Often, they could not define their growing dissatisfaction. Everything seemed so nearly perfect on the outside. More money, Caribbean vacations, private schools for the kids. What more could they want?

On one hand, they felt ungrateful. They didn't know, they weren't sure what was missing. On the other hand, they began to question the dream. They felt itchy about their husband's assumption of authority. Gingerly, they tried out their own powers, tried to transfer a small piece of his power to their turf. But they continued to walk around him cautiously, unwilling to be disruptive. However, they knew absolutely that there was more to life than what they were getting.

A few made tentative requests, asked permission to find a little job, perhaps. And they were enormously grateful if he agreed.

I call this *Stage Two*.

I know these women because I was one of them. Although my husband did not work for a corporation, I carried his suits to the cleaners, entertained his professional colleagues, and took major responsibility for household tasks to relieve him of those "petty details."

Then one day as sure as Sleeping Beauty awoke, I asked him if I could take a course at a local college. I had been thinking about finishing my graduate degree. I asked for his permission.

My husband is a kind man. He must have sensed the intensity of my request. He loved me. But he also knew that with two small boys and a new infant daughter, his agreement would impose certain changes in our family life. Perhaps he might be opening the door to trouble, since I would no longer be endlessly available. He hesitated, then he said yes.

However, he set three clear restrictions. The course had to be given in the evening after the kids were tucked in. It had to be only one course to see if I could handle the assignments without taking time away from the kids. And I had to approach this as an experiment in case it didn't work out.

"Thank you, thank you!" I was ecstatic. I flung my arms around him like a little girl whose daddy had granted her permission to stay up past midnight.

This script I played out over two decades ago frequently takes place in Stage Two, although the dialogue has been largely rewritten by a society whose views on women have changed. Nevertheless, corporate wives whose loyalty to their husbands is paramount still play out this permission-request today. As their itch turns to irritation and they seek to understand their own needs, their roles as corporate wives grow hollow and empty. They begin to ask for more.

In Stage Two, the corporate wife is still not sure of herself. She knows she's discontent. But she can't define her needs. She is scared. She does not feel worthy enough to ask for much. But she's trying to find her place in a situation that gives her less pleasure and more financial rewards every day. What's the matter with her, she wonders? As she evaluates his instructions, his decisions, and the sacrifices she makes for his corporation, she raises disquieting questions about herself.

Most corporate wives start out in Stage One. But a few are closer to the line of Stage Two. Or Stage Two hits them early in the game. Or they juggle Stage One and Stage Two simultaneously, moving forward two steps, then back one. Unsure, hesitant, reaching for something better, they play tag with their personal aspirations. And some, exhausted as dogs chasing their tails, quietly slip back to Stage One, that well-rehearsed position they know so well.

It is not until Stage Three that many wives find their own voice. At this stage they ask for what they want. At this stage they become clearer about their goals. At this stage they take action to achieve them. They do not ask permission, they tell.

"I'm going to take a part-time job three afternoons a week," Charlotte, a former physical education teacher I interviewed, told her husband when her last child went off to kindergarten. She did not, like me, ask permission, although she did ask her husband how he felt about it. "I had already hired the baby-sitter and accepted the job at the gym. I figured if I presented it as a *fait accompli* I'd get less flack," she confided to me.

As I interviewed her, she described her start in the business world with a grin of satisfaction. "It was an uphill battle all the way. One night I couldn't make it to his company dinner and my husband was furious. Treason! He didn't speak to me for a week."

Today Charlotte owns a string of health clubs for women and credits her success to taking forceful charge of her life.

Risking and making demands is part of Stage Three. It can cost a wife her marriage.

This did not happen in Charlotte's case. Her negotiating skills were superb, and her husband became less rigid. "But it took me a few years to bring him along. He wasn't exactly cooperative and I fought with him every inch of the way up. But a funny thing happened. As I gained power, I noticed he began to admire me and respect what I was doing. Everything improved. Especially our sex life! I guess I was lucky," she summed up with a playful toss of her head.

Is it luck that gets a corporate wife successfully through Stage Three? What about the failures? The families torn apart, the couples who split? The wives who never effect any changes, whose efforts dry up on the vine?

Stage Three is clearly the most dramatic stage of all.

It is all conflict and resolution. Mystery and denouement. It is Act Three of a wonderful, satisfying play.

In Stage Three all the pieces collide. Passions erupt. The drama explodes!

If Stage Three works, it is all applause and curtain calls. If it fails, it is tragedy. In between, a number of endings are possible.

"Here's what I want," she may say. And he may answer, "No!"

"Here's how I can get it," she may propose. And he may refuse. "You can't! I won't let you! I won't stand for it!"

So in Stage Three we see the clash of wills. If Stage One is all satisfaction, and Stage Two is rising discontent, Stage Three is eruption.

Stage Three is all ifs.

If she has brought him along slowly, unthreateningly, *if* his ego is not bruised, *if* he cares enough to relinquish power to her, *if* she is loving and steadfast in stating her requirements, *if* he has seen it coming all along and is willing to help her achieve her goals, they are on their way to a happy ending.

But *if* he refuses to let her grow, *if* he stands in her way, *if* he sets up booby traps, *if* the corporation is his first priority, *if* there are deep wounds between them, *if* he is burnt out, *if* she is too tentative, *if* she is too ambivalent, then the marriage can rock so hard and shudder so fiercely a death rattle can be heard. That marriage will likely end.

Is this a tragedy?

Many women I talked with said no, protested they would never have survived another year as a corporate wife. "The marriage *deserved* to die," one wife insisted. "I couldn't have grown up, couldn't live that way. I felt stifled, I was choking on corporate life."

A thirty-eight-year-old mother of three told me, "I had to do work that meant something to me. I went back to teaching. In four years, I moved up to principal. And I began to feel my work was as important as his. He laughed at me. He made four times my salary, so I guess it proved I was only worth a fourth of him. Well, the cost of staying in the marriage became too high. I divorced him."

To breathe freely, some wives in Stage Three must risk the end of the marriage. "I didn't become a person until I got divorced," a set designer told me.

A number of women I talked with, once married to corporate executives, were careful to explain that the demise of their marriage was not entirely due to the demands of the corporation.

"I plunged ahead. I outgrew him," an advertising executive said. "He was a powerful guy at The Corporation. But I zoomed right by him—intellectually, emotionally, and professionally. Know something? Those top guys, even CEO's, aren't all that bright," she said.

"They roar a lot, but they haven't got too much up here," and she tapped her temples.

Many women in Stage Three do *not* divorce their husbands. When the crunch comes, they retreat. Having failed to achieve their goals quickly and expediently, they slip back to Stage Two and allow the corporation and their husband to continue to call the tune. It is worth the marriage, they conclude. So they buckle under. They complain, they grumble. But rarely do they dare to make demands again.

A few of these corporate wives discover unhappily that their brief sojourn into the land of Stage Three has caused irreparable harm. Once they articulate their demands, their husbands turn mean and angry. Buried hostilities erupt.

"How dare you complain after all I've given you! I work my butt off for this family. What the hell more do you want?"

These women become so shaken, they cannot recover their footing. So they wind up muttering, bitching behind his back, or silently undermining their husband in a long and undeclared war.

An unsuccessful sally into Stage Three may return the couple to the status quo of Stage Two. Or it may not. Perhaps the husband has now found his excuse to divorce her. He finds another woman, more compliant and obedient, a clone of his first wife, only twenty years younger, the adoring bride she used to be. The first wife took the risk and lost the marriage.

I have talked with women who lost and some are bitter. They are full of regrets. They blame him. They blame the corporation. They blame themselves. They weep unabashedly. They are convinced they have lost everything—husband, status, financial security. A way of life that was pleasant, even agreeable in many ways. They remember the good times with nostalgic reverence. Dear God, look where I am now. They join the army of divorcees on the prowl for another husband. They feel they can't make it without a man. Without a man, they are nothing. Having perceived themselves as an auxiliary, second-rate person all their lives, their divorce only underscores their poor self-esteem.

"If only I hadn't said this. If only I hadn't done that."

In this play, Stage Three has a tragic ending.

Many of the women I interviewed, divorced and married, described their corporate husbands as uncooperative, hard men. Men who balked about performing the smallest task they labeled women's work. Men who refused to relinquish the tiniest grain of power to their wives. These men were brilliant negotiators in the corporate world. They could stand toe to toe with a man and arrive at mutually agreeable concessions. But no woman could change the rules or make them come to terms, least of all their wives.

Such a husband *will not, cannot* change his priorities. It is the corporation first, and he is used to giving orders. At home it must be his way, or not at all. What can she do? She retreats. Or faces the humiliation of divorce.

However, there are supportive husbands out there, too. Many of them younger men who are flexible, caring, and willing to give their wives a boost. Men who want a real partner, a full adult person who brings her own excitement to his life.

These men, often under forty, see corporations in real terms. They know precisely what they are up against. They are pragmatists, realists, and they do not deny the demands of corporate life: the pains of relocation; the loneliness of weeks away from home; the temptations of out-of-town sex; the strain of long hours and impossible assignments; the frustration of tiresome meetings that force them to miss family birthdays and graduations.

These corporate men have measured exactly what they can live with. And they are distinguished by their overriding concern for their family. It's *family first* for them. *Then* the corporation.

Sometimes the family must make sacrifices, perform unpleasant tasks for the sake of his job. But there is a line this corporate husband will not cross. His wife is half of an honorable partnership. And although the feathers fly on occasion, it's not a battle of "who wins."

Is it the luck of the draw? You pull a "good" corporate husband or a "bad" one? Is that what it comes down to? I think not.

In talking with women in their twenties, thirties, forties, fifties, and sixties, I heard one resounding theme throughout: *"Good" corporate husbands are not born. They are molded and changed by their wives.* A few of these women exhibited a strong sense of themselves. But a larger number changed and grew along the way, negotiating safely through the perilous white waters of Stage Three, with fortitude and good will as their oars.

The women I interviewed throughout this country were young and old, widowed, single, married, divorced. Women with small children, with no children, with grown children, with grandchildren. Some held jobs, some did not. Every one of their stories is a human document of risk and pain, of tragedy and celebration. Stage One. Stage Two. Stage Three.

I have tried to establish their world, to go beyond the trappings. For we know absolutely that things are never what they appear to be.

This book came together when I saw the work of the Dutch artist, M. C. Escher. His prints of contiguous birds, reptiles, and fish begin as one figure in the upper left-hand corner and change slowly to develop into another figure. A fish to a bird or a reptile. Each figure starts out as one species. But it ends up another.

I exalted when I saw those prints!

I was well past my hundredth interview when the metaphor came alive for me. Like Escher's figures, the women I talked with began as one species and, defying a logical order of cause and effect, they emerged another species.

Escher's designs and motifs fascinated me. His juxtaposition of light and shadow seemed to me symbols for the joy and pain that change the order and balance in women's lives, producing an infinite number of outcomes. Like an Escher print, each interview was a print of the small changes that linked the woman to what she was and what she might become.

Some of Escher's figures are not animal or human. They are black and white triangles, geometrically and mathematically precise, that become transformed into living creatures. The concept awed me! From inanimate to alive. Some women claimed they weren't alive while they were immersed in being corporate wives.

Another observation. I interviewed each woman at a moment frozen in time, at a click in her life, like a square torn out of an

Escher print. Some young women, in their twenties and thirties, were starting out and looking forward to adventure on the good ship Corporate Life. Some were in their forties and fifties, at mid-life, struggling to emerge whole. And some were near the end of the trip, looking back and assessing the process.

Who was the fish? The reptile? The bird?

Who would fly?

Come meet them.

2

Stage One: Jane

See Jane.
See Jane smile.
Smile, Jane, smile.
Smile *wider*, Jane.

See Patty.
See Patty sip her Dom Perignon.
Sip, Patty, sip.
Sip *faster*, Patty.

See Mary.
See Mary scan her party.
Scan, Mary, scan.
Scan *harder*, Mary.

Three beautiful women. Jane. Patty. Mary.
All in Stage One.

Jane is thirty-one. A new corporate wife. This is her first company party. She's scared. Her palms are sweaty. Is she dressed correctly? Four hundred dollars for this emerald silk Halston from Saks. They could feed the whole family for a month on that. But tonight is special. This invitation makes it clear that Bob is on the fast track. She must make him proud of her. She looks for the little clues that tell who is a social equal and who is not. She wants to learn. To fit in.

Where has Bob gone?

She peers past the butlers holding gleaming silver trays of hors d'oeuvres, around the knots of tuxedo-slick graying executives with their wives magnificently turned out and bejeweled. She sniffs decorously the aromas of French perfumes. And her heart flutters.

Where is he? Being left alone makes her anxious. Is she perspiring? Will it leave stains under her armpits? Across the room, she catches her husband's eye and smiles. He winks back, and she feels enormous relief spread over her. She's doing okay. She turns to Patty whom she's just met. And she smiles wider.

Patty is forty-eight. A slick and polished corporate wife for eighteen years. She knows how the game of social climbing is played. How to rub shoulders with the right people. She is wearing the diamond bracelet Ted bought her for their twenty-fifth wedding anniversary. It makes her feel secure as it slides sensuously on her slim wrist.

Patty is thinner and blonder and richer every year.

She leans into her third cocktail before dinner. She can handle it. And of course she knows corporate wives never get drunk in public. She sips faster, emptying her glass. And she turns to Mary, her hostess, complimenting her on the gorgeous calla lilies arranged on the tables.

Mary is sixty-five, with a halo of white hair framing her handsome face. She has worked hard alongside her husband for thirty-six years, viewing him and herself as a team. Her husband will be retired as chairman of the board next month. Thus this party. Her last hurrah.

She scans the living room, dining room, library, and patio swarming with the two hundred guests she's invited, and she feels a glow of satisfaction. Yes, Jim's dreams for them have really come true. This eighteen-room, Country French home in Far Hills, New Jersey, on twenty-two acres of wild rhododendron and mountain laurel. Jim's exquisitely tended flower beds groomed by his gardener-chauffeur. The trips to Singapore, Bali, China, the Philippines, Japan, and every major European capital. The fascinating people she's met.

Scanning, she catches sight of the photos on the grand piano. Their four children all grown up, their grandchildren healthy and lively as colts. Yes, she thinks, corporate life was a blessing.

She recalls the pinched face of her dear mother, may she rest in peace. If only she could see me now. Her little Mary with the pug nose and freckles and the map of Ireland across her face. I did fine, Mother. See?

She scans her party harder, concentrating on every detail.

From her living room window, Jane watched Bob pull out of their driveway to take the sitter home. And she knew absolutely they would make love tonight. He was flying high with the success of the evening, and success always proved to be a surefire aphrodisiac.

"You were perfect," he had told her in the car coming home, and his right hand stroked her thigh, signaling his mood.

"I was?" She had looked up at him coquettishly, hungry for more of his compliments, a hoarder of her husband's reassurances.

Now she hung the Halston back into the garment bag and slipped on her black lace nightgown, the $69 one from Victoria's Secret. The secret, Rose Anne had brazenly declared over their Chinese lunch last week, was that it guaranteed you'd get laid. Fine. She was in the mood.

She tiptoed into the kids' rooms to smooth Robbie's blanket and to reach over the crib railing to touch the baby's soft warm cheek.

Ah, life was good! She felt so cared for. The message her mother had given her, that the highest achievement in life was to marry well, to attach herself to an ambitious, dominant man who would take care of her, was good advice. Bob made her world delicious.

The corporate people were so nice to her tonight. It was perfectly clear. *I have a husband on the way up.*

She lay back on the pillow. Scarlett O'Hara waiting to be taken.

After they made love, they talked. Ordinarily, Bob didn't confide easily, but lovemaking relaxed him. It used to annoy her a bit that he snapped on the light and immediately reached for a Marlboro. She disliked smoke in the bedroom, but it seemed petty to complain. At least he didn't roll over and go to sleep like Rose Anne's husband Warren. And she and Bob could talk about anything. After lovemaking, the big tycoon became a little boy. Silly little things. Goofy, actually. Like whether to get his hair permed. He was so damn worried about it.

"You think they'll object? Think I'll look okay? Will you come with me?"

"It's a perm, honey, not an execution," she giggled.

Funny how insecure he was about the little things. A man who made tough decisions every day, who spent thousands of corporate dollars. A man The Company called up in the middle of the night, on weekends, to reroute the charters, to reschedule tour agents, to reshuffle emergency vehicles. All stressful situations you couldn't afford to mess up. Like a doctor, Bob lived with a beeper and handled it all smoothly.

But whether to perm his hair made him anxious. Was he afraid it was the wrong corporate image? Or was he pushing to get it done before their party?

The party. For months everything revolved around the housewarming party. The new sectionals were in place in the living room. The vertical blinds installed. The graphics flew across the dining room walls. Everything new and shiny. Spelling success.

The only items not new were the guests, his high school and college buddies. The old crowd. For weeks he was as fussy as an old lady. This party would show off his new home. His furniture. His wife. His kids. At thirty-four, he'd made it into a top corporation. He held a position of power. Was pulling close to $60,000. They had more money than they ever dreamed of. This party would say it all. However, it would also be the kiss of death to the old crowd.

Because after the party, they wouldn't be seeing much of them anymore.

"We've outgrown them, Babe. We have nothing in common anymore. They can't keep up with us."

She agreed. "And they're jealous. So damn jealous."

She cuddled closer and told Bob about her Chinese lunch with Rose Anne. How it had left her irritated and annoyed.

When Jane pulled her white Volkswagen convertible into her driveway, she let the breeze lift her pageboy coiffure. Lunch with an old friend was supposed to be fun. But Rose Anne had talked too loud over their Moo Shu Pork and her girl talk was boring, although she pretended to listen. Rose Anne was from the old crowd, the ones they were dropping. Bob was right, they were a drag. She flicked her bangs out of her eyes and lingered at the wheel, feeling sorry for Rose Anne.

They were the same age, thirty-one. So Rose Anne should have known better. Marrying, at twenty-eight, a divorced man with two teenage children to raise. A going-nowhere guy who'd never make it up the corporate ladder. And now she was bitching. Quiet little Rose Anne, with her saccharine Southern drawl, had lost her mellifluous purr and replaced it with a yapping whine. Whine, whine, whine. What fun was that?

Their new friends were fun. They knew how to spend money. How to dress. How to eat. How to travel. All Rose Anne did was bitch about money. How she hands over her paycheck to support *his* kids in *his* house. Well, the daughter of a corporate executive should have known better. But she was just like her mother, a deep-down spoiled Southern belle with unrealistic Presbyterian ways.

Jane hopped out of her car and gave the clean white hood a tender tap. Really, what did she need a new car for, even though Bob was itching to replace it with a new sports model.

She remembered Rose Anne describing Warren before the wedding.

"He's gorgeous! Six-foot-three, 250 pounds. I feel so small and protected next to him."

And now for two hours all she could talk about was how hard her life was while she peered jealously at Jane's diamond ear studs.

"His first wife was a strong-willed career woman," Rose Anne had whined. "Devoted more time to her real estate business than Warren and the kids. So I figured I'm going to be Miss Susie Homemaker. I was brought up to think that's the wife's role. Keep the house spotless. Have dinner on the table when he walks in, a drink in your hand mixed the way he likes it. I'm from the old school," she had told Jane.

In the beginning, Rose Anne saw Warren's corporation as a symbol of security and status. She remembered the advantages of being the daughter of a district manager at The Corporation, how nice Daddy was treated. Warren's corporation would look out for her. Besides, Warren looked like a winner. Big, tall, confident, he was intimidating. Corporations chose big bruisers because their appearance gave a sense of power. And like her daddy, Warren dressed well, he was meticulous.

"I had to relearn how to iron, Jane. He likes the tips of his collars just so." Over fortune cookies she continued bitching about picking up after him.

"He just drops his clothes on the floor and expects me . . . Ugh, men! At the office, Warren has people running around him to do the dirty work. He carries that attitude home."

Jane tried to change the subject. "How's your art class?"

Rose Anne had smiled wanly. "I had to drop it. I'm sewing drapes for the girls' bedrooms."

Jane tried again. "How was the party at Phil's?"

"We didn't go. Warren was tired and he grumped and griped about having to shave again. So we stayed home. Know what I did? I worked on my hands and knees scraping paint off the stair railing. My mother would die if she saw me."

Jane searched for something upbeat to say. A surge of pity went through her. Poor Rose Anne. Spoiled Southern Belle marries man with high hopes for his success. Now she's a damn slave to him. Cuts the strings off his new clothes. Irons his shirts, raises his first wife's kids, scrapes paint off his stair railings.

Embarrassed to sit there a captive to her friend's outpourings, Jane stared into her hands. When she looked up, Rose Anne was sniffling. Right there in a public restaurant, with everyone staring at them, proper Alabama-bred Rose Anne was breaking down over the almond cookies.

Jane patted her hand. But Rose Anne pulled it back to hide her chipped nail polish. Jane's hands were soft and manicured in that new shade called "Country Russet." Her diamond ring sent a galaxy of sparkling lights across the Chinese wallpaper.

"The thing is, Jane, where is Warren going? I'm investing in *his* career. My secretary's pay goes to *his* house and *his* kids. I wish I could quit and stay home like my mother. Like you. Have a baby, maybe." Her hands made a fist. "I just don't know."

The whole lunch was depressing. But it made Jane feel—in a strange way—absolutely elated about herself and Bob. Their life-style was solid, satisfying, secure. They had such fun! God she was lucky! She and Rose Anne, both corporate wives. But one was stuck with a loser in the $35,000 range. While she! She had married the Golden Boy!

Bob was ambitious. Competitive. High-powered. She admired those traits: his drive, his push to get ahead. He put in an 80-hour week for his family. He even wanted to buy her a new car.

"How does it look for my wife to pull into Maison Petit's lot in an old VW and park next to those snappy sports cars? What color you want, Babe?"

Jane hugged herself. Bob was so good to her. The house they bought four years ago for $90,000 had gone up to $190,000, and now they had this California ranch in a fancy neighborhood. The kids' closets could stock two aisles of Toys-R-Us. And she was investing in expensive jewelry, learning about the good life.

So it annoyed her to waste an afternoon in a tacky Chinese restaurant with Rose Anne. She understood Bob's intolerance of people who didn't measure up. He was demanding, impatient, short-tempered because he was a perfectionist and he couldn't stand stupidity. That's why he's a success, she concluded. That's why we have a lot of material things. She snuggled against Bob as he squashed out his cigarette and turned the light off.

Mother was right. All a girl had to do was pick a winner. The rest was duck's soup.

Someday, she'd give a party like Mary.

Someday she'd be the wife of the chairman of the board.

You know Jane. You've met her often. Young, likable, attractive, she's Miss Congeniality with an easy laugh.

On the go every moment of the day, Jane is raising small children and tending to her home. Busy, busy, busy. Above all, her primary concern is her husband's comfort. He is her first priority. He is the wage earner, the boss, the head of the household. Jane has no problem with that. The Women's Movement has brushed by her like a butterfly, but she won't allow it to alight on her. With a successful husband to provide for her needs, she sees no benefits to her of all that equality talk.

Jane is content to have a man look after her. She clings to home and hearth, which spell safety to her. Her husband's success will become her success. She has no aspirations of her own.

Jane looks upon the corporation as a powerful, wealthy uncle. If she and Bob behave well, the corporation will provide them with marvelous benefits. So she is willing—no, eager!—to do whatever is called for. At this stage, pushing her husband ahead appears to be her primary job. She has no complaints, and the few minor irritations seem petty. Hasn't the company been good to them? Don't they live better every year? More money. More purchases. More status. Her dreams are for her husband's success and she is convinced that a devoted wife can do wonders in that direction.

Mary's party has confirmed that their future is rosy. Bob can achieve wealth and prestige through the corporation. Achievement, of course, means Bob's achievement. To be his wife is all she wants.

When she compares herself to Rose Anne, she feels impatient with her and the old crowd. They don't have enough drive, they aren't geared for success. If she seems insensitive to Rose Anne's plight, it is because she feels that could never happen to her. She feels invulnerable. She perceives few dangers ahead. She is convinced that corporations reward the smart boys. And luckily, she has married one smart guy who has what it takes.

So Jane is aglow and fearless. She is in love with her husband. Sex is good. Money is rolling in. This new power and status are giving her confidence. Her life is all promise: a succession of sweet dreams. At this stage, she equates material success with happiness. The more they own, the happier they will be. She measures the world from her sliding glass doors. Yup, that is how it works: worldly goods confer pleasures. Jane is transparently, unreservedly happy.

It would be easy to comment that Jane's assignment to Stage One is based on her youth. But youth alone does not establish a woman in that stage. At thirty-one, Jane is unmarred and uncomplaining. But Patty at forty-eight and Mary at sixty-five, both veteran corporate wives, are also in Stage One. They continue to be pleased with corporate life. They are commited to corporate policy, grateful to the corporation. Patty and Mary may be separated from Jane by many years and different life experiences. However, they are, like Jane, in Stage One: contentment.

Perhaps they are even a bit smug.

Follow them home after the party.

3

Patty and Mary

Patty placed her diamond bracelet back into its velvet box and yawned. She removed her makeup and slid on her nightgown. At forty-eight, she felt content. The mirror confirmed that she was still that pretty, pale blonde who looks cool as iced tea when everyone else is sweltering at ninety-five in the shade.

She hadn't started out that way.

Twenty-five years ago when she married Ted she was a chunky brunette with flabby thighs and thick, dark eyebrows. To this day she feels grateful to Ted for picking *her*. Without him she would still be ringing up paint in her father's hardware store in Ohio.

Patty had enjoyed Mary's party. She enjoyed most parties that, she felt, showed her off to advantage. Smooth and confident now, it amused her to remember the frightened, mousy introvert she used to be.

It was Ted who forced her to be sociable and improve herself. Now when she attended functions and mixed with the other important corporate wives, she felt at ease and in control.

When Ted first introduced her to actors and television stars, the broadcast people and production moguls he worked with, she was terrified. What could she say to Rodney Dangerfield, to Tony and Emmy winners? But Ted taught her how to speak, to chat lightly, amiably, without really revealing herself. That was the secret to Ted's success. He appeared low keyed and mild mannered, but they both knew that it was an M.O., a carefully planned strategy to make things happen for himself.

She watched him get into his pajamas, his tanned body, at fifty-two, still hard and slim. Nothing sloppy about Ted. His emotions never spilled over, he kept himself in check. He was guarded. He knew the trick of speaking without informing. She had learned it all from the master. Learned how to use power in that quiet, unpushy way of his that got results.

Power. That was his greatest gift to her. Patty loved the power of being his wife.

However, she rarely made a decision without checking with him first.

"Do you mind if I skip the hospital budget meeting?" she asked, sliding off her satin mules.

"Mind?" He climbed into his twin bed and turned his back as he spoke. "Whatever you want, dear. Good night."

Dear. He called her dear in public and dear in private. Never her name. Never Patty or Pat, just dear.

A good man. Decent and generous. Their restored carriage house cost $350,000. Last year they finished the decorating with the antique armoire she bid $8,500 for at Parke Bernet auctions. Any material things she requested were hers. If she asked prettily, politely, he'd agree. "Of course, dear, whatever you need." And she'd hand him the bill. He was equally giving to their two sons: the best tennis pros, the best clothes, the best summer camps.

Where did it all come from? The Corporation. Patty was glad she had put Ted's goals first and spent twenty-five years helping him get there.

His power filtered down to her.

How many women could call the publisher of *The Wall Street Journal* and ask a favor? How many wives could wheedle a five-figure donation out of Quaker Oats? Get through to anyone on the phone? If she needed a helicopter, it was hers. If she needed a ballroom, it was hers. Since Ted became chairman of the board of trustees of the medical center where she did her volunteer work, she gained even more power. Got Myra's father-in-law into an old-age home. Got a bed for a cancer patient. Raised $25,000 for the volunteer corps. Ted's connections made everything possible. Reflected glory was delicious.

"Can I phone William Morris this week? We need a comedienne for the dinner dance."

"Sure," he agreed.

She knew she could push buttons and most people were thrilled to oblige. Last month she had sixty-five stylish women volunteer to stick stamps on letters for the privilege of a cold tray lunch in her home. She was sought after. The president of one of the world's largest insurance companies was a personal acquaintance. They had met rock stars.

She was in the mood to talk, but Ted's back said no, though his breathing told her he was not asleep.

"Worried about buying the new stations?" her voice was a gentle nudge.

He turned on his back and folded his hands behind his head. "No. But I have to be tough and protect myself," he answered cautiously. There were few he trusted, but he was expert at playing the game.

"Anything you want me to do?" It was an offer. Did he want to make love?

"No thanks." He rolled over.

Actually Patty didn't mind. Twenty-five years had adjusted her to Ted's low sex drive. She once figured it out mathematically. Sex took fifteen minutes. At once or twice a month—about twenty times a year—that added up to five hours of her time. Sex was overrated. And like Ted, she distrusted passion.

She used to be jealous of the movie stars he met, the bright attractive women who were willing to sleep their way up. She used to worry about the drinking and cozying up at parties. But the corporation had a rule about out-of-town conventions. No intra-office funny business. Hard work. Eighteen-hour days. And you didn't make a fool of yourself.

Ted's too smart to mess around, too careful. Besides, if it's going to happen, it's going to happen. She'd rather not know.

She snapped on her tensor light to flip through the new *Vogue*. God, how lucky I am. I have a lot to be thankful for. No worries about money. They had health, travel, exposure to the best. And power.

Last week when she was introduced to three company presidents and forty new people, it was exhilarating. Her voice purred with delight, dripped with honey. She laughed and wagged a finger admonishingly, and mugged with the best of them, tilting her face at the smartest angle.

The Corporation made Patty's life sweet.

The morning after the party, Mary asked her maid to gather the vases of calla lilies for shipment to the home for crippled children. She did this after every party.

"Keep the best one for the dining room table," she said, giving the instruction with good-natured ease. A practical, no-nonsense person, Mary was alert to details. After thirty-six years as a devoted corporate wife, she had learned to be a perfect hostess, to give orders to people who worked for her—bartenders and maids—to choose menus, and to back up Jim in every possible way.

Fourteen company transfers in thirty-six years. The assignments in Bali, Singapore, Italy, Japan, Australia, and Pakistan had taught her to "make do." To be resourceful and smile. To be there when he needed her.

"You put your husband first," her mother had instructed her, "even before the children."

So she never considered the moves as sacrifices. Nor did she cast herself in the role of Christian martyr. Compromises and adjustments were in order if you wanted your husband to succeed.

In the forties when Mary married Jim, women were usually considered appendages to their husbands. Mary had no trouble with that role. What other options were there? Her small, sweet singing voice was passable for church choir and high school plays. But Radio City Music Hall was not breaking down her door to sign her up.

This morning there was still much to do to put things back in order. But she took a moment to sit down at the piano and let her fingers ease into an old favorite: her theme song over the years. In her head Mary Small was singing it on the radio so she sang along. How did the words go? Something like

> Pack up your troubles
> in your old kit bag
> and smile, smile, smile.

She paused and sighed with satisfaction. A fitting ending to thirty-six years with The Oil Company. No regrets.

She could look back now at the hard times and see that the line led directly to this point. Retirement. Security. Stability. We wouldn't have any of it without The Company, she thought. And I was Jim's partner the whole way.

"We're a team," he had explained forty-two years ago, a bright junior engineer fresh out of the Navy. "And you're my Girl Friday."

When they got their first transfer to the Philippines, he hugged her and babbled about the great opportunity. It was a shock once they got there. No one to talk to. Nothing to do but sit around in the heat and wait for the men to come home. Jim was a workaholic. Wasn't every successful man? Whatever it took to finish the job, he'd do it. Out there at six A.M. checking construction of the new plant, dealing with short orders and slowdowns until midnight.

Even a two-week holiday in Paris gave them little peace. "If you were in the Mohave desert, you'd still call your office," she had teased after he'd sent three cables and made five transcontinental calls.

But he laughed and said, "You're my girl, Marylove. I married a good sport."

Even when the corporation's plans caused disappointment for the kids, when Danny had to change high schools four times, when they missed Elliot's birthday and Winston's graduation, she felt it her duty to be with Jim. The kids groaned, but they seemed to understand, and each one got his own color TV or some extra special gift to ease the pain. Relocating fourteen times, never settling in was hard on them. But she didn't complain. It was her destiny, her duty as a wife.

After college Mary had no ambition to pursue a career. In those days it was career or marriage, and she chose Jim, a handsome guy with a twinkle in his eye and a tweaky Irish sense of humor.

On her wedding night, she felt she was the luckiest person in the world. An ordinary girl with no special gift or real interests: too tall and horsey. "I don't need fame, God. I don't want to compete. All I want is a good marriage, kids, my husband's success. Okay, God? Is that too much to ask?"

This morning Jim heard her singing. He sat down beside her on the piano bench and took her hands in his. "Remember the tough times? I dragged you to some god-awful places. You were lonesome a lot." It was true. They had developed no close friendships among the corporate people, or any others. They socialized, but as Jim moved up, they steered clear of personal relationships in the corporation.

"Well, we never stayed in one place long enough for friends."

"You should have kept up your singing, Mary." He squeezed her hand tenderly. "You'd of liked that. You had a sweet voice, you could have gone somewhere."

"Aw, c'mon, Jim. I have more than most women." She was not the type to demand a lot. She eschewed personal power. "A silly little job to fill up my time? What for? My job was you!" She beamed at the man, genuinely satisfied to be at the sweet end of the journey. Kids grown up and married. Seven darling grandchildren. A fat pension, bonuses, stock options, health benefits for life, consulting work if Jim wanted it. Enough money socked away to live well, with plenty left over to help the kids.

All compliments of The Company! They had earned the velvet-lined nest and the golden egg. Not like her poor sister Theresa, scratching by on her paltry Social Security check.

If Mary asked for nothing along the journey, it was because she was brought up to believe she had no right to ask. Decisions were made by the wage earner, the man who brought home the bacon. Her job was to cook it and make an attractive home wherever they were sent. She knew her place, her role. Every December she sent out their three hundred Christmas cards.

Luck was with her. Jim never let her down. Could she let *him* down? Under the stress of relocations, she kept a stiff upper lip. She kept the payoff in sight. Around the fourth move in nine years, she understood the objective. To stick it out. Secretly, she measured her husband. Like herself, he was quite ordinary. Not creative. Just a stick-to-it type who'd be steady and solid.

This morning, with the sun streaking across the Persian rug, it seemed a good time to go on a trip down Memory Lane. "Hey!" She poked his shoulder. "Remember our chow kidar? That crazy old watchman? And the Yacht Club? When you fell overboard in your tux."

Scenes from thirty-six years tumbled out.

"Remember Australia and the fire in the bush?" He laughed, then his face fell. "Remember the scandals when twenty-seven oil companies had to pay $633 million for overcharging?"

Mary nodded. Through all the federal charges of corporate crime, she had remained loyal to The Oil Company. At parties she defended her husband's company against detractors. "We're not fat oil barons," she explained politely to the vehement do-gooders. "We have fact sheets to prove it. Our Ethics Committee's policy is no bribes, no foreign payoffs. In Pakistan we refused outright. No two thousand rupees, not a cent!"

"Remember New Guinea? That was the worst."

"Oh, those hideous crabs underfoot. The sogginess, the snakes, the insects." They had been sent to a mining town carved out of a jungle, a muddy filthy camp that never heard of fresh milk or bread and butter. Two years. A record for corporate families. Gossip was the only diversion. The women began the bridge games at ten in the morning. By noon, someone sang out, "It's gin and tonic time." And the drinking began. Light bulbs in the closets to avoid mildew.

The ten-foot snake her houseboy chopped up with the rake. Ugh!

"But Naples was fun, Jim." She reminded him of the good times when the kids were with them in the American schools. How she became fluent in Italian.

Grouse about the uprooting? Not Mary. She viewed it as Jim's big chance. His opportunity for advancement. For her, a new culture to explore. Hong Kong. Latin America.

"Pakistan!" She poked him in the ribs. "You tried to learn to speak Urdu, remember? There were no books." In 1974, the hot, wet season was the worst. They were exhausted fighting dysentery. The camel-drawn carts. The political troubles. The harsh brutal lives of the Muslims to please their Allah. "I had seven in help," she reminded him. A bearer, who was their head man. A sweeper, a gardener, a driver, a laundryman, the chow kidar, and the cook.

Ninety-five families all belonged to the Sind Club, the Boat Club, and the Yacht Club, membership encouraged by The Company. The cocktail parties with long dresses and jewelry. "We were high society there. We hung together. The two of us against the world. Remember the smell of hashish in the streets? Watching them harvest the poppies?

"Then we came home to more stress. The environmental protection committees, the economic opportunity laws, every agency out to break the oil companies' backs."

Mary was stalwart through it all. The object was to stick to it, stay in the game. His briefcase came home every night. Funny, she mused. Even then he never thought of striking out on his own. Not the type. There was security with The Oil Company.

"Remember Alice? You liked her," Jim said.

"Australia. I learned to garden there. I wrote Alice two letters after we left and that was the end of it. No time for friendships."

He flung his arm around her shoulders. "Well, now it's time to enjoy ourselves." There were all the perks and sweeteners to gobble up in retirement. Their house in Florida on the water, their thirty-seven-foot, twin-engine boat, their two-and-a-half acres in Vermont. "We made it to the end, Mary. Let the Young Turks come on. We're free!"

Free.

Free of the cold sweats when the performance reviews came up. Free of the corporation's rating system where Jim's immediate superior goes over his weaknesses and places him on a chart plotting his career. Will Jim move up? Or out? Free of the stress to keep proving he's better than the guy pushing up behind him.

"Free," she answered.

Mary felt satisfied and hugged her husband back. Their corporate journey together was over. She'd wanted to be a good wife and mother, nothing else, and she'd done that.

"So what do you want now, Mary?" he asked sincerely.

"Want? I just want things to stay this way forever."

Jane—Patty—Mary. Each one, comfortably entrenched in Stage One, derives her status, money, and power from her husband. These are dependent women. Not one of them finds her role unpleasant. They do not work at paying jobs. Nor do they pursue studies or talents for themselves. They clearly see their work as serving their husband and his interests. Beyond this, they require no more.

At thirty-one, Jane is atwitter with activity, aglow with the prospect of her husband moving up. She has already outstripped her old friends in the race for acquisitions and is eager to climb into the next social league. Whatever it takes to push her husband ahead, she will do. Her commitment is singleminded. Move up! Up! UP!

Patty, at forty-eight, likes having a man look after her. She is unswervingly grateful to his corporation and aware of the enormous power her husband's position confers on her. His corporation has changed her, stretched her, improved her. Therefore, she is loyal. She is also by nature a contained and passive person. This fits in well with her dedication to keeping her spouse's favor and receiving the bounty of his largesse.

At sixty-five, Mary is at the end of the corporate journey, past the hurdles and the tests. She has been her husband's partner, his Girl Friday, his uncomplaining comrade for thirty-six years. No career conflicts here. His career was hers. No tensions about sex roles. He had his job, she had hers. Through thick and thin, Mary stuck it out for the big payoff. And now, it has come to pass. They are free.

Generations apart, shaped by different times, they still share certain characteristics. Although the circumstances of their lives varied and their backgrounds were different, they drew a composite picture for us. Neither Jane, Patty, nor Mary had *every* one of these qualities, but a composite tells us a lot about who they are.

THE WOMEN IN STAGE ONE

Dependent

1. They are dependent women who rely on their husbands to support them and their children financially. They see their husbands as the sole breadwinners in the family, the kingpins, entitled to certain rights and privileges. They are dependent upon the kingpin's generosity.

Security

2. Their security is tied to their husband's success. His goals become their goals, his values, their values. Identifying so closely with their husband's corporate views gives them little room to complain. Security above all.

Expectations

3. Their personal expectations are few and easily met. They view themselves as helpmates, team players, and Girl Fridays. They will do everything to better their husband's work because they have no work of their own and no sense of separate or personal identification.

Dutiful

4. They regard duty and responsibility as primary virtues. They respond to unpleasant assignments, even relocations to primitive far-off places, without complaint. They regard the good wife as obedient and duty-bound to be supportive. So they do not whine about hardships.

Passive

5. These women are compliant by nature. They react to what life hands them and they play out the cards they are dealt. They rarely take initiative or implement action. They serve their husbands by being receptive sounding boards and good listeners. Passive, silent partners.

Self Esteem

6. They have low self-esteem. They describe themselves negatively, as uncreative persons with meager talents and no special gifts. Therefore, they do not try to develop themselves. They do not feel entitled to much.

Status

7. Their status is proportional to their husband's position and salary. As he moves up, they tag along as Mrs. Success. Each survives by investing in her husband's status.

Uncompetitive

8. These wives let their husbands do battle for them. They are unambitious and prefer to stay in the background. They do not strike out on their own. They shy away from earning recognition or glory for themselves.

Sex

9. Sexually, they are undemanding partners. Willing to perform when called upon, they are unassertive partners who let their husbands take the lead and set the frequency and intensity of lovemaking. Faced with a spouse with a low sex drive, they merely adjust.

Risk Takers

10. Since safety and security are primary goals, women in Stage One do not rock the boat by making changes in the status quo. They want to keep what they have. So they regard sexual fidelity as in-

violate, and any act of assertiveness as risky business. They want no part of mutiny. They cling to their snug harbor.

This composite of Stage One paints the picture, but it leaves out that exquisitely revealing third dimension, a depth of perception that a hologram supplies. Let's fill that in before we go on.

Generally, I found the women in Stage One to be lacking in vitality. Their voices were soft and diffident. Many times I had to lean forward to catch what they said. Or I'd have to turn up the volume on my tape recorder to make sure I got it all. Often, I'd ask them to speak louder.

If you believe in body language, these women told me something in their posture and their dress. They sat on sofas and chairs, legs crossed, hands folded in their laps. And they rarely gestured, and never extravagantly. They dressed conservatively, mostly in skirts and suits, though younger women wore slacks, no jeans. Their demeanor was ladylike, nice.

As a group, they were the most guarded. There was a sameness to their expressions and examples. Many interviewees want to please the interviewer. However, these women did not gush forth with information. I really had to drag it out. They lacked a spirit I saw in the other stages. They lacked an awareness of their own needs. Which perhaps explains why they seemed to me less articulate than the women in Stage Two and Stage Three.

Perhaps because their power was derived from their husbands, they could not afford to be expansive. They might embarrass their husbands or slip and say the wrong thing about their corporations. In several interviews, the wives told me they asked for permission before they could speak to me. And in one case, it took forty minutes of my telephone persuasion before a husband would allow his wife to be interviewed.

Stage One women were the most quiet, careful group, full of hesitations in their responses, which they peppered with pleasant reassuring smiles. Like the political candidate in a television appearance, their lapses and corrections were highly informative.

The outstanding finding that applied to almost every woman in

Stage One was that these women lacked zest, lacked passion, lacked energy. Perhaps the years of getting and spending took its toll, depleting them. I suspect they secretly fear they could not make it on their own. So they pin their hopes on their husband. They hang on to a childlike trust that he will take care of them if only they play out the script satisfactorily to the end.

Many of them do. They hang on, like Mary, to the end. Blotting out their pain. Accepting with resignation what corporate life dishes out. Focusing on the benefits. The money. The security. The status at the top.

However, a fair number of corporate wives tumble, slide, fall, or jump into Stage Two.

How do they fare?

How do they change?

What happens to women in Stage Two?

4

Entering Stage Two:
Anne

To understand how Anne got to Stage Two, you only have to know the story about the Gucci luggage. They bought the three matched pieces, an extravagance they could ill afford, to make their first corporate relocation in style. There would be other moves, bigger promotions, fatter raises. Gucci luggage would be a good investment in their future.

It was. It took them through seven years and three more moves. But tonight, her mind was not on luggage. She was trying to comprehend what Clint was telling her.

She moved her coffee cup aside, and smoothed the place mat.

"No, Clint, I *cannot* have an answer by Monday." She had never spoken to her husband this way before. Anger flushed her face and made her hands tremble. She could feel her heart thumping in her chest. Could he hear it, too?

"But I have to tell them Monday, Monday morning," his voice was as reasonable as ever.

"No. I need more time. I don't know if I can do it again." Uprooting her, selling the house, moving across the country, no! Not again, at thirty-nine.

In the past, Anne had been bland and uncomplaining, all loyalty to the company. *Whatever you say* had been her response when Clint needed her to do something special, important. But this Friday night hostility seized her like a high fever. Her voice turned threatening and abrasive. As she listened to the rain pelting the roof, she felt like Chicken Little. The sky was falling in on her.

She gave him the zinger.

"I'm not moving again. Not for The Chemical Company. Not for you." Saying it made the rest tumble out. One by one she handed him her complaints. "I'm tired of moving. It wreaks havoc on us. It's terrible on Melissa. I'm scared. I don't want to go." She lowered her eyes, a little ashamed to be saying all that.

"But you never complained before. You coped so well, you were terrific. You were such a good trooper for the last relocations." He was confused. Surprised. Irritated. Why was she balking? Now, when the biggest promotion of his career was in the offing? "If you want me to rise to the top, we *have* to move."

Usually, that did it. A little rumble, a flash of lightning, but no torrential downpour. He could count on Anne. She knew you could make only one boo-boo for The Company. And refusing relocation was a biggie, a doozy. It never entered his mind that she wouldn't welcome the news. "Texas! You'll love it!"

She just sat there. Silence. Her head in her hands.

So he brought the Gucci luggage up from the basement. One. Two. Three pieces. He set them beside her chair.

She lighted up another filter Satin. She said nothing. She was reviewing sixteen years of marriage.

After Vietnam, as a bride of twenty-two, she pushed her young husband to get out of retail. Assistant manager of a shoe store was the pits. Long hours, weekends—and the chain made promises to Clint they didn't keep. She scoured the want ads, circled the leads for him. But he hung back. He didn't want to change jobs. He was fearful, insecure. *She* was the ambitious one. Self-confident. Optimistic.

When Melissa skipped off to kindgergarten, she began to nag him about going back to college. She encouraged him to take night courses in accounting. She made a deal with him. An offer he couldn't refuse. She would go back to work. She had her B.S. in computer science. And she would put him through college. It meant putting off having another child. It meant working full time for five years while he got his degree. It meant, finally, that she even covered for him at the shoe store on the nights he had to leave for class.

She wound up working her own job nine to five, and selling shoes three nights a week. Tough years. But it would all be worth it.

She was always tired. Melissa needed her. The house needed attention. Her job was demanding. But she saw it as their only way out. To turn Clint into an accountant. To make him over into a go-getter. An achiever. So she pushed and pushed and pushed. She pushed him ahead.

What she had done, she realized now, was to put all her eggs in one basket: Clint.

Ironically, what got him out of retail was that the chain went under. By luck he had just earned his degree, and The Company was taking on newcomers. He was full of fears. But she bolstered him, gave him pep talks.

She lifted her head and measured her husband. You'd never know it to see him now.

Now he represented the company image. Now he delivered speeches at universities and organizations on energy and soil conservation. Four promotions, fat raises. If he would agree to travel. Of course! She was all for it. They went where the company sent them. Relocated without hesitation. It was the way to the top. She stopped working and invested her future in her husband.

From then on, the relationship changed.

He gained confidence and began to make decisions for himself. She was glad to see him grow, but it bothered her that he didn't come to her anymore. She felt left out that he didn't consult her, ask her advice. Her suggestions were met with a pleasant shrug. Was he patronizing her?

He took charge of their checkbooks, their budget. He made some investments that miraculously panned out.

"How did you know that stock would go from three to seventeen?" she asked. She knew nothing about stocks. How did he learn so much, so fast?

"Know? No brainwork. Just a smart connection, honey. Tips. Contacts."

True. He had made a lot of contacts. He was exposed to some sharp operators. He picked up fast. And along the way, Clint developed a captivating charm, a simple but eloquent style. Monogrammed silk shirts. Italian shoes. He even acquired a taste for diamonds. Diamond cuff links. A diamond pinkie ring. For Christmas he gave her a diamond pin.

It was the Gucci luggage that started it all. She stared at it. It represented power. The power Clint had over her now.

He doesn't come to me. Doesn't lean on me anymore. Doesn't depend on me. He and The Company are calling the shots. The company has the power I used to have. They tell him what to do, where to go, when to leave his family.

Panic clutched her throat and she put her hand to the muscles tightening in her neck. She felt as if she were suffocating.

I'm losing control.

"They told us we'd get four weeks notice and they lied to us. A weekend to decide?" She could tell he *had* decided. That he was only announcing it, pretending to talk it over with her.

"I thought you'd be excited," he said with disapproval. "What's the matter with you?"

"I'm not going to pull up roots again for him," she thought. He's pushing me around. In two years we'll have to move again. Where? For what? What do I get out of it? I'm losing my identity. I was always in control of myself. And all of a sudden I feel like I'm falling apart. I'm getting kicked aside.

"What I say, what I want, doesn't matter to you."

"What do you want? Tell me."

"I don't want to uproot my life again. Leave everything behind and start over. I want to be me. Ooooh," she wailed, "I don't even know who me is anymore."

Clint got up and stood behind her chair, his hands pressed down on her shoulders. "Get control of yourself."

It was the wrong gesture. She wanted him to wrap her in his arms and say *whatever you want, baby, whatever you say*, the way he used to. She wanted him to value her opinions and come to her for help. Had he outgrown her usefulness to him? The company, not his wife, now ruled him. The company came first.

"Your time is all taken up with the company. What's left for me? You're never around. Is that what I get for all those years of working two jobs? For putting you through college?"

Oh! Her hand flew open-palmed across her lips and smacked them shut. She had *sworn* she'd never say anything so gross. And here she was turning into a sniveling housewife.

It terrified her to hear her own words. They frightened her and she began to cry softly into her hands. Confronting her feelings was a new experience.

I'm getting short changed, she thought, but held her tongue. I'm giving up more than it's worth. I'm only his sidekick now. I make all the sacrifices and he reaps all the rewards. He has a full and satisfying life. And I'm alone, completely dependent on him, his paycheck, his attention. My survival is up to him. I've placed myself in a terrible position. Terrible.

Was she having a breakdown? Was she going crazy? She never admitted such wild thoughts to herself. To divert attention from herself, she decided to talk about Melissa.

"What about our daughter?"

"She's doing fine."

"A lot you know. Melissa's confused. One minute she loves moving. 'What's the kitchen like, Mommy,' she asked last time. 'Can I go swimming there in the winter?' Miami meant sunshine to her. But then she got anxious and her grades dropped that marking period. She nearly flunked history, her best subject. Well, this year she put in seven months working out in chorus, twice a week. If we move, she'll be out in Texas for the performance."

"Kids survive. She's tougher than you think."

"Melissa has us to fall back on. Who do I have?"

He looked at her sternly, sat down and slapped his thighs with a sad sigh. "What's the matter with you? You were never like this before."

"I have feelings, too," she replied weakly.

She wavered between wanting to please him and needing to express what she was experiencing. She wanted to restore peace between them. But a whole surge of feelings was surfacing, pushing against her throat like a painful swelling. Could she continue to swallow her feelings? Go on pretending?

Last night in bed, she had wanted to please him. But the scenario of every other weekend imposed its pressures. A weekend home meant the entire two days she would be uptight. From the time she picked him up at the airport, she could hear the clock ticking, urging her to cram every moment full.

In bed, she couldn't relax. He wanted her to go down on him. He was getting bolder, more experimental. But it turned her off. For one thing, she didn't enjoy it, so she resisted. It gave her no pleasure. On another level, it frightened her. She wondered: *where is he picking up this stuff?*

Conventions. Travel. Long periods of separation. Does Clint cheat on me? It ran through her mind that her husband had acquired sophisticated tastes, that he was exposed to the high life in food, travel, and clothes. Were women one of the fringe benefits? A vision of a highly paid call girl coming to his hotel room clutched her. Call girls, whores! They were teaching him sex tricks and he was bringing them home for her to perform. Her vagina turned to cardboard and her thighs clamped shut. She knew she wouldn't climax. She was glad when it was over.

The rest of the weekend was no better, a stalemate. The weather continued to bring them thunderstorms and heavy rains. He paid the bills, griped about the new sofa she bought, said it was too hard and uncomfortable. Their time together, a precious commodity, was measured out in household tasks, petty arguments, a lousy movie, and trying to make the earth shake.

Saturday night she prayed that sex would be spectacular because this is it baby for two weeks! Make him remember you when he returns to hotel life. But Saturday night he wanted to have sex before she was ready, and she didn't want to tell him and break the mood. Or insult him with instructions. It was too embarrassing to ask him to touch her there, especially since she had refused him last night. So she let him do it to her fast and she pretended. A few groans. A healthy whelp at the end was all it took to convince him.

Why couldn't she talk about it? Why did talking about sex make her feel dirty, demanding?

Why don't I break the silence? Express my feelings?

Sunday, she took a stab at it.

Unaccustomed to acknowledging feelings of dissatisfaction, she was at a loss about how to express them. She could do it by being self-deprecating, glib, by sort of laughing at herself. Or she could turn it into a talk, maybe risk taking herself too seriously. It was a wobbly tightrope. Scary. Her feelings were too new, too frightening.

"Well?" he asked Sunday afternoon as she packed two of the three Gucci bags for him. "Feeling better?"

It seemed like a perfect opening. So she stopped packing and sat down on the edge of the bed.

"I'm feeling depressed. Resentful."

"Resentful?" Amazement widened his eyes. "Of what?"

"I'm alone. How do I know what you're doing when you're away?"

"Doing?" He was getting angry. "I'm working, dammit, busting my balls for you."

"You travel in mighty high company. Fancy executive women travel with you. A lot of opportunity for fooling around. Who's to know?"

"Are you crazy? Is that what's bugging you? Christ!" He backed up against his bureau and faced her.

She waited for his denial. When none came, her throat tightened harder. "I don't want to sell this house all by myself. Transfer to a new place. Uproot Melissa. It makes me angry. I resent it one hundred percent."

"You used to love moving on. You read the company's Relocation Program Package inside out and backwards. You knew what was in store." It was an accusation, a how-dare-you.

"I don't want to do it anymore. We're no longer two people. There's a third party in our life—The Company. It's what *they* say. You have to be available to them every minute. They own you.

They separate us, move us, control us. They run our lives. I feel like I'm floating in space. Someone else out there is controlling my destiny."

"I don't know what the hell all this is about. But let me tell you something. If you want the financial security, that's the price you pay." He glared at her. There was no sympathy for her.

"I want you to stay home. I don't want to move to Texas. Stay home. Please, Clint. Don't go," she was pleading, begging. She despised herself for it, but there was no bottling up her feelings anymore.

"You picked a great time to lay this on me. I have a plane to catch, remember?" He walked toward her and charmingly got on his knees to take her hands from her lap. "Keep your mind open, Anne. Be flexible. I'll call you tomorrow."

Dismissed. She stood up and lighted another filter Satin.

Because he objected to her smoking, it irritated him further. "You smoke too much, it makes you jumpy. Cut down, will you."

He was right. In the last six months she had gone from three cigarettes a day to two packs. She was also taking a Valium every lunchtime to calm her down. And a glass or two of white wine before dinner. Yup, she was falling apart. And all he could say is, be flexible. She could taste the resentment. "I'm not going to stay home and cry my eyes out."

"What the hell does that mean? Some kind of veiled threat?" He resumed packing. "I've got enough on my mind, I don't need this shit."

God! She had blown the whole thing. Accomplished nothing. Just got him angry. She decided to try once more to clarify her feelings.

"When I said my husband's career comes first, where he goes I go, I meant it. I believed it when I said it. But I believe now," she snuffed out her cigarette, "that I was dishonest with my own feelings. Why should I move to a no-man's-land? Why leave what I have? I feel different."

"Is that so?" He snapped the two Gucci bags shut.

Thinking back from day one, she could see the mistakes she had made. She had given him his chance to succeed. But what did it do for her?

"I feel neglected, unappreciated. I feel like extra baggage to you. I thought the rewards would come. But I see I'm losing control. The rewards are coming to *you*, not *me*."

That did it. He turned on her hatefully. "You know what?"

"What?"

"You're turning into one jealous bitch. A jealous complaining bitch, that's what you're turning out to be."

The third Gucci bag stood there between them. Empty. At attention. Waiting to be used. Just like her!

She gave it a violent kick and it bounced against their night table knocking over the lamp and the clock.

He picked up his two bags and fled down the stairs.

"Take a cab. Take a goddamn cab!" she yelled after him. "I'm not your chauffeur anymore."

Jeezis, the whole thing had gone wrong. She didn't want him to leave this way. Blowing up at him was stupid. Where did it get her?

She ran down the stairs after him to make peace.

If I say no to the move, won't he say I'm holding him back? Won't it make him resentful? Will he punish me for it? Will The Company pass him up if I refuse relocation? Will he lose his incentive to succeed? Will he be denied promotions and raises? Will he leave me behind?

She reached him as he was dialing for a cab. "Clint?"

"What now?"

"I'll drive you to the airport." She waved the white flag of retreat.

They drove to the Eastern terminal with a cassette playing. Loretta Lynn was singing: *Don't come home a-drinkin', with lovin' on your mind*. To avoid conversation, they pretended to be listening to the song. They didn't speak. Anne's outburst hung in the air between them.

The next morning when she woke up, she felt strange. Immensely relieved. In spite of the unpleasant ending to the weekend, she was convinced that her feelings were real and deserved attention. But she'd have to think about them, acknowledge them in a new way that was neither scattered nor defensive. She would also have to learn how to express them with more care, not to enrage him.

She used to be the moon to his sun. Could they get back on that footing again?

She took out the third piece of Gucci luggage, the twenty-six-incher that was her favorite. I think I'm going to take a weekend off by myself, send Melissa to her girlfriend's.

When Clint called on Thursday night, she told him.

"I'm packing. Going off for a weekend by myself."

"By yourself? What? Where you going?" Undisguised disbelief. A hint of amusement.

"I don't know. I'll figure it out on the way down the turnpike."

After she hung up, she went upstairs to pack. The Gucci was a good investment after all.

Anne's first venture into Stage Two is like that of many compliant and contented corporate wives who stick a toe in the water to test the temperature. Up to this point, she had not been able to acknowledge her feelings of discontent. She had felt that it would be disloyal to complain. So she spent years burying her resentments and denying them.

In Stage One, she had a role to play, an image to live up to: the Good Wife. A woman who helps her husband at all costs. She valued herself as the Good Wife. She knew what the job called for and how to behave. How to react. How to feel. Which is why she had returned to work when Melissa went off to school. Why she had worked five years holding down several jobs: her own nine to five; her husband's, three nights a week, plus full responsibility for the household and raising her child. Isn't that what the Good Wife would do? It never occurred to her to complain during those years. Because the Good Wife pushes her husband ahead no matter how tough it is on her. The rewards would come later when Clint became an accountant.

What provoked her to dip her toe into Stage Two was the realization that there would be no reward for her. Clint had grown. Clint had developed. Clint had succeeded. Clint was reaping the rewards.

Where was she? Stuck in the Good Wife role. Way behind him. Unappreciated. Unnecessary. Unrewarded.

Confusion is a principal ingredient of Stage Two.

Anne felt out of control. She was becoming unglued. First she denied her new awareness. Dissatisfaction is not part of the Good Wife's role. So she put a cork on her complaints. She disliked wives who whine; she would not become one of them. Therefore, she denied her feelings of discontent and buried her resentments. I'll go along, it will change, she said to herself. Things will get better.

When they don't, many women, like Anne, enter Stage Two. Perhaps through an explosion of feelings. For a long time, they have been irritated and itchy. But they plod ahead, enduring. It is their pattern. They are unable to face their feelings squarely because they have a track record of covering up, smiling, pretending. So it is a giant step to say words like: *No, I won't, I can't.*

Afterwards they feel guilty, ungrateful. Aren't their husbands decent, hardworking men? They feel like ingrates. So they tread gingerly around their powerful men who pay the bills and call the tune.

Confronting their buried feelings is the entrance level to Stage Two. Expressing them is even scarier. To go from *Whatever you say* to *No, I won't, I can't* is to plunge headfirst into Stage Two. Unprepared. Therefore, many women thrash about wildly, express themselves poorly. This is new terrain, the water is icy, and the spray of newly confronted feelings leaves them gasping for breath. It is easy to panic.

Like other women, Anne botched it the first time out. But corporate wives—like doctors' wives and movie stars' wives—all in the same lifeboat, suffer the same pain. They do not feel *entitled* to their own feelings. So the pattern of denial persists for many years until they truly explode!

Their first dip to test the water, whatever provoked it, is frequently not a rousing success. It takes a number of tries, starts and stops, two steps up and one step back, to make it work. It takes a growing and persistent need to express themselves. It takes a heightened awareness to redefine themselves in new terms and to accept the fact that their present position is no longer satisfying. The women in Stage

Two must feel pushed to an intolerable level before they can take action and move into Stage Three.

If Stage One is all comfort and compliance, Stage Two is all complaints and confusion, disruption and disquiet. Wives reassess themselves. Look around. Take stock of their cupboard and ask what Anne asked: *What's ahead for me?*

Other wives in Stage Two, unlike Anne, write themselves different scripts. Some recant and quickly retreat to Stage One, fearful that their husbands might divorce them. Some break down or find solace in drugs, alcohol, or love affairs. And some, a brave and beknighted number, emerge stronger and smarter. They enter Stage Three.

However, every woman in Stage Two does battle her own way. Behind closed doors, each woman struggles, however briefly, to be sane, whole, healthy, and in control.

There is the confusion of discovering new truths. The bewilderment of confronting past dishonesty. The embarrassment over new feelings. Is it okay? Is it right to feel this way? Stage Two women distrust the words that come out of their own mouths. Are they overreacting? Making a fool of themselves? Are they way out in left field?

Bonnie Sue stuck her toe in by asking one fatal question, then scooted back to the safety of Stage One. Too late.

Risa was abused by a husband while he supported her in luxurious style.

Tracy took a hard look at her corporate husband and made the decision not to have any kids.

Carol suffered a mental breakdown which she attempted to treat with vodka, Valium, and love affairs.

Stage Two is no holding pattern. Some of these women don't stay shaky forever. They conduct themselves with a newfound urgency and a growing passion.

5

Bonnie Sue and Risa

Bonnie Sue and Risa didn't make it into Stage Two *while they were married*. Almost to the end of their marriages, each remained "The Good Wife," compliantly and submissively ensconced in Stage One.

It was only after they found themselves duped and deceived that they entered Stage Two and began asking the disquieting, essential questions. Only after the marriage ended did they voice complaints and reassess their roles as women.

"I didn't see it then, but I see it now," Bonnie Sue said.

"I wonder how I could have been so dumb for so long," Risa told her friends.

What kept these women in Stage One until their house of cards came tumbling down? Does Stage One ensure a life of security and status? Bonnie Sue and Risa used to think so. They know better now.

Bonnie Sue

Everything Bonnie Sue had ever done trained her to be a good corporate wife, so it was shocking to see how far she had fallen. How

44

to explain it? Two years after the divorce, her manner was still diffident.

Bonnie Sue had located herself in a landscape of Southern sensibilities. No razzle-dazzle background here. She had been brought up in a household where emotions were held in tow, where privacy was valued, where there was dignity in not announcing your complaints. She spoke in a well-modulated voice, she behaved like a perfect lady. It was impossible to imagine a four-letter word escaping from her thin lips. Amiable and pretty, she found it easy to be a nice girl.

At seventeen, fresh out of high school, she was married to an air force cadet. At forty-four her world caved in. She will tell you this calmly. "I happen to be a Christian and I believe nothing happens by accident. God has a plan for me."

But when she read the note that morning, her heart began thumping right out of her chest. She read it again, right there standing in the driveway. It looked like another invitation stuffed under their garage door. When she pressed the automatic opener, it fluttered to her side. It had his name on the envelope.

"Thank you for your calls, your flowers, and your love." It was signed Clarice.

She called him at work. "Who's Clarice?"

Silence. "What do you mean?"

"I have her note here. In my hand."

"Hey, honey. She's an old friend in Building Four. In her fifties. Lost her husband, poor old girl."

"Oh?" She wanted to believe him.

"Well, it's a long story. I'll explain it to you when I get home." He sounded rushed. "Gotta go. Runway's waiting for me."

Bonnie Sue knew how hard her husband worked. He was under a lot of pressure piloting five different aircraft for The Agricultural Conglomerate executive runs. He had to be qualified, he was constantly traveling and training. What she didn't know was that he had a lover in Chicago.

When he came home he explained Clarice and Bonnie Sue was satisfied. Besides, he was taking her to Hong Kong and there were many preparations for the trip. They laughed about Clarice, and she buried the idea of his infidelity. Not her husband. He was a man of conscience and integrity. She trusted him completely. She had been faithful to him for twenty-five years.

The trip to Hong Kong was glorious. He kept urging her to buy clothes, so she ordered a custom-made silk kimono, a white suit, and three silk dresses. Their other trips to Hawaii, Australia, Aspen, London, San Francisco, and Rio had been wonderful, too. But this trip was special. He couldn't do enough for her. They made love like honeymooners.

When they got back, she proposed an idea to him. It was not like her to make requests, but she'd see how he'd take it.

"Remember Phyllis? The one in cosmetics?" He nodded. "She wants me to work part time for her. What do you say?"

"You're bored, aren't you?"

"Well, the kids are grown up and you're away so much. There's not a lot for me to do."

"It's okay with me." He wanted her to keep busy.

When the kids were small and he wasn't around, she covered up for him when he missed their birthdays. When he missed Christmas, she made new excuses and rented a Santa Claus outfit for herself. When the kids griped, she told them, "We all have a cross to bear." He was a good man. Never forgot to send her flowers on her birthday, their anniversary, a holiday he wasn't home for. She put nagging thoughts aside.

Six months later, out of the blue, he told her.

Without the grace of an introduction, he sat down and while taking off his socks he said, "I love her."

Her heart knew it immediately. It turned over and broke. "Who?" She tried to fit in a little smile.

"Clarice."

"Clarice? The fifty-year-old widow in Building Four?"

Clarice was thirty-three, an M.B.A. out of Harvard Business School. They traveled together. He flew her and other executives to exotic places. He married her as soon as the divorce became final.

Their daughter was married, a few months later, in a fancy country club setting. Bonnie Sue had no money to contribute from her small settlement. She was not invited to the reception. Clarice would be there, of course.

"Do you mind, Mother? Daddy says it would only complicate matters with both of you there. We want it to be a nice wedding."

"No," she said, "I don't object. I don't want to be anyplace I'm not welcome."

Bonnie Sue put the phone back in the cradle. Quietly, with ladylike control, she wept into her pillow. Until great sobs thrashed her and her knees folded up into her chest. Compliant. Passive. Powerless. Where did it get you?

"Shit!" she said. "Bastards!" she screamed. And then she said the word she hated. "Fuck them! Fuck them all!"

A few months later, she consulted a therapist.

In a ladylike tone she began to apologize to the doctor. "I'm not usually a person who washes my dirty linen in public. I'm not a complainer."

"It's okay. You're allowed to complain."

"I am? Well," Bonnie Sue replied. "I never knew that."

Welcome to Stage Two.

Risa

Risa entered Stage Two very close to the end of her twenty-three-year marriage. She was forty-three.

Like Bonnie Sue, she did not enter Stage Two by choice. Like Bonnie Sue, the end came in the mail. Like Bonnie Sue, it had never entered her head to speak up for herself.

"He told me I was frigid, I believed him. He told me I was stupid, I believed him. Whatever he told me, I believed."

Twelve years ago, when Victor had made the big move to The Corporation, she was all for it.

"I've been devising systems for the best of the littler guys, why not move up to the big boys?" He was confident, eager, and optimistic.

Headhunters had been after him for six months. But he played it cool, demanding a hefty increase to leave his company and go with The Corporate leader. He wanted perks he never thought they'd go for: a hefty benefit package, a car, an expense account. And in two years he was a phenomenal success, in charge of twelve major accounts where most of the men had four or five.

So they bought their twelve-room Tudor. Each girl had her own beautiful room and a playroom. And they had an office, a maid's room, a twenty-foot kitchen, a living room, and a dining room out of *House Beautiful*—it was heaven!

Risa was not surprised by her husband's sweep to the top. He could make anyone believe anything. He was an actor, a charmer when that was called for. But he could turn hard, even cruel, and ride roughshod over his employees. He fired a twenty-year system analyst over one mistake. Told him to clean out his desk on a Friday afternoon, that he was finished. A pragmatic workaholic, he expected perfection from everyone. He could reduce his secretary to tears, then turn so concerned and apologetic that she'd remain loyal and stay on. He could sweet-talk anyone; he was seductive, handsome; it was hard to refuse him.

He was also a consummate manipulator. He knew how to use power.

When he was rude to her, Risa forgave him. When he was short-tempered and impatient, she figured he had had a hard day.

"My head was so deep in the sand, I didn't see what was in front of my eyes," she admitted to her sister, her confidante, over shrimp salads in the last booth at Gilly's.

"I let it go on and on. I accepted it. Whatever he did was fine."

"Why didn't you argue when he spent a fortune on the pool? Why didn't you put up a fuss when he put you down? Why didn't you complain when he didn't show up for your party? I saw him cut you to ribbons at Thanksgiving, Risa. You just sat there and took it. Why?"

"What could I do? I didn't argue because if I did he'd say: *You sound like my mother. Shut up.* So I did."

"What about the girls?" her sister asked. "My kids talk back. Teenagers are always giving parents lip. Why didn't they open their mouths?"

Risa folded her napkin and lowered her head. This was the part she felt most ashamed of. "They were intimidated. They didn't want to cross him. You know Victor. He can turn mean. They just wanted to stay out of his path." She paused. "I should have stood up for them, but I was afraid to start a fight."

She remembered the fight over the boat when she tried to speak up. He was going bananas then, spending money, getting rid of cash. They had bought the condo in Hilton Head for summer vacations.

"I want you to go to the boat show in Annapolis with me."

"You want to trade in the fishing boat?" She liked their little twenty-one-foot open boat. The girls liked to fish off it.

She saw irritation rise in him. "No, no, no. Who said anything about trading in? I want a cabin cruiser to keep there. With twin one hundreds. Something around $30,000."

"But you're never there. The first summer you spent nine days there out of twelve weeks. The second summer you were there fourteen days. And last summer you missed nine weekends out of twelve. What do you need it for?"

"Don't tell me how to spend my money!"

"I only said . . ."

"I'll spend my money any way I like!"

She swerved to avoid a blowup. "Will you be coming down more?" she asked hopefully.

"Christ! Don't bug me! I have a new company to set up in Baltimore. A company apartment to furnish. I'm up to my eyeballs. Besides . . ." He snickered. "Risa likes nice things. I have to work for them."

She didn't say another word.

He had the power because he held the purse strings. Every month he gave her a check for the household accounts—telephone, gas, electricity, gardener, maid—and she paid them all promptly. The rest he stashed away. She had no idea how much he made or what he did with the money. Although she signed their joint income tax forms every year, she never read them, never asked: What do we have? What do we own? Where is our money? He once told her everything had to be in his name so he could remain liquid. He was wheeling and dealing. Their phone bill was four figures.

Of course he bought the cabin cruiser.

He also put in a seventy-foot pool. He maintained three fashionable wardrobes: one at home in Boston; one in Baltimore in the company apartment; one in Hilton Head. He nagged her to buy clothes, said she looked dowdy. He bought each of the twins a car for their seventeenth birthday. A Datsun 280ZX and a TR3.

"Isn't that extravagant?"

"It's in The Company name."

But the girls weren't fooled. Although he bought them expensive gifts, they were scared to death of his wrath. He demanded to be waited on. He gave them orders.

"Bring me a drink." "More ice." "Christ, doesn't anyone around here know how to mix a scotch and soda?" He dominated them. They took it because he had all the power.

Even when she designed the gardens for the pool, and moved the dog houses for the two golden retrievers, built patios and decks and planted flowering shrubs, he put her down.

"What the hell is this, the Taj Mahal?" It wasn't the money. He didn't like her taste. "It stinks. I'll do it over with a decorator."

Still, there was much to admire in the man. He was an achiever, aggressive, a winner. If he lied now and then, if he used people to move up, well maybe that's how successful executives operated. She wanted to be fair, to see his side.

What eroded her was the way he pulled her apart. Mocked her needlepoint: "Hang it in the laundry room, I hate the stuff." Criticized her appearance: "Knock off twenty pounds, you look awful." He controlled her behavior with orders:

"Don't wear a bra when I'm around."

"Don't lock the bedroom door."

"Don't wear a swimsuit in the pool."

He swam nude at Hilton Head, which disgusted her.

"We have two teenage daughters, please," she begged.

"Don't turn them into a prude like you."

When he threw the crab casserole at the kitchen blinds, she knew he was coming apart. When he started knocking off half a bottle of Johnnie Walker Black, she saw his disintegration. When he brought home the adult sex books, she watched his descent into hell. But she *still* held her tongue. Maybe, just maybe, it was only mid-life crisis. It would pass.

The sex part was hard to talk about, even to her sister. But she needed to tell someone.

"One night he threw a couple of packages across our bed. I thought they were gifts because after a fight he'd buy me jewelry. Never on Mother's Day or my birthday or our anniversary. But after a blowup, he'd go to Jordan Marsh for something expensive."

"What was it?"

"Dirty books. *Screw Magazine, Penthouse,* sex devices, a vibrator, pictures of sex with dogs, gang sex, an old lady and three little boys. You know what he told me?"

"What?" Her sister's face was ashen.

" 'Wake me up when you get interested.' When I wouldn't do what he wanted, he called me one stupid cunt." She was wringing the linen napkin, twisting it in her lap. "The crazy thing is the man was never impotent. Never. He said he was training me. I think he was trafficking with whores."

Risa's sister shook her head mournfully. "Did you ever ask him to go to a marriage counselor?"

She nodded. "Know what he said? 'I don't need help. *You* do!' So I said, 'Please, Victor, I can't take this anymore.' He just looked at me, cold as ice. *'If you don't like it, leave.' "*

Her sister laid a consoling hand over hers. "He knew you wouldn't leave. Power sniffs out weakness."

Risa nodded. "He had all the power."

Power, she thought. The money and power went to his head. The more he got, the crueler he became. She was too ashamed to go on telling her sister how abused she was. *Abused? Was she an abused wife?* She laughed it off. Who could believe that a woman with a maid, a gardener, a pool, two houses, and a new Mercedes was abused?

The end of the marriage came in the mail.

It had been piling up for weeks in Boston, while he was in Baltimore and she was in Hilton Head. From the end of June to August, she couldn't reach him. He didn't call, and his secretary made up lame excuses when she phoned his Baltimore office. Would he be coming to Hilton Head? She didn't know. When would he call? She couldn't say.

When she returned to Boston, the mail on the hall table was halfway up the mirror. To pay bills, she sifted through it. A phone bill from Baltimore had slipped through. Normally he paid it through the business.

When she opened it, she found the phone calls. Over and over, the same number. Long calls, forty-six minutes, thirty-four minutes. At night. Sundays. Saturdays. Business calls? She punched in the phone company for the listing. *L. Riccardo.* L? Was it Louis or Lucy. The answer came quickly as she sifted through the rest of the mail.

The title to a Buick station wagon in the name of Laurie Riccardo. Her hands trembled and she started to cry, babbling like a child who has lost her bus fare home. "No, no, no." She was glad the girls were out to a movie. She sent the maid away and locked herself up in his office. She went through his files.

It was all there, had been there right under her nose if she hadn't ignored it. Thirty-six thousand dollars worth of checks to L. Riccardo, Laurie Riccardo, Riccardo Decorators. Of course. She was his decorator for the Baltimore corporate apartment. He set her up in her own decorating business. Bought her the wagon. And what else? What jewelry and furs and houses did her husband buy her? Who was Laurie Riccardo?

It was an ugly divorce. Private detectives. Filthy tactics. Lies and recriminations. It took three years to unravel the skein of Victor's deceits.

The first day she sat down with her lawyers, they suggested she rationally prepare a list of her complaints.

"We'll explain Massachusetts law to you. But first we have to know everything. Start with your complaints."

"Complaints? I never complained when we were married."

They smiled like the seasoned attorneys they were. "Try to remember everything."

She didn't have to try hard. They flowed out like the swollen tears rolling down her cheeks. Complaints. Hardships. Abuses.

"And did you explain those feelings to your husband?"

"Explain? I didn't know I had them until now."

Risa entered Stage Two in the presence of two of Boston's finest divorce lawyers.

6

Executive Woman versus Corporate Wife

At 6:02, brushing her teeth in the bathroom mirror, Kim could have passed for a pert high-school senior. But when she slipped on her Brooks Brothers suit and Ferragamo pumps and swung her Mark Cross briefcase onto the seat of the 6:58 express, she became a corporate executive. She had allotted twenty minutes to instruct her housekeeper, fondle the baby, and kiss her husband good-bye. Kim is one of the new breed of eighties women. Wife. Executive. Supermom. She does it all. It is her season of excellence.

Kim is also the Other Woman to worrisome corporate wives.

Is she strictly my husband's colleague, they wonder? Will she seduce my husband? Wreck my marriage? Corporate wives feel threatened by the bright new executive woman.

Amid the confusion and unrest of wives in Stage Two is puzzlement about the woman their husband spends time with. She is that new species of tigress whom even saintly and secure corporate wives fear. Male colleagues may resent her incursion into their bastions of power. But corporate wives regard her with another level of suspicion. She is the other woman in their female-male balance of power. The third leg of the triangle. She represents a kind of extra-marital connection. She keeps them off balance. So corporate wives feel edgy about her. Damn her!

Who is she?

She is under forty, clever, and confident. She is well educated, ambitious, assertive. *And* she sees the corporate husband daily, more hours than his wife does. She enjoys private jokes and business intimacies with male executives. They admire her.

Wives in Stage Two, coming out of their lethargy into a new awareness, begin to recognize that their own lives are drab. They may envy the position of the female executive. Who is this woman who is in the thick of the action? Who shares the passions and tensions of their husbands' corporate life? As they feel their own power eroding, wives in Stage Two may resent the executive woman who is on equal footing with their husbands.

There are the sexual fears, too.

They travel together. Stay at the same hotel. Is it strictly business? Or is the executive woman using every female ploy to get to the top? Stage Two is a nervous time for the corporate wife. The advent of the executive woman does not make it easier.

When she measures her position against executive women in her husband's corporate life, she notices that her powers are waning. Sexual and financial decisions are not in her hands. Dependency seems less attractive to her now. When Walt Whitman was singing the body electric, he must have been foreseeing the New Executive Woman, not the corporate wife in Stage Two who is feeling short-circuited, played out, used up.

Suddenly a panic sets in. One she cannot voice yet. But it settles on her like talcum powder. She has become a weakened woman with little power. Even a loyal husband in a pleasant marriage might take a long hard look and discover he has outgrown his bride of twenty.

The female executive, full of fire and passion, engaged in work her husband respects, gives the corporate wife in Stage Two a big dose of self-examination. Compels her to face her image in the mirror.

The wife may rationalize that the executive woman turns hard, loses her femininity, pays a huge toll in family life. Change places with her? Never! But underneath the sour grapes are some deeper, darker emotions. The executive woman shakes up the corporate wife who must take a new look at herself. Reassessing her position is what Stage Two is all about. Even if she can't deal honestly with herself yet, even if she can't voice her feelings, her dependency strikes her in Stage Two and makes her turn a critical eye at what she has become.

The female executive may be the catalyst that forces a wife to plant her feet firmly in Stage Two. Kim makes wives nervous.

Kim: The Whiz Kid

Kim arrived home at 8:45. Late, because she stopped to get her hair trimmed, which threw the nighttime schedule off. The housekeeper complained that dinner would be burned through. The baby was cranky because Steve was trying to keep her up for Mommy. Her husband, a radiologist with the medical center, was sulking.

"I would have done racquetball tonight if I'd known you'd be late," he said.

She played with the baby for ten minutes, treasured moments of her day, then listlessly sat down to dinner. She was too tired to eat. Today had been a bummer at the office. And she could see from Steve's face that the radiology department had not danced a jig either. They were both beat.

When Kim started with The Corporation's jet program at twenty-nine, she was one of seventy attorneys quickly weeded down to twenty. She knew that meant the law of the jungle: survival of the fittest. It didn't scare her one drop.

In a year of working her tail off, she was singled out for the fast track and pushed ahead to the $40,000 level. It didn't hurt that she found a mentor in Donald, senior vice president in charge of rate cases. He assigned her some tough ones. Putting in a seventy-hour week, she did him proud.

But now she was having trouble with Donald. His wife was driving her nuts.

"What held you up?" her husband asked over the lasagna.

"Haircut. You like it?" She wanted to keep the conversation light. The housekeeper had big ears.

"Nice. But don't cut it shorter."

She laughed. "You liked me better with hair down my back, right?" He nodded and pushed his overcooked dinner around on the plate.

Long hair was four years ago. Kim caught on fast. From day one, she understood the corporate image. One vice president actually gave a speech on it, recommending Brooks Brothers. *Dress corporate* was the message. Neat. Traditional. Ivy League. Kim was goal-oriented. Like the new crop of executives, she knew how to fit in. Knew that deals were made on the tennis courts and over lunch at the Harvard Club. Loyalty, not brilliance, catapulted you ahead. If it meant short hair and Brooks Brothers, it was okay with her.

Later in the evening with the den door shut and Susie tucked in, they talked above the low buzz of the television. She sprawled out across the leather sofa with her feet in his lap.

"The baby ran 101 today. Didn't you call home?" he asked.

"You know I call twice a day. She's teething, that's all."

"You look beat. Bad day at Black Rock?"

"It's Donald's wife. She called twelve times today. She's got back trouble. Stomach trouble. Hives. She's always calling him. Where is he? When will he be back? If he's not around, I have to listen to her chitchat. What can I do? The boss's wife." She lowered her eyes. "I may ask for a transfer."

What Kim wasn't telling Steve was that good old Irish Catholic Donald, older than her father, had a crush on her. No passes yet, but she could feel them coming. There was a lot of sleeping around. She didn't want to be drawn into that. Sleeping your way to the top was for incompetent women. They did it in the mistaken belief that it would smooth their way up the ladder and ensure faster promotions.

But if you knew you were good, like Kim, you didn't skate on thin ice. Kim was no moralist, no righteous do-gooder. She had simply figured it out. If you lose favor with the man you're sleeping with, or he loses his footing, it's curtains. Let incompetent women make it on their backs. Kim was too smart and too realistic not to

earn her stripes by excellence. She knew they called her the Sixth
Floor Whiz Kid.

Too bad Donald's wife was getting in the way. A middle-aged
mentor with wife trouble was bound to make a move on her pretty
soon. Better transfer out before it got too hot in the kitchen.

"I'm kinda sorry for his wife," she told Steve.

"Why?"

"Six kids. Upstate Irish Catholic. Her red hair gets teased to plastic
in a beauty parlor every Thursday. She plays golf at her country club
and wears a mink stole."

"Maybe she likes her life that way. Every wife isn't competitive.
Some women aren't out to be assistant vice presidents at $100,000
a year."

He *was* in a bad mood. Must be their low-simmer quarrel which
had been going on since Susie's second birthday party. She was
trying to keep it under control so it didn't escalate to a rolling boil.
But Steve, a virtual nine-to-fiver on salary at the medical center and
a pretty easy-going specimen, was giving her flak. Funny. She had
deliberately married a quiet, undemanding guy in the belief that two
highly competitive people under one roof would be disastrous.

He began the evening of Susie's party.

He slid the remains of the pink and white birthday cake with the
smudged roses back into the refrigerator and turned around to face
her.

"Let's have another baby."

"Another baby?" She flicked off his remark and got busy with the
cups and saucers. But she knew there would be more on the subject.
Another baby! That was the last thing on her mind. When she made
the mistake of getting pregnant almost three years ago, her career
stopped dead.

"No more turnarounds to D.C. and Chicago, we can't let you do
that, dear," Donald had said. That was the trouble with a mentor.
He took a "fatherly" interest. Called her out of meetings to teach
her something. Introduced her to bigwigs over lunch. But a mentor
wielded the power of parental authority and nixed a lot of things,
too. Throughout her pregnancy he gave her only nice little assign-

ments, nothing too taxing. It set her back two years. When she geared up and reentered, the fast-track people were way ahead and she had to re-prove herself.

She looked up again and said to Steve, "Don's grooming me. They're watching me. Don wants to bring someone along. And if that someone is me, terrific! I have to be ready."

Steve sulked. A whole week went by before they made love.

Now he looked at his wife and gave her toes a loving squeeze. Beautiful, brilliant Kim. The hot shot. She had dark circles under her eyes and a vertical line between her brows. Was she on uppers? He prickled.

"You're working too hard. Lay off the stuff, huh?"

Kim used to smoke dope in college. But now she was clean. An upper sometimes to keep her energy up, but never when she was in the middle of a brief because she didn't want to crash. No alcohol either. Too many executives were landing in The Corporation's dry-out center. These days she was into grapefruit juice. Several stress related health problems were cropping up.

"I'm thirty-four, but my gums are eighty-four and my teeth are getting loose." Her dentist had recommended deep scalings, a gingevectomy.

"You know you're grinding your teeth in your sleep?" Steve told her. "How did your physical go?"

"I didn't get high marks," she admitted. "My plumbing isn't wonderful because I don't have time to go to the bathroom."

"Easy to fix. Take the time. What else?"

Her gastroenterologist put her on milk of magnesia. "Colitis. Incipient ulcer. Same old stuff." She paused. "It's your mother's fault. Needling, needling me all the time, telling me Susie'll grow up to be a moron because I'm out working. I laugh it off, but it builds up internally. Her damn chipping away."

"Don't blame my mother. You make your own stress."

He was right. She had no free time. She didn't even go shopping anymore, she ordered by mail. She was time-crazy, a typical Type A with every second allotted to be productive. Even the baby was scheduled on weekends for quality time. Three hours on Saturday and four on Sunday. Quality time was more important than being there any old time.

Methodical and conscientious, she was neurotic about preparing lists. Her housekeeper got one weekly and one every day. Her secretary, too. Impatient with inefficiency, she could be manipulative, even vindictive when crossed. But Kim could also be soft and loving. She was generous and thoughtful about giving gifts. She kept lists of everyone's birthday and anniversary.

She sat up and cuddled up to Steve. He was a darling, a teddy bear. But he didn't understand that a woman had to be twice as good as a man to get to the top. Secretly she wondered why he wasn't more competitive, more ambitious. When she got real mad at him, she muttered *wimp!* under her breath.

She didn't want to fight. She wanted to make love. "I have priorities, that's all," she summarized.

But he held on. "Another baby is what we need. It's time. Susie would be three, even if we get started tonight." He smiled and she smiled back. He wanted her. Good.

"Tonight?" She gave him a devilishly seductive look.

It was the last day of her period and she knew she was safe. Her body needed loving. She wanted it. But her mind ruled out baby. Absolutely not! She let his hand creep under her panties and she resolved to put off any debates about another baby. It would be the same rehash and end in the same fight. Family versus career. Which came first?

She had spelled it out to him once before. Shouted, screamed at him in the heat of argument. "I don't believe in family to the exclusion of all else! Damn it! Let them call me ballsy. So I'm aggressive, ambitious, competitive. If I had a dick they'd admire me. The hell with them! Fuck them!"

He grabbed her wrists and forced her to sit down. "You're pushing yourself into burn-out country. Why do you do it? Why?"

"I'll tell you why." She struggled for composure. "Hear this! I really *love* my work. I do it for *me*. A sense of satisfaction. The intellectual stimulation. The ego. I love to see the limo waiting when

I land in Dulles. I love the power I wield. I love to make decisions that count. *I love my work!"*

No, I'm not taking off six months to have another baby.

No, I'm not changing my priorities.

No, I'm not going to wind up like Don's wife or your mother.

"Let's go to bed." She grinned and they took the stairs holding hands.

First thing Monday morning she'd put in for a transfer. Make up some cock-and-bull story for Don. There was always Timothy. Good old Tim, her backup mentor. He'd welcome her with open arms.

What was *his* wife like?

What Kim didn't know yet was that Tim's wife had neither red plastic hair nor a mink stole. What she did have was both feet in Stage Two.

After sixteen years as the perfect corporate wife, Tim's wife was going through an awakening. After sixteen years of loyalty, Tim's wife was questioning her eroding position. After sixteen years of comfortable compliance, Tim's wife was seized with feelings of envy, shame and guilt.

She *envied* the respect Tim showed when he talked about his women colleagues. She envied the competence of those women. She envied their lives which she imagined could not be as dull as her own.

She felt *ashamed* of herself for diddling away her time with busy work. Her needlepoint gave her no pleasure. Her golf score was a monkey on her back. Her charity work was boring. Was she less capable than other women? Less gifted? Less courageous? She had stood in a corner watching a young woman called Kim at a company party. Watched the energy, the magic of that young woman. And she felt ashamed of what she had let herself become.

Last, she felt *guilt*. Guilty for not exercising her own powers. For not stretching herself. For allowing Tim to take over her life. For not having made a single important decision in sixteen years.

Tim's wife was edgy, nervous, distracted. She was itching to make changes. The trouble was she didn't know how. Where to begin?

She thought about Kim.

Tomorrow, she'd have her hair cut short and styled that way.

Tomorrow, she'd look over the fall courses they were offering at the community college.

And if she had time, she'd drop in on her husband for lunch. Get to know Kim.

7

Babies, Lovers, and Other Considerations: Tracy and Carol

Executive women like Kim are not alone in their anxiety about when and if to have children.

Tracy, a corporate wife for ten years, tiptoed around that decision until she reached thirty-two. Her goals were worlds apart from Kim's. Although Tracy worked in retail throughout her marriage, she never had a career commitment she couldn't walk away from for Glen's career. And unlike other corporate wives who complained bitterly about relocation, she really loved it. In eight years they moved four times, and each time Tracy rose to the challenge and excitement of meeting new people and discovering a new city and a new job.

Tracy started out in Stage Two.

Most of her crowd did, too. College-educated, Jewish, suburban women hammered out by the revolutionary sixties rarely turned out to be coy, compliant corporate wives. They skipped Stage One entirely. They had a different perspective about tasting the world. And Tracy was a bit of a Bohemian gypsy with her dark beauty and kooky clothes. Hitting the road with Glen every two years was fun. As long as they didn't have kids, she got a kick out of relocating. The Pharmaceutical Corporation did it all, took care of everything. Sold their house and smoothed the way. Professional movers packed them up and all she had to do was point to the garbage and say, "That stays."

She didn't blame their frequent relocations for their not having babies. She didn't blame lack of money—it was rolling in. She didn't blame her new mail-order business that she could take with her anywhere.

It came to her in an epiphany. The realization. The overriding reason. *I don't want children because Glen would make a lousy daddy.*

She would not put it that baldly to her mother and dad who were dying to become grandparents. She would not repeat those harsh words to her friends who were having babies left and right. It took her a long time to admit it to herself. But at the $50,000 level she took a long hard look, and she knew absolutely that Glen had turned pure corporate right down to his John Chancellor P3 glasses and his trim preppy haircut. Short of lying or cheating, he'd sell his soul for The Corporation.

Corporate husbands were a special breed. Hard-nosed workaholics dedicated to their company, they ate, slept, and breathed power. Power was their turn-on. An insatiable hunger controlled them. They needed power, more power, more, like a druggie needs a fix. No way could she see Glen rocking a cradle, changing a diaper, reading a bedtime story, finding time to fit a child into his life. And to be honest, she had never regarded having children as a necessity. She and Glen worshipped at the altar of freedom. Now that they had the money, along came the freedom to do your own thing. Selfish? Hedonistic? They didn't think in those terms. They were happy. They were having a ball.

"You mean you turned down the headhunters *again?*" Tracy was incredulous and her dark curls bobbed with disbelief. "Double your salary doesn't shine up your walking shoes?"

"Hell, no." Glen took off his gray trousers and hung them in the dark slacks section of his meticulously arranged closet. "Leave The Corporation? For what? For ticky-tacky down the road? For the other giant who treats employees like meat." He chuckled with satisfaction.

"We're the best, Trace, an elite group. Know what I tell headhunters? 'Take a flying leap.' "

"Snob!" she teased and turned so he could unzip her. What a night. Another posh dinner, this time Lutece, drinks, a limo and two nights at the Drake. "They did everything but kiss your feet."

"Why not? I'm the star. The client. I walk on water. The Corporation drops millions on television time. So let the TV moguls quake. No other Fortune 500 company can touch us. We've got the muscle. We make things happen. We've got the chambers of commerce, the boards of symphonies and theaters. No one has our clout."

They had been together since she was sixteen, a high-school junior, and he was in prep school on his way to Cornell. Even then she knew he was a winner. He was incredibly organized, a perfectionist on top of every detail. He was goal-oriented, knew where the target was.

In five years at The Corporation, he was on his way to the Pantheon. They began to think of it as *our* company, *our* corporation. The money doubled and doubled again. But it was not the money he worked for. It was the power. Power and the competitive need to win. He made good decisions, got more clout, a heady experience for a guy under thirty. When he was invited to attend a meeting with the president, it blew his mind.

"Some day I'm going to have his job, Trace. Watch me. I'll be tougher than John Welch at GE. Harder than Klopman at Burlington and Grove at Intel." His mind kept track of the biggies like some guys tracked baseball scores.

"Not CEO?"

"Nope. The president's spot, in the president's suite. President is the real heavy." He had the wallpaper picked out. Knew where the plants and the ficus would be. In one year he'd make it to associate advertising manager and be responsible for four brands. There was no stopping him. That commitment. That intensity. That need to win.

It was what attracted her from the start. But now she was feeling edgy about it. For one thing there was the scare about the heart attack last year. Which knocked them both out flat.

He had always been a mild hypochondriac so she didn't worry when the first pains came. But when two guys in their forties landed in intensive care, Glen hightailed it to the doctor about his own symptoms.

"They're not chest pains," the cardiologist assured them. "It's in your esophagus." He gave him all kinds of tests, the electrocardiogram, the works. And his diagnosis was esophageal muscular spasms. "They can imitate heart attacks. No danger yet. But," and the doctor smiled ruefully, "it's remarkable how many people at your Corporation suffer from that symptom. It's pure stress."

Stress? Not Glen. He seemed to thrive on work.

"Is it the damn gestapo that's always watching you?" she asked as they drove home, her face full of concern.

"Naw."

"Is it another bout with antisemitism?" The Corporation was said to keep Jews out.

"No, no."

"Is it Lee?" He was the guy behind Glen. "Is he waiting for you to make a misstep so he can walk right over you?" She wanted to charge someone with the crime.

"Don't be ridiculous. Lee's a gnat, no threat at all."

"Then what is it? Why are you feeling such awful stress?"

"It's nothing, a fluke, forget it."

But she knew the answer. His own hunger to succeed was sticking in his throat. The hunger for power. More power. More.

Tracy asked him to talk about it, his feelings, his fears. But Glen had no time or inclination for talk. She tried to drag it out of him. But he couldn't express his feelings and he was a terrible listener. When she tried to get him to open up, he was in the ozone. He brushed her off. "I'm okay. I'm fine."

However, the bout with the cardiologist turned him into a dedicated hypochondriac. Whereas before he'd complain mildly of assorted symptoms, now he began to monitor his health with a vengeance. Secretly, he checked his weight twice daily, his intake of calories, his nutrition. He *was* worried about a heart attack. To avoid it, he started on Nautilus, pumped iron at a gym, played tennis, and took up golf.

"How about I buy clubs and play golf with you? It would give us more time together."

He threw his head back and laughed. "Hey, knock it off. I play to win." He never got angry. Never raged. He could be cold and calculating, but he was always in control.

The man she married was devoid of passion. Why? Because whatever little he had was siphoned off for The Corporation. It made Tracy angry. She felt a frustration she could hardly contain and she was not one to keep it inside. So she began with a list of secondary complaints. The small frustrations that sent her up the wall. She had always gone through life expressing herself. Now she bombarded him with her feelings.

"Win, win, win, that's all you think about. It's ten, twelve hours a day and then papers to go over at night. I'm sick of it."

"C'mon, sweetie, don't get yourself riled up."

"I want us to go to the theater. Subscribe to the symphony. You have no time. I want us to work on the record collection. You have no time. I want us to shop together for the new sofa. You have no time."

"Didn't I go to *Chorus Line* with you?"

"That was a freebee and we went with four company people."

"We joined the philharmonic, didn't we?" He tried to placate her, but his patience was running thin. He shuffled his papers around so she'd get the message.

"Philharmonic!" she raged. "You went once! And we left early so you could polish some goddamn presentation." He was already in the ozone. "Listen to me, goddammit!"

He stopped shuffling and his voice softened. "I'm listening, I'm listening."

"You're a taker, Glen, not a giver."

He turned her raw accusation into a compliment. "Sure. I took you along, and hasn't the ride been good?" He smiled.

"You take everything. I have to fight for anything I get from you. You take my time, my energy, anything you want. Maybe it works to be ruthless at the office. But at home I want more." She knew she was right. All the corporate women she knew were givers, the men takers.

"What do you want? You know you can have anything you want. Did I ever deny you anything? A new dress? New furniture? Anything you ask for, I say sure, okay, yes."

Goddammit, he didn't understand a word she was saying.

"Buy, buy, buy! That's not what I'm talking about." The rage was bringing tears to her eyes. "Ooooh. It's my own fault. I get so little from you because I ask for very little. I make few demands."

It occurred to her now that he had known that when he married her. That she would be a giver. That he could do all the taking. A perfect pair.

But things had changed. She was never one of those corporate wives with no life of her own. She had always worked. They had kept separate checking accounts. His money was his, hers was hers, plus their money market funds together. But *he* paid the bills. *He* oversaw every move they made. *He* had all the power. "I don't need a lot, but I deserve more than I get from you."

"Didn't I buy you your brother's car? $8,900. That kooky outfit you wanted for the party?" He still was not angry and it infuriated her to see how calm he remained.

"Damn you! I want *passion!* The kind of passion you give out to The Corporation!"

Ooops. There it was, right out in the open. Laid bare. Passion. Sex. She was complaining about sex.

He stood up. "Want a glass of cider?"

"Sit down and *listen!*" she screamed.

No, I'm not going to talk sex. He knows how I feel. That would be a trap. He's not going to change. He is what he is in that department. He can be loving, even tender. But he's not romantic, not emotional. He's logical and calculating. Devoid of passion. God, I'd love him to be wildly romantic in bed. But I can't expect that. I'll never get it from him.

However, Tracy knew where passion lay. Wasn't Glen an example? Work! *I'll get my kicks from my work.* Just like he does. If I don't have his children, if I don't get his passion, if I don't get his time, I'll have my work. *Work of my own.* Her breath quickened and she seized the moment. She had been planning to enlarge her mail-order business. She had ideas about how to expand her lines into gifts and take on other catalogues. She was creative. A self-starter. If she could get some business help from Glen, she could proceed.

She would not make a scene. Would not be disruptive about his assumption of authority. Forget the sex part. Don't talk about passion. Don't discuss children. Don't discuss power. *Talk money.* He'll understand that. He's reasonable and he's not tight-fisted.

"Okay. I'm listening. What's your gripe?" He sat down all ears. "Tell me."

"I don't ask for much, do I?" He didn't answer, but he was paying attention. "I want something. Very badly."

"It's yours," he said, all generosity, eager to get it done, finished.

"You do your thing, Glen, now I want to do mine."

"Which is?"

"Enlarge my mail-order business into gifts, household items, small appliances. I can drop-ship and take on other catalogues. I've never had more confidence in anything I've done. I believe in this project and I have the retail experience behind me. I can execute it. But I need your help to get started."

"Sure. Anything you want, Trace. I'm all for you. What do you want?"

"Well."

"Be precise. How can I help you?"

"With financial backing. I'll need funding." She paused. How would he take it?

"Write it all down. Show me what you want to do and what it'll take." He drew himself up. "I'll see that you get it."

"You will?"

"Of course. I'm all for it. I want to help. I'll even check your copy." He stood up. Interview over.

"That'll be great!" Her anger dispersed like dust particles and floated away. "You know," she explained in a gush of zeal, "I function well alone. My work is alone, I enjoy my time alone. I don't need a lot of people. Just some good music and my work." Do this for me and I'll stay out of your hair was her message.

"Then you'll be happy? I want you to be happy."

"Thank you." She gave him a radiant smile. He was a generous man. With his backing, she could do her own thing. Expand her business. Pour herself into her work. That would be her reward. Money made it all possible. "You won't be sorry," she promised. She felt triumphant. She had won.

So they wouldn't have kids. Children need a lot of giving. Emotional giving. A mommy and a daddy. *Two* parents. Glen's first priority would always be his company. Not much left over for a baby. He wouldn't be there for a child. She'd wind up trying to be both parents. Twenty years of child-rearing on her shoulders alone. He'd make her a baby, but she'd raise it.

No way. Let other women rounding thirty quit their jobs and have babies, worried that their biological clocks were running out. Let other wives give up their work, their job, their dream, in order to be mommies. Not me. I'll run a business. Travel with Glen. Be a corporate wife. Live well. And have the excitement of heading my own company. Having babies is not for everyone.

"I'll start small, work right from the house, okay?" She was out of her skull with delight. Eager to spill her plans now that she had his promise to back her. "I'll need a vertical file, okay? Maybe a small personal computer to keep track of the orders. And a copying machine."

"Just put it all on paper, Trace." And he shot out of the room.

"I will. I will," she called to his back.

In Stage Two, Tracy has come to acknowledge her feelings as real. Many of these are new feelings. A new view of who her husband is and where they are going. She has asked Glen to pay attention. She has voiced a flood of complaints. She feels entitled to speak up.

Unlike women who start out in Stage One and move gingerly into Stage Two, Tracy was a child of the sixties who knew how to express herself. She had no trouble letting it all hang out. However, her confusion in Stage Two is typical of corporate wives engaged in the struggle for a new honesty. There is the tug of war between Good Wife and New Awareness. A fussy period of coming to terms with the man they've married and the woman they've become.

Scratch the surface of Glen, the perfectionist, and Tracy discovers a bundle of anxieties and insecurities. A man fearful that at any minute someone, somewhere will find out how imperfect he is. So he must never let up, waste time, or show anyone the soft side of his underbelly. His restraint and control render him passionless. A fact Tracy deplores, but can no longer deny.

She cannot change him; she sees that clearly.

She also recognizes his hypochondria as an overpowering need to be loved and approved by others. She sees that his self-esteem is based on how others perceive him. Basically, Glen, for all his tough, is insecure. The corporate image bolsters his ego. He clings to it like the drunk hanging on to the street lamp. Tracy understands. A person like that needs constant reassurance.

Glen gets much of it from the corporate system of status, money, and power. It is what he fights for all the time. More reassurance. Bigger and better trappings of power. A position of command and control. These confirm his worth, his rank. But it is not enough. He needs to take more from Tracy. He becomes a taker. He consumes her time, her energy, and her emotional support in his need for unending approval.

When Tracy asked him for help with her business, she chose the path he would most likely respond to. She did not ask for his time; he has no time. She did not ask for his emotional involvement; she made it clear she would work alone. She asked him for something he could afford: financial backing. Would he be generous to her financially? Would he show his support? Would he write her a check? Of course! In writing her a check, he would reinforce his image. He was a powerful man and a generous husband. His ego was properly stroked.

Tracy was angry, but she, too, had been socialized to be "nice." However, at this point, she questioned her husband's assumption of authority. What gives *him* the power to decide? Why do his choices impose behavior on her?

She begins to feel her own needs more urgently. She becomes more aware of what she wants. It is scary to acknowledge these feelings. However articulate she may be, Tracy doesn't want to provoke a real clash of wills. She is not willing to be disruptive. She can't even define what she wants. Not exactly. Because Stage Two is all scratch and itch. She is dancing around herself, doing an Indian War Dance with her true self at center, the bonfire licking her feet. One thing for sure. No kids.

Carol

The cannon that shot Carol headfirst into Stage Two was discovering that her husband had a mistress. Smack! Crash! Pow! Her world crumbled like a toothpick castle. She was forty-one then and that was seven years ago. But the humiliation still backs up like vomit in her mouth.

Her husband's lover was a thirty-one-year-old divorcee with three little kids. She was his tennis doubles partner at Rockledge, their posh country club.

"I should have seen it coming. I wore blinders," she wept to everyone for months.

And even now, at forty-eight, with Ed back home, her breakdown past history, her bouts with alcoholism and agoraphobia, her years of analysis with three psychiatrists, she still totters unsteadily in Stage Two.

What threw her off, she had cried to her women friends, was that they had never fought, never raised their voices even with their two daughters. Plenty of sarcasm from Ed, but no rip-roaring open clashes.

"I should have read the signals. The lipsticked cigarettes in the Caddy's ashtray. Our feeble sex life. His extended business trips to Las Vegas and Palm Springs. I should have questioned his high lifestyle at the Beverly Hills Hotel and the Polo Lounge." But The Investment House had tentacles everywhere, a corporate giant of immense power and prestige. As vice president, dealing with millions in portfolio bonds and commercial paper, Ed had to go where the action was, had to be with the top honchos.

For all the years he climbed the corporate ladder and she smiled and played corporate wife, for all the years she played suburban mommy and did the PTA bit, the chauffeuring, baked cookies, was class mother—she was willing to be whatever Ed wanted her to be. When she had married Ed at nineteen, the fifties message was *push your man ahead.*

From the start, Carol was a round peg in a square hole as a corporate wife. At elegant corporate parties, she couldn't think of a word of small talk, and her hands trembled as she brought the champagne to her mouth. The Investment House people intimidated her. The women were intensely competitive, blatant social climbers. Their luxurious fashions spelled power, and they courted the "right" people for their husbands. She had none of their imposing smoothness. She was an outsider in their cliques of haughty, indulged women who seemed to sneer at her.

She was painfully shy. She felt safe only when she was glued to her tall, handsome husband's arm. People liked Ed. He was sociable and sexy, gregarious and fun.

"You're a lucky lady," they told her.

She smiled until her face cracked. Little did they know.

"Look at that. Another package from Saks," he snorted when the UPS man arrived. "Can you fit it in your closets?"

"You're the one who wants me to be the elegant hostess next week. I'm rising to the occasion."

"Your bills are putting me in the poorhouse." He liked the expression. Poorhouse. Once her youngest, Tina, had come crying to her. "Daddy says we're going to the poorhouse."

It was true. Shopping was the only thing that gave Carol satisfaction. She spent days in Saks and Bloomingdales buying and canceling, charging and returning. Her monthly statements were lengthy documents of transactions, of credits and balances.

When she complained that the house looked shabby, Ed called in a famous decorator and gave him a hefty budget to redo the living room, dining room, center hall, and den. When she complained that the pool needed attention and the grounds looked scruffy, he hired a landscaper-designer and an oriental gardener. When she complained about chauffeuring the girls to dance classes, cheerleader workshops, and karate instructions, he bought each girl a car on her seventeenth birthday. Anything money could buy.

The truth was that Carol was tumbling into a paralyzing depression.

On the one hand, she was blazing angry. Her hostility was burning a hole in her stomach. On the other hand, she could not voice her furies. She kept her resentments bottled up. Her complaints came in mild whines, carefully couched in housewifery terms centered on domestic issues that Ed smoothed over by spending money. The pleasure of buying a $2,800 Galanos gown was largely in seeing his face when the bill came.

The repressed hostility turned rancid and plunged her into a depression. Her first psychiatrist took her back to her childhood view of herself as gawky, clumsy, and inarticulate. A second analyst lanced the pustules of a painful eight-year education in a Roman Catholic convent. However, the more corporate functions she attended and the more that was required of her, the less she could perform. At forty-one, her $400,000 house now decorated to the nines, the pool and cabanas a showcase, the kids were grown, what was there to do?

"Would you like me to get a job, help you out with money?" She returned the sarcasm of his "poorhouse" remarks.

He laughed derisively. "You? What could you do?"

She was relieved, not angry, at his comment. She would have died if he said sure, go to work. Who would hire her? An over-forty housewife who had never worked. What *could* she do? Sell pantyhose in a mall at minimum wage?

The discovery of his affair plunged her over the abyss.

She stopped eating. At five-foot-nine, she went down to ninety-eight pounds. She became terrified to leave the house. A trip to the supermarket sent her into an anxiety attack of dizziness and sweats. She stayed home and went on compulsive buying sprees via mail-order houses and telephone. A third therapist diagnosed her as agoraphobic. She ordered food by phone and had it delivered. She turned to baking and spent eight-hour days ordering and sorting her ingredients, mixing and baking and wrapping and freezing.

She screamed and screamed. She threw things and hollered into the empty house. She asked all the questions that had been unasked for more than twenty years. To achieve a catharsis, Carol unleashed her dragons.

They didn't declare war until the affair came out in the open.

"Get out! Bastard! Fucking filthy bastard! Out! Bastard, bastard, bastard! Fucking, fucking bastard!"

She hurled their wedding picture at him, tore his clothes out of his closet, kicked his shoes down the stairs.

He took an apartment ten miles away.

When she started putting away half a bottle of vodka a day, she went into therapy five days a week. The girls were devastated. They made excuses to go on trips or to sleep over with friends.

"Everyone in town knew about your father's mistress. I was the object of gossip and whispers for years," she told them.

Buried in the deep soil underneath her fury was a cold terror about her economic security. If they divorced, would the house be taken away from her? Would she be left with nothing? She spoke to a lawyer, found a few bank books. Ed agreed to give her $40,000 a year, tax free. Could she manage on that?

A tremendous guilt engulfed her.

"God," she sobbed her heart out to her friends. "What'll I do?"

In a series of breast-beating *mea culpas*, she blamed herself. "It's all my fault. I should have done more for myself. I should have been a pair of ragged claws. I was weak and dependent," she told her analyst. "He kept me that way. . . no, no, no!" she shouted to correct herself. "I did it to myself because it was easier. Safer to avoid a struggle than to take a risk."

Some days the anger overwhelmed her. When someone phoned and asked where's Ed, she'd say, "Ed? He's out fucking."

Her women friends and psychiatrist saved her life.

For six months Ed continued to live in his apartment. Then around Christmas, he just came home. A couple of suits moved back in. There was no discussion. One sentence: "I don't see her anymore."

She took him back. To cut down on her drinking, she smoked two packs a day. They established separate bedrooms. Separate lives. A public stance.

One day over coffees, the woman across the street exchanged confidences with her.

"My husband and I have an arrangement," she told Carol.

"How?"

"I look out for myself."

Carol gave her a quizzical look and the woman roared. She was an Italian beauty. Carol admired her. She was a wonderful mother, chairperson of the Muscular Dystrophy drive, a community leader. She kept a lovely home, entertained lavishly, lived well.

"How?" she repeated.

"Affairs, dummy. Men. Lovers." And she filled Carol in on her new lover, a professor at the local college whose name she protected, but whose lovemaking techniques she spelled out in rapturous terms. "He gets lots of free time. Why waste it?" She gave Carol a wicked wink.

Carol tried not to act astonished. But that night alone on the cold sheets she nearly shouted it out loud. "Of course! Why not! Look at her. Isn't what she's doing fantastic? Why am I missing the boat? What am I saving it for?"

She and Ed were into the fifth year of their truce. No sex. No passion. No companionship. And she thought: *if fucking is okay for him, why not me, too?*

Her first two affairs were retaliatory acts with a couple of professional lechers who performed well. But she was too nervous to find it satisfying. Her next affair, three months later, was with the man who installed the new burglar alarm. It was easier, more casual. Less guilt-ridden. Even, admit it, less retaliatory. Now she understood about "I look out for myself."

Within a year she found a new lover, an exciting boy of twenty-six, her daughter's age, who stayed at her place over the weekends whenever Ed was away. He was a graduate student in marine biology.

"You taught me to enjoy sex," she told him as he unzipped his jeans. "I didn't know anything about passion until I met you."

He flushed with modest delight. "You're puttin' me on."

"I mean it."

"Thank you, ma'am," he tipped an imaginary hat, then tickled her bare feet. "You're a lot of fun, babe."

"Babe?" Once long ago, Ed had called her babe when they had been the golden people and life was delicious.

The price of dependence was pain! The status of protected wife meant phony emotions, few rewards, an absence of passion.

It took a twenty-six-year-old boy to teach her oral sex. Why not?

"I like it, I like what you did to me. But I could never ask for it," she told him afterwards and cradled him in her arms.

"Ask!" he told her.

And she did.

Carol was poorly prepared to arrive at Stage Two and unlike Tracy, she panicked, broke down, fell apart. It took her years of analysis to work through to a level of heightened awareness.

Unlike Tracy, who could harness her strengths and find passion in work, Carol could not do it alone. The breakdown, the drinking, the agoraphobia, the anorexia all pushed her to hit bottom.

Some corporate wives hit bottom before they pull out. They are quietly stashed away in dry-out centers or rehab hospitals, hidden from public scrutiny. Nevertheless, they are casualties. Basket cases. They have to bleed before they heal. Only then can the scar tissue form.

Actually, Carol wavered in Stage Two, sliding back to Stage One, wobbling back into Stage Two, complaining and complying in her utter confusion, a rattled boxer flung against the ropes. Good Wife versus self-interest. Where could she be safe? Safety is uppermost in the minds of corporate wives in Stage Two.

If Ed's affair hadn't crashed through the roof of her house, she would probably have continued playing nice corporate wife, undermining Ed, slipping into a deeper depression rooted in her dependency. That dependency spells impotence is one of the discovered truths of Stage Two. What a woman chooses to do with that knowledge is the story of what happens to women who venture into the hazardous zone of Stage Three.

Carol's affair with the twenty-six-year-old graduate student ended without bitterness. He took her to some of his classes. In the spring catalogue, she filled out a form to enroll as a nonmatriculated student. She got a B + on her first term paper and declared computer science as her major.

Her ex-lover helped her out a few times with her homework.

8

The Dangerous Journey: A Thrilling Metamorphosis

Remember M. C. Escher from Chapter 1, the Dutch artist who changed fish into reptiles and then into birds? Who transformed inanimate geometric figures into living creatures?

In Stage One we observed wives content with their status quo.

In Stage Two we observed women starting out on a journey, beginning their metamorphosis, slowly changing the outlines that defined them. We saw them redrawing their parameters and re-shaping their positions in the journey through Stage Two. A barely observable line moved in one direction. Another line moved in another direction. Altering themselves, they changed their form. Like an Escher figure, they became another creature.

What are their most outstanding characteristics?

THE WOMEN IN STAGE TWO

Reassessment

1. They *reassess* their position in the family hierarchy and find it seriously lacking. Like adolescents, they begin to question "Daddy's"

authority over them. Are *his* goals, *his* rules always the right ones? Of course not! Then why is he the final authority? Their reassessment compels them to reexamine their lives.

Confusion

2. They are *confused* and they feel shaky. Never having questioned his assumption of authority before, they now begin to probe into sensitive areas. They ask delicate questions. They find that his answers are no longer satisfactory. They experience rising discontent.

Complaints

3. So they begin by voicing small *complaints* wrapped in sweet smiles. Gingerly, diffidently, they tiptoe around their husband. They begin with trivial issues, perhaps about small household matters, in order to keep a lid on their real feelings.

Testing

4. Wives do not have confidence. They *test* the waters cautiously. Voicing complaints makes them uncomfortable and guilty. Shouldn't they be grateful? They have so much materially. They feel unworthy of asking for anything else. Which only confuses them further.

Feelings

5. Although they cannot yet deal fully and honestly with their disquieting feelings, they begin to trust themselves a little bit. They confront their *buried feelings* in private because they do not yet feel entitled to them. And they discover new levels of truth.

Fear

6. They are *frightened*. Acknowledging new feelings makes them nervous and shaky. They may begin to rely on drugs or alcohol to get them through the day. They may have a brief discreet affair, one that can't jeopardize their marriage. They are still too fearful to make sweeping changes, too frightened to give up their security and safety.

Power

7. They perceive correctly that their *powers* have diminished, their identities have been lost. Their husbands have catapulted smartly to the top and *gained* power, while they have *lost* power. The early "team approach," in which husbands respected their wives' input, now withers and dies. The wives feel powerless.

Dependency

8. Wives in Stage Two find *dependency* has lost its attraction. They feel depressed and they acknowledge that their present position no longer satisfies them. They are irritated and they want desperately to make changes. But how can they move out of their established dependency?

Permission

9. Often they ask for *permission* to make a small change, it is their strategy to avoid appearing demanding, because they still need to retain their husband's good will. "May I take a little part-time job?" "May I open my own bank account?" They are self-deprecating and terribly grateful if he approves. It seems like a giant step forward to them.

Urgency

10. A growing urgency propels them along, pressing a hard hand against their back. They are no longer content. Now they are contentious. Their feelings overflow. Powerful needs are uncorked. What can they do about it? Despite their compliance, wives in Stage Two *are* changing. Ever so slightly and very slowly, at first. Imperceptibly, perhaps, like a line barely altered by Escher. But as they move further into Stage Two, they raise harder, more disquieting questions. They recognize their discontent as their true feelings. Will I live out my life this way? Will I be dependent on his good will forever?

When a woman enters Stage Two, she finally hears her discontent. It becomes louder and clearer until she has to deal with it. That's when she speaks up and the lightning flashes.

It is not until Stage Three that she sees the sky crack wide open with the electricity of her new feelings. It is not until Stage Three that a *living creature* emerges and the metamorphosis can be completed.

Stage One is a *childlike* stage in which "Daddy" tells her what to do and how to do it. Where her pleasure is derived from pleasing Daddy. Daddy knows best. Daddy will take care of his little girl. You do not question the authority of Daddy, you are grateful he is there for you.

Stage Two is *adolescence*. That rebellious period where compelling new feelings are awakened; where complaints are aired; where fearful questions are asked; where the old rules established by a husband's authority don't hold up; where the corporate wife flings her arms out to see how far she can reach, testing, not always with knowledge of what she is doing.

Stage Two is a tricky period for corporate wives because, like adolescents, they are so needful, so scared. They cannot cut the hauser and sail out to sea yet. They haven't the skills, the convictions, nor the confidence. They are not yet ready to leave their snug harbor, but they know there is something better. How can they reach it?

The fish is changing to a reptile!

New awareness makes them more wanting. They complain. They argue. They resent.

"Stop treating me like a baby!" adolescents cry. And wives in Stage Two cry out similarly.

To make matters worse, Daddy does not want to give up control. He's the parent, the boss.

Despite the discomfort of Stage Two, many wives do make important changes. From fish content in their comfortable pond, they crawl out of the water onto the land and become a higher species. They are the reptiles in the Escher paintings and while they move slowly and cautiously, they breathe air now. They fill their lungs and move onto this new terrain. There is solid ground beneath their feet.

A bit here, a bit there, they alter themselves. They acquire flashing new perceptions of where they've been and what they might become. In Stage Two, women discard their babyish behavior of Stage One.

They are changed, different, and they try to behave in new affirmative ways.

As in adolescence, there is a lot of floundering during this period. Discomfort increases, displacing the comfort and mindless security of Stage One. These corporate wives are scared and miserable.

Many corporate wives reported that they did not really feel *alive* until they were in Stage Three. Like Escher's inanimate objects, they felt like objects pushed around on a chess board, with their husband in charge, playing the game. Even wives in Stage Two, who griped and complained, continued to let their husbands make their decisions. They remained dependent women behaving according to his pleasure, adjusting to his goals. It was he who held the power, he who told them what their roles were.

Stage Three requires a strength and confidence some women lack. It takes a special kind of courage.

Stage Three can be the greatest adventure any woman can experience. Never has she played for higher stakes!

9

Born to Stage Three: Darlene

Darlene is thirty-one, exactly the same age as Jane whom you met in Chapter 2. Like Jane, she is married to a man in corporate life. Like Jane, she views the corporation as an opportunity to move up. Like Jane, she intends to get there.

Here the comparison ends.

Darlene is worlds apart from Jane.

She was a black child of the sixties. The civil rights movement belonged to her. She observed life. She watched. She listened. And she figured it out early in life. Mama made babies and scraped by on Daddy's janitor job. But not Darlene. Bright and gutsy, she knew in sixth grade that she would live on her own terms, set her own course, and pursue her own goals. Her mother's example taught her that she would never, never, *never* rely on a man to get her there.

Like Jane, Darlene had dreams. But Mama had warned her, "Dreams is okay, honey. Long as ya do for yourself."

From Mama she learned to be practical, to stretch a dollar with a smile. By twelve, she was street smart and wise.

By high school, she knew what she wanted. And she went after it with a soft touch. She excelled. She made people like her and want to help her. She was sociable and quick. Mr. Steiner, her social studies teacher, helped her win a scholarship to Essex County Community College. She enjoyed her success. It taught her that she could achieve, and she liked the taste of rising in the world. She also had a long streak of pragmatism that ran, like an iron bar, down her back.

Her mother was a religious woman, pious and humble. She often told her: "Darlene honey, see it clear. No place where the sun always shine. No perfect man. No perfect job."

And Mama was right.

She married Calvin—three years younger than she and barely out of high school—when she was twenty-one. Cal joined The Company. It sounded like heaven: a paycheck every week, job security, health benefits, reviews and raises. Cal was a hunk, six-feet-six, and The Company was avid to show its commitment to affirmative action. They didn't even tell Cal to get rid of his Afro, and he wore it like a badge of honor.

But in less than two years, Cal turned cranky, impatient. "I don't want to wait for the year 2000 to move up." Other guys were edging into managerial spots, passing him by. He developed a personality conflict with his immediate superior and demanded an examination of his rights through The Company's grievance procedures.

Cal's performance reviews became "inaccurate." He was passed over for a third promotion. He became enraged, paranoid. He began to document every move he made for his own protection. As his anger rose, he slipped into a muddy depression. He felt that his troubles were not of his making. He felt powerless. Frustration, anger, depression pulled his performance down. Would they fire him? Probably not. The Company had a reputation for moving people sideways, for making them uncomfortable. But firing a highly visible Black might be sensitive.

"Why don't you quit?" Darlene asked. "Change jobs if you're so damn unhappy. Get out."

But inertia glued him there. The power of The Company spelled security. Another company would mean starting over. There was comfort—even if perverse—in a known level of pain.

For two-and-a-half years Darlene and Cal were at odds. She wound up consoling him, advising him. They avoided going out with Company people who, he complained, gave him no respect. He leaned on her emotionally. They nearly separated.

And Darlene came to see Cal as a square peg in a round hole.

"I know he won't move up," she admitted to her sister, "he hasn't got the knack of sociability or whatever it takes."

Like the little girl at her mother's kitchen table who watched and listened, she now studied Cal. His negative example told her two things she *didn't* want. *I won't be locked into a job I hate. I won't hang back as a sidekick to my husband.*

Throughout Cal's struggle, Darlene was making good decisions about herself, feeling her own powers. She did well in her first teaching job. But the second grade routine soon became boring. Should she quit? Why not? She felt capable and strong. She also needed to get away from Cal.

"I've been leading and he's been following. The stronger I get, the worse he gets," she told a friend.

She knew she could outstrip him and she felt no guilt over it. She felt competitive, ambitious, itchy to get going; Cal felt depressed, stuck, beaten.

One Thursday night, she saw the look on his face, grabbed her jacket, and said, "So long. I'm going to the movies."

One weekend he disappeared, returned Monday with no comment.

Over a pepperoni pizza they tried to talk it over.

"Today it takes two salaries to make it," she explained with the patience of a second grade teacher. "Most couples are supporting a mortgage and car payments and they're overextended."

She saw defeat in his eyes. Is it a macho thing? A reflection on men that they can't do it alone, without their wife's salary?

She tried a more positive approach. "I like working!"

She avoided saying that she was feeling her own powers. It wasn't just the salary she brought in, it was all the rest of it. Getting dressed up every morning. Driving to work with the Supremes cassette turned up. Quit teaching and have babies like her poor Mama? No way. She was cut out for better things. It bothered her that her husband was in a rut, that he couldn't shake off his problems, that he was digging in deeper every year. But she couldn't hand him his own confidence. And she had a powerful need to develop herself, to push harder, to find her full potential.

She shoved the pizza box aside.

"I'm quitting teaching, Cal. I'm handing in my resignation."

"What? Why?" He was puzzled and he looked a little scared.

"I'm bored."

"What will you do?"

"Fly!"

"Fly?" He was confused.

There was a tint of pleasure in playing it out this way. In fact, she had planned it all down to the last detail. Had chosen the moment. "The best airline. I'm going to train the end of June. Stewardess. More money. Travel. Lots of benefits." She enumerated them for him and he returned her a glum approval.

"Stewardess, huh. If that's what you want, okay."

They both knew the separation could lead to other kinds of pressures. Being apart could strangle a marriage. Or give it air. It was transparent that he resented her freedom. Resented her decision made without consulting him. Resented that he would be left behind.

She reached across the table and took his hand. "I wish I could be a pregnant and barefoot wife for you, but it's not me."

"I wish I could be a corporate exec for you, but it's not me." He pulled her around. She fell into his lap and snuggled against him.

But in the morning there were truths to face up to. Cal doesn't want to compete. *And I do.* Cal is blocked because he never went to college. *And I did.* Cal's afraid. He needs security. He doesn't have the will to change jobs. *And I do.*

She felt good about herself, and good things were happening to her.

"I feel zippy, Mama. I feel gorgeous. I feel confident."

"Go on, honey, do for yourself. Only don't forget. No place where the sun always shine. Put it clear in your head, girl."

A year later when her father died and left her mother to raise the three younger girls, she quit flying and came home. She took a job as an assistant editor with a publishing house. It drove her crazy to sit in her cubbyhole with her formica desk. After three years she quit that job, too. Darlene was never afraid to quit a job and strike out fresh. She figured: *why not? I can deliver the goods. I have what it takes.*

She looked around. Seriously. Intently. Thoroughly. She measured herself against the teachers hanging on for retirement. Against the stewardesses who turned out to be no more than glorified waitresses. Against the editors who brought home armfuls of manuscripts, twenty extra hours of reading when they left on Friday afternoon.

Where should she look? Where should she go?

She had the innate skills to be successful. She was pushing thirty, with three careers behind her: teaching, flying, editing. Where could her talents be best appreciated?

It came to her in a flash of recognition. The Company!

An article in *The New York Times* had described *a new elite of corporate women.* A survey of the largest corporations in America had revealed that half of those married women, "the new elite," earned as much or more than their husbands. Seventy percent had no children. The essential nature of these women was their ability to set their own goals and rise *independent of a man.*

"That describes me," she thought.

She acknowledged her new priority. Work, not a man, would be the great love of her existence. She would forego raising children. Self-determination would mean success.

She knew their corporate policies inside out. Cal had educated her. They were hiring women, hiring blacks, recruiting a new sales force of tigresses. Excitement beat in her throat. Just because Cal was la-di-da, that didn't exclude her from a turf that suddenly appeared verdant. The myth of meritocracy clutched her. She would beat The Company at its own game.

She measured her advantages.

The skill to be political. To look out for herself. To remain outwardly cordial. To pinpoint a good situation. To be savvy.

Miraculously, Cal did not object. They'd be in different buildings. Different departments. No crossing the same chain of command.

As long as they kept their personal lives out of business, Company rules did not prohibit hiring married co-workers.

The Company had a strong corporate culture, a way of doing things that focused on a sense of mission. They created "heroes" through the company paper. They had "rituals" that could spin her to the center of the action. Their work hard/play hard dedication to sales and customer service appealed to her. Her social skills had been honed as a teacher and a stewardess. Her communication skills had been polished as an editor. Put them all together they spelled a career at The Company.

"Would you mind?" she asked in her most charming deferential voice.

"The Company runs at a near frenetic pace," he replied by way of warning.

"I can handle it."

And she did.

The training program was clearly a series of carrots held before donkeys. A 100% *Club* was The Company's treat for meeting a quota. *The Golden Circle* was a classier reward given to those ringing up the most money. A trip to Hawaii, Madrid, an exotic company-paid vacation. Promotion and recognition would come in three years. Or else. Perform or Reform.

Darlene had no trouble with that message. She understood it. Even admired it.

From the first day of training, she took a quick survey of her sales team. They were arranged around the conference table, wearing their proper images. For white guys, it was pure jock: blonde hair, blue eyes, muscular. But additionally, the sales force was now hiring blacks and women. Darlene was five feet eleven, taller than some of the studious black men who were wearing glasses. Not a hunk, like Cal, among them.

She caught on quickly to the company taboos. Held them up against the lens marked "New Elite Women." Could she hack it? She scrutinized her every move, measured her effect in smiles and gestures in the bathroom mirror. In place of dangle earrings it was conservative studs from now on. Gold balls or six-millimeter pearls. A tiny diamond would be a nice Christmas present to herself. Her wardrobe was easy. Darlene had a slim model's body that moved well.

"I'm on display," she told her mirror every morning. "How'm I doing?"

Guys could get loose and get drunk and unraveled, but not a woman. Guys could fool around as long as it was done with discretion. But a woman who flaunts it is removed to "special assignment," The Company's Siberia.

For a guy who daringly stepped over the line, it's goodbye, Charlie; he, too, is whisked away. In the good ole, *ole* days, rumor had it that guys had call girls come in for conventions. Now even the men were clean. Stress and surveillance were everywhere.

"When I'm out socially, I'm still at work and I never let my guard down," she told a sweet young thing straight out of Rutgers.

What surprised her was the drugs. Not pot, which was considered passé and for kids. The drug of choice was cocaine. Snorting coke at parties was the "in" thing to do. Older executives drank to be sociable. The under forty young lions did coke. A lot of their money went to it. Incredibly they made their connections out jogging.

Darlene kept herself clean. She didn't need coke to energize herself. Work turned her on.

The new inductees were treated well. The young women fresh out of college, with no work experience, were naive, all rah-rah-rah for The Company. They were easily seduced by the carrots. But she, with three job experiences behind her, saw the challenges for what they were. Corporations were not humanistic by intent. But to be so was good business. The *Company cares for you* motto was a crock, she thought.

Of course, the superstars operated by their own rules, they were the exceptions. The guy who knew how to cover his ass, how to pull out a ready alibi, was respected. If he could bend the rules and get away with it, swell. But the guy who couldn't do it—*well*, he got chewed up. They'd have a meeting and "forget" to tell him.

She found a mentor, Judy, a Jewish woman, forty-four, who

showed her how to study the board like a chess game. "Know who the players are and where the moves are. Where the crossfire is coming from."

It was Judy who explained the difference between the *handout* plan and the *bonus* plan. "Your husband's on the handout plan. He gets a review and a raise if he's a good boy. You're on the bonus plan. With bonuses you can double your salary. It's up to you."

"What about promotions? I don't know what I'm worth."

"Whatever they offer, ask politely how they arrived at that figure. They'll give you a lot of double talk. Act contemplative."

She wanted to be where Judy was, on the path to the new elite, and Judy was generous to her, eager to push a younger woman ahead. She tooted Darlene's horn at every opportunity. And Darlene caught the rhythm of it. All the superlative reviews in the world won't get you to the next rung unless a mentor on the next level is pulling you up.

Judy knew a lot about the hazards of stress and anxiety. She taught Darlene to pace herself. "Avoid red meat, no sugar, no caffeine." Judy, divorced, her children grown, lived alone. "When I hit the door, I'm tired, hungry, lonely, and my batteries are run down. That's when my personal life turns to shit. So I go back to some conventional wisdom."

"Which is?"

"Be good to yourself, Darlene. I've seen a lot of casualties fall by the wayside. Look out for yourself."

The same message as Mama: "Do for yourself, honey."

Judy, comfortable in the $50,000 range, was not unaware of being a woman. Macho was alive and well throughout the company. "They exclude me from the locker room repartee. They have their little secrets. They patronize me and clean up their language for me. They don't say shit or fuck it to me." She laughed. "They still like women to be decorative and submissive: the old why aren't you home planting petunias, sweetheart?"

For all her toughness, Judy began every day with meditation. "I dispel anger that way. I talk about my feelings to myself. If I fail, I try again. I tell myself, 'Bag it, lady!' when I'm feeling sorry for myself. 'This is what you want. Don't grouse.' "

Darlene took Judy's advice to heart. Instead of diamond earrings, she bought herself a stationary bike for Christmas because Judy stressed physical activity. She joined a twice-a-week aerobics class. And in three years she gobbled up all the carrots.

A company-paid trip to Rome was followed by a promotion to managerial level. And now, to cap it all, came a chance to move up another rung if she'd relocate to Washington, D.C. Should she go?

"If that's what you want, you figure it out," Cal grumbled. She was already making more than he and her trajectory was flashing in neon: up, UP, UPPPP! A blow to his ego.

What to do?

She wanted the marriage. She wanted the career. But there were practical limits to what family life could withstand if she commuted to D.C. Cal would not leave The Company, would not relocate for her. That was out of the question. Would she become one of the casualties Judy had described?

Give it all up? Never! She had come too far. Had learned too much. Had tasted a little power.

"To move up, you have to move around," a V.P. with four kids had once told her. And she yes-yessed him with a compliant smile.

Now it was her turn. It would put a lot of stress on the marriage—financially, sexually, socially—upstaging her own husband.

But I like money. I like my comfort level. For three years I played my game by their rules. I stopped being a rebel. I fit in. I gave them the image they wanted. I conducted myself the Company way. So it's phony. They pay me for acting phony. It's an ability. I've learned to be tactful, to swing with the punches. I can deal with a boss even though I hate his guts. My goal is to make money. Integrity? I can argue a superior right down to his socks and still let him leave feeling fine. Another consideration: After forty, my face won't look so good. I've been blessed with youth and guts, but I can't ride them forever.

She weighed the pros and cons. The new elite seemed closer, within easy reach.

It's been a nice social club for men for too long. I can give them one helluva ride for their money. If I have to stay up all night for the next two years, I'm going to get there!

It would hurt Cal to say all that. She didn't want to hurt him. But she concluded that it would be better to yank the Band-Aid off in one fast tear than to drag out his pain.

"I have to do it, Cal. We'll work it out."

He sagged a little into the sofa, a huge teddy bear with sad eyes.

She came over to him, nestled against his hulk. "I have to accept it, Cal. Have to have a career of my own, a life of my own. I want the marriage, too."

He nodded.

It offended her sensibilities to ask permission. But this was no time to stand on principle. "Do you mind? Can I go?"

And the big lug gave her back the lie she wanted. "Sure. We'll work it out."

Stage Three is the danger zone. Look out!

There are unknown galaxies to crash into as they swirl in the heavens. Wild air currents to sweep you away. A universe of billions of options twinkling and demanding choices. In Stage Three *the choices are not made without struggle.*

We saw Darlene's struggle: *Should I leave teaching? Or hang on? Should I bolster Cal's ego with polite wifely lies? Or look out for myself? Should I acquiese or compete? What direction should I take?*

In Stage Three every road sign carries a warning: Danger. Watch Your Step.

In *Stage One*, wives are compliant and agreeable, so there is no real struggle.

In *Stage Two*, women reassess their positions and hear the rumbling noises inside them. Like hunger pangs, they are the sounds of discontent. They are confused by those sounds. They are troubled to touch tender hidden feelings. They question their dependency and what it costs them. They may even voice a few tentative complaints. But they do not effectively change the course of their lives. They do not take action.

In *Stage Two*, there is confusion.

In *Stage Three*, women select the active, ongoing struggle.

Struggle? Not such a tough struggle, some argue. Thirty-one is all youth and zeal. If Cal had been successful like Jane's husband, Darlene would have behaved differently, would have been content to let Cal take care of her. Marriage to a loser forced Darlene to choose work. No struggle in that. Hold the applause.

Struggle? What kind of woman emasculates a man with her ambition and competitiveness? Why work for The Company? Why not another company? Wasn't that a hostile act to show up Cal? Darlene is a bitch.

Struggle? All two-salary couples struggle. Most are in a bind over whose job comes first. Usually, it is the one making the most money: the husband who has the power. Since Darlene made more money, she had the power. No struggle. Facts.

Struggle? In an unequal marriage where the wife has grown more than the husband, the marriage can remain the same, end, or change. Darlene's marriage—childless by choice, a commuting marriage by choice—is bound to go down the drain. She'll get what's coming to her.

Most people like Jane. They react to Darlene with dismay and disapproval. What she has chosen to do goes counter to their experience of the Good Wife. If you believe a wife should be dependent and make do, letting her husband support her, Darlene has made poor choices. If you believe a Good Wife hides her ambition, buries her competitive spirit, suppresses her own growth, Darlene made poor choices. If you believe the wife who outearns her husband should withhold her power and pretend—like a fake orgasm—that he makes her come, that it is his power to give her pleasure, then Darlene has made poor choices.

If you believe any of those, you probably also believe in a secret recess (admit it!) that men are babies who need to be coddled, lied to, coaxed, wheedled, and manipulated.

Darlene gave her husband the highest compliment. *I accept what you are, Cal. I want the marriage. Now you must accept what I am.*

What is the alternative? Is sabotaging herself the proper stance?

Is abdicating responsibility for her own life a wiser choice? Is economic self-determination the death knell for a married woman like Darlene?

Wives in Stage Three struggle with these concepts. Then they take action.

10

Smarter than He Is: Georgia

Like Darlene, Georgia discovered that she was smarter than her husband, that she could become more powerful than he was. Unlike Darlene, she took twenty years to discover it. And she was extremely uncomfortable with her discovery. She had been brought up to look up to a husband, to rely on him, a classic Stage One bride. She married Ross one week out of college. He was the handsome only son of a famous, dynamic father who headed an international cosmetic company. Ross would lead; she would follow. That was the plan.

For the first two decades of marriage, it worked out fine.

Raising two rambunctious boys kept her anxiety-ridden and, yet joyful. As the years pulled her along, each new adventure in their upbringing became a test of her talent and organizational skills. She was the creative member of the family. Ross was the mover and the shaker, in charge of the ship.

She had been an art major at Bennington and her paintings and drawings were hung throughout the house. Ross complimented her on each new one; he delighted in everything she did in their home.

"Georgia's creative touch," he'd point out to their guests.

For twenty years he appreciated her artistic side and admired her approach to child-rearing, entertaining, fashion, and home decoration. Life was full, life was sweet. Indeed, motherhood and wifedom were the bookends that held her up.

When the children were small, she made them creative birthday parties. Eschewing the ordinary, she held Dwayne's eighth birthday party at the Museum of Broadcasting, and seated the entire third grade in the private theater to view the original 1960 version of *Peter Pan* starring Mary Martin. Since no food was allowed, and neither her charm nor persistence could persuade the powers-that-be to turn the opulent hi-tech lobby over to her caterers, she invited the parents and kids for refreshments at Mortimer's, the East side "in" place. Hot dogs and pastry pizzas for the kids served from a cart. Fresh oysters and sliced Scotch salmon for their parents served from another cart. The ceiling was layered with helium balloons that said "Dwayne," in silver and royal blue. And every kid brought home as a favor an original cast album.

When it came time to select a prep school, Georgia attacked the problem with the same thorough care. Ross turned the project over to her.

"You do the spade work. Bring me your five top choices and I'll narrow it down. Okay?"

She investigated seventeenth- and eighteenth-century schools whose mission and philosophy were well established. Then she checked out newer schools with outstanding faculty, labs, and libraries. She charted their computer programs, athletic activities, their study-abroad semesters. Exeter? Deerfield? Groton? Phillips? Cheshire? Above all, she rated the prep schools on their ability to place their graduates in top Ivy League colleges. No snobism here. Practical horse sense. A prep school would offer her sons a total environment for learning. And a boost in the world.

She did not resent the fact that Ross delegated "the spade work" to her. She viewed it as another challenge to creative parenting and an opportunity to select for her children the extras in life. They could afford it. Ross was now in six figures.

Hadn't she done the summer camps the same way? Her annual visit to the Camp Shoppe, that exclusive Eastside outfitter of the rich, packed the boys off correctly every year right down to the boilerproof name-tapes sewn into every shirt and sweater and brief and sock. It amused her to see the nannies arrive in limos with the children's measurements. It made her feel superior not to entrust the purchase of a single T-shirt to anyone but herself. The bill spilled into four figures. Ross wouldn't mind.

For twenty years Georgia felt adored by "the three men in my life." She was engrossed, powerful, appreciated. Her sons would be achievers, leaders, like Ross. And her husband was rapidly moving to the top of his father's corporation. They were financially secure, way ahead of their contemporaries. She was thrilled to live through Ross's achievements. He made her feel very much a part of his success, that her role was vital.

From the start she had responsible domestic help, a remarkable live-in housekeeper who kept things running smoothly, so she never felt caged. She continued to take drawing and painting lessons. She had access to the museums of New York and memberships in the Metropolitan and MOMA. She felt alive, attractive, sexy.

Although it worried her that her husband was often away, she and Ross had a powerful sexual bond. They made love vigorously and frequently. Sex was fun. If they quarreled over her overbearing, tyrannical father-in-law who believed women were not to give their opinions at the table, they made it up in bed. And her few fears: Did Ross see other women when he was away? Could the children be kidnapped for ransom?—seemed unfounded and childish when she lay beside Ross. His lean, powerful body excited her. Nevertheless, for insurance, she made sure she got to know all the secretaries, and she instructed her housekeeper never, never to open the door to a stranger.

Child-rearing validated Georgia. She would not let uneducated help raise her children or make their decisions. Scrubbing floors and serving dinner were proper tasks to be delegated. But she alone was in charge of shaping her children's lives. A powerful responsibility.

The bottom fell out unceremoniously, at dinner, two weeks after their twentieth anniversary. The housekeeper was off. Ross had brought in smoked fish and imported cheeses from Zabar's. They were alone.

There was no fanfare. No explanation.

She was chatting, munching on the sturgeon, describing her new dinner suit for the upcoming Christmas party at Sign of the Dove, when she saw the glazed expression on his face. Not listening, hadn't heard a word. It irritated her. To gain his attention, she tried a question. "Should I wear the diamond pin you gave me for my birthday?"

"Huh?"

"Huh," she snapped. "Huh. Is that the best you can do?" Her voice turned raspy.

He looked her straight in the eye. "You're boring. Did anyone ever tell you your conversation is boring?"

He had never insulted her before. Certainly not in the vicious way her father-in-law publicly and crudely degraded her mother-in-law. Oh yes, once he had tried it a long time ago to impress his father, and she had put her foot down. No doormat, Georgia.

"Don't speak to me that way. It's rude. Understand?"

He never tried it again. But now—true, it was in private—he had insulted her. Deliberately.

It was shocking. She? Boring? She had a high opinion of herself. She was confident, she was attractive, effective, artistic. Boring? The taste of fishy vomit rolled up in her throat.

Through the years she had been vaguely aware that he was doing important things. She thought she was, too. She overheard bits of telephone conversations about mergers and buy-outs, stock options and venture capital. But always, *always*, Ross would sit at the table and love to hear her go on about the dumbest little things his dear children did during the day. Loved it! The most trivial details delighted him. He was not interested in being a disciplinarian, he left that to her. And he did not talk a great deal or take business home with him. But how he'd loved to listen.

And now . . .

"Boring? You never thought me boring before," she accused.

"Listen to yourself. Don't you ever have anything important to say?" He rose from the table and walked out of the room.

That night they did not make it up in bed. She slept in Dwayne's room. I'm losing control, she thought. I've spent my whole life raising our children and making a home for us. Now what?

She got up and wandered into Newton's room, that perfect boy's room she had decorated with loving care. She sat on her son's bed and felt the silence accusing her. An emptiness she had tried to suppress wagged a finger at her. That part of her life was over: mothering. She felt a loss of something valuable.

What is it? My identity.

Good God—with the child-rearing over, what do I have for myself? What will I do? Now that the kids are grown, what do Ross and I have together? She struggled for some answers. Golf, she was a competitive golfer. No, he hates the game and I love it. Art? No, he's uninterested. Music? Athletics? Travel? Friends? What life do we have together?

At forty-two, Georgia stared into the dark, into her future. What was there ahead? Like a frightened child, she crept under her son's comforter, clutched his pillow, and pulled the covers over her head.

Stage Two set in like creeping fog.

How had it arrived? When? Complaints tumbled out, flooding her memory. Anger turned her knuckles white.

Perhaps the first signs—if the truth be told—came soon after the boys left home. Between summer camp and boarding school, less and less mothering was required. She missed all that positive feedback and stroking.

For six months she made a hobby of resetting her jewelry. She had a feel for antiques and she purchased several old pieces from estate sales.

Then she refurnished the den and the dining room of their brownstone, replacing the contemporary pieces with nineteenth-century French and English antiques. That whole process took two years of conferences with decorators, visits to galleries, selections of designer fabrics and hand-painted wallpapers. Her creative side was satisfied. Her time was pleasantly filled.

But Ross seemed to care less about the trivia of her day. And she herself felt a growing irritation with him, with herself, with the tentpins of her life which were coming loose. Like the start of a cold, discontent invaded her body, sapping her strength. She prescribed for her lassitude doses of art classes. Like megadoses of vitamin C, they would ward off a serious malady. Museum lectures at the Met on French country furniture. A life drawing class on Saturday mornings. But her discomfort grew. She buried it in sandcastles of busyness. It seemed ungrateful to complain to her husband. And what could he do about it anyhow?

In the dark of the night, she now understood that she and Ross were alone, and their lives would be interfacing without the glue of their children.

Everything had changed.

Truths danced under her eyelids.

Everywhere, in magazines, movies, and television, women's roles were changing. Two close friends, married, had opened boutiques, both well-heeled wives. Why not jump on the bandwagon? I've played my role, done my job to perfection. Supermom is over. This is the eighties. And I'm young and vigorous and capable. Why have I held back?

For twenty years I've had a fine relationship with Ross and a damn good marriage. Am I going to let it all go down the drain? Reluctantly, she reevaluated the time spent refurnishing her home and resetting her jewelry. Two years. Pleasant enough, but treading water. Why continue? I've taken a few false steps, wasted a couple of years. Maybe, just maybe, Ross is right. *I am a bore.* The admission stung her.

She was still angry at him. But perhaps he had done her a favor.

Unless I make changes now, quickly, I'll lose everything. My husband, my marriage, my self-respect.

Georgia seized the moment.

Complaints and arguments were unproductive and not her style. She was smart, effective, creative. What could she do that would combine her talents?

Suddenly she felt enormously hungry. She went down to the kitchen and made herself a sandwich of the leftover Zabar's. She brewed a cup of tea. And at four-twenty in the morning, Georgia pledged to go to work. Work! At forty-two, she felt healthy, financially secure, in her prime. Why not?

That very night, she stepped out of Stage Two, a brief untidy encounter. She took the *Times* off the top of the refrigerator and studied the classified ads. What could she do?

It came to her that before she went out to the job market, she needed training. She enrolled in the New York School of Design without consulting Ross, without asking his permission. Ross was neither for or against it, though it irritated him that she hadn't asked. His attitude was, let's see what happens. At least their conversations became more interesting. She seemed more alive, infused with enthusiasm. Their lovemaking turned lustful. That part pleased him.

But one year later, with a hairy, nervous feeling, she took a job as an apprentice to a New Jersey decorator with a reputation for restoring carriage houses and country homes for the horsey Hunterdon County set. Her knowledge of French and English antique furniture had impressed him at the interview. He liked her thorough attention to details. One year later, he turned over two clients to her.

Ross hadn't seemed to mind when she returned to school. But having a wife whose attention was focused on earning her own money clearly annoyed him. She was often not available. He had to leave messages on her answering machine. And some nights she arrived home after him, too tired from the commute to New Jersey to prepare dinner. She bought a microwave and left him instructions.

"My remote picked up your message, Ross, but I won't be home 'til eight, so stick the pizza in the microwave, okay?"

That message left him angry and resentful. Her big deal job was costing him too much. With the kids gone, they no longer required full-time help and she expected him to pitch in. The worst slap in the face was that she was making decisions without even consulting him. She snapped at him, she demanded he perform tasks that she used to do, and she was getting too damn uppity.

She even opened her own bank account. And the mail coming in from investment brokers was addressed to her! What the hell did she have to know about IRA's? That was a husband's job and he had always taken care of their finances. Now she was asking all kinds of questions, reading magazines like *Money*, pouring over his *Wall Street Journals*.

Ross sensed danger, a loss of power. He was no longer the last word. She argued with him and did what she wanted. She criticized his decisions.

"What's happened to you, Georgia?"

"Well." She snickered. "You can't complain that I'm boring."

"You're turning into one sour apple!"

"Sour apple, hmpf! I call it getting smart."

For twenty years, she was all sweetness and light. Then came a brief period of undefined discomfort. Now, Georgia seemed to be fighting for her life.

Stage One . . . Stage Two . . . Stage Three.

In the past when they were about to have a quarrel, she had often given in before it turned into a real bang-out fight. She had avoided confrontations, burying her anger and resentments for the sake of peace. She'd found solace in lunch with her sister. Starting a new canvas. And Ross, to compensate for any ill feeling, would buy her a pretty nightgown, a leather belt.

She felt flirtatious. It crossed her mind to have an affair. There was this attractive older man, a wealthy client who let her know he found her attractive. Steel gray hair, Paul Newman eyes. His hand held hers too long and he hugged her in a less than fatherly way. But she clung to her fantasy, her dream of Georgia and Ross, the perfect couple. An affair would defile that and rock the very foundation of her fantasy. Ross was her true love. He would always be there for her. Or would he?

He was not a bit supportive when she asked questions about Ginnie Maes. He laughed and told her to stick to her fabric selections. She had deep periods of loneliness and self-doubt. A loss of the intimacy she and Ross had once shared. She felt jealous of a small town friend who didn't have money, but enjoyed a real closeness with her husband that was missing from her own life. She began to feel angry at Ross, envied him his glamorous life of eating in the best restaurants, flying first-class to their plant in Puerto Rico while she froze through the January blizzards.

But she was also sensitive to what Ross was going through. Her personal growth was glorious for her, but he was experiencing a loss of the wife he married. *I'm a different person. He may admire me, but I've cost him some difficult adjustments.* She resolved to be kinder, easier, less demanding. She would not mimic the worst traits of businessmen who become hard and clawing. *Poor Ross is out there working for me and our kids. He has a powerful dad to live up to and that's a tough act to follow. You're too critical, Georgia, too tough on him. Ease up.*

But when he taunted her, all her good intentions flew out the window. They bickered, they quarreled, they fought.

"You're so damn competitive," he sniped.

"Come off it. What's really bugging you?"

"You used to be efficient. This house is a mess."

"You mean I didn't wipe out your drawers this week?" Her voice turned to acid. "Poor baby. Well the hell with your drawers. Wipe them out yourself. I'm not your mommy. I don't provide those services anymore!"

"What services *do* you provide?" His eyes accused her.

"Go to hell!"

A cold war was heating up. The more complaining he became, the more resistant she became. Their voices rose, their tempers flared. Instead of enjoying her wonderful period of achievement, he was pure resentment. Instead of helping her, he resisted. When she asked for financial information, he patronized her. And there were no mentors around to fill the gap.

For six months, Georgia dealt with Ross by avoiding him. On the one hand, she felt gloriously alive working. Her creative and organizational talents were harnessed and she was wild with the pleasure of her work. On the other hand, Ross and she were at each other's throats. Is this what it costs to take charge of your life? Was the price too high? Would she end up a successful interior designer with a marriage on the rocks?

It came to a head when Georgia made the decision to open her own business: Country Antiques. A close friend of her father's was helpful. Her sister pitched in. Her mother gave her $5,000 which, with her own savings, got her started. She didn't ask Ross for a cent, which she thought would please him. It did not. He felt left out, abandoned, exiled.

Unhappily, at the same moment, disaster struck The Corporation.

His father, in a fit of temper, insulted Ross over a decision to let a multinational company buy them out. Ross said no. Daddy said yes. Ross was out of a job.

At the very moment that her future was rosy, her husband was, at fifty, a has-been, an ex-CEO, a man without a job. He did not speak to his father. He sat for hours in the den brooding. While she, delirious with the joy of winning this client and that commercial account, tried to play down her success. Her life was on the upswing, while Ross had the pins knocked out from under him.

They were in different places. Different moods. They had become different people.

For the first time in their marriage, sex could not patch up their troubles. During the day, they argued and he resented her suggestions for getting out of his lethargy. At night in bed, he turned his back on her. Poor Ross, she thought, he's turned fifty, lost his position of power, and his wife is flying high. A hard time.

She tried to see it from his view. She softened her approach, tried to mend fences with his obdurate father. She refused weekend appointments with clients. She watched television with him, brought him a cup of coffee.

It was a relief to see Ross finally pull out of it. He went into corporate financing, wheeling and dealing. He had played it safe all those years in his father's company. Now he was on his own. He asked her for help interviewing, meeting personnel. He included her and she was flattered. He was a tough taskmaster, but she was so pleased to see him pull out of his slump that she took his barked commands and his lack of appreciation as a temporary pressure of starting up.

But once he got settled, he cast her aside without so much as a thank you, ma'am. He wanted her out of the picture, excluded, and he minimized her contribution. He moved to larger quarters, farther away, and he made it clear he wanted her out.

"I don't need you now. Stay out of my hair, okay?"

"You used me," she accused. "You used me to start up. I was your chief cook and bottle washer. I answered your phones, Xeroxed your papers, decorated the space, painted the logo on your walls. I befriended your personnel. Now it's get out time, right?" She was furious.

"Right. I want you completely out of the picture. I make the decisions around here. Go back to Country Antiques."

"Bastard!" she screamed. The pain and anger made red splotches across her cheeks. It was a damaging blow.

Money problems erupted. It bothered Ross that Georgia held on to her money, that she was unwilling to put her earnings into the family pot.

She tried to explain it, but it came out defensive, an apology, as if she were trying to justify her crime. "I have a strong need—maybe it's insecurity—to hold on dearly to what I've earned. I want to keep my money separate. I save some, I spend some."

Money got tighter. So tight Ross actually asked her for some, which she gave freely. But he found it demeaning.

"You should have offered."

"Offered? Too damn bad. I had to ask all our married life." She enjoyed the role reversal. Even in the good years, she had to ask if she wanted a smashing dress. Or save from her household money. He was a slow payer and all decisions about their finances had been in his hands.

She gave him exactly the amount he asked for. But there was icy resentment on both sides.

She began to see many marriages breaking up. Women her age left with little security. She saw her husband getting into a financial bind. Having her own money was a kind of insurance. Her values had changed. She was no longer interested in jewelry. She worried about losing her sex appeal. Everything was changing.

Money seemed the one power that was unchanging. She was not willing to hand it over. Not after his insults, his sniping, his lack of appreciation for the support she had given him. Insecurities raged inside her. When push comes to shove, she thought, I can manage financially. But at a much, much lower level. She saw her fledgling business as a splendid opportunity to build power for herself. There would be strains and conflicts with Ross, but what could she do?

Many nights, unable to sleep, she wandered down to the kitchen for a cup of tea. Am I doing the right thing? Who will take care of me if I don't look out for myself?

Georgia really wanted to achieve, wanted it badly. She now recognized her own growth and was convinced she could be successful. There would be setbacks. But she learned to accept responsibility for her failures. Her business goofs weren't fatal and her client list was growing. She liked the power of making decisions, liked hiring assistants and delegating jobs. She felt enormously gratified to be participating in the exciting world of business. She met interesting monied people who sought her friendship. But in every cup of tea taken in the middle of the night she read the same unresolved question. Should I back off and save my marriage?

Other questions loomed large and frightening. Are our sexual problems attributable to his fiftieth birthday? He hardly touched her anymore. Passion had seeped out of their lives.

She suggested a simpler life. Many of his business associates were winding down rather than starting a new business. Nothing was going to divert him from his goal. They had become two immovable objects.

I've paid through the nose for success, she thought. To develop myself has cost me a lot.

One night they talked it over. The marriage. The kids. Their work.

"We have nothing in common except our children," he told her. "Should we remain married?"

She tried to appear unruffled, but her mouth grew dry. "We've achieved too much to break up a nice thing," she answered weakly. But in bed, with his back turned to her again, she wondered if he was right. He does his thing, I do mine. I go to concerts and plays with women. He's content to sit in front of the TV and do nothing. He's burned out. And I'm raring to go.

Does he have another woman?

Georgia liked male companionship. Was her sex appeal running out? To test herself, she had a one-night-stand while she was on a buying trip—meaningless, no emotional involvement. She wanted to kill the dream, to test whether this hero, this one-man-in-her-life fantasy could be killed. It would be a step toward freedom. But she didn't enjoy it, didn't have an orgasm, and it didn't seem very clean. So she held on to her fantasy.

Georgia and Ross reached a stalemate.

Locking horns didn't work. Complaints didn't work. And a return to compliant bride was impossible. She envied more frivolous women who enjoyed lovers. But something about the way she was brought up mitigated against it. Self-respect, perhaps. Yet she craved more intimacy. More fun.

"It's later than you think," she told herself. "He wants a return to the status quo. I want to bite into the world. We're out of sync. If I stay home and clean the goddamn closets, he blossoms. Well, there are times in my business I could have used a wife, too."

Marriage and career. It looked so easy in the magazines. "Will Ross change, give in a little? I'm so tired of making the sacrifices and adjustments. It's always me. Why can't he bend, change a little?

"He won't," she concluded. "I took the risk, took a chance. What did I really win?" She had spoken to friends who broke up their marriages. They were lonely, so lonely. "I wouldn't want to be a single woman again, out there unprotected," she thought. "But I will not bend anymore. And I can't go back."

Her sister, married to a successful Chicago physician, was her confidante. She phoned her. "I hate to dump on you, Frannie, but it's getting worse."

"Fly up. Take a few days off and it'll all look better," she promised. Big sisters can be a comfort.

"I like my life now. I like having power, making choices. I get a kick out of my business and I like handling money. I'm a person now, Frannie, I can't give that up," she wailed, curled into the corner of her sister's velvet sofa like a lost child.

"Why can't you use the very skills you've developed in business to improve things with Ross? Your ability to handle people, apply it to Ross. As long as there's basic respect and attraction, you can do it." Frannie was an up person, practical, a problem solver.

"How?"

"Try to get what you want in a more subtle way. Soften your approach."

"I feel cheated, Frannie. They told us self-actualization would be whipped cream. Wrong! You can't take educated women in their forties and expect them to stay mommies forever. This feeling of constantly sublimating, giving, giving, giving, sticks in my craw. I'd lose respect for myself if I . . . "

"But Georgia, listen! I don't think it's necessary to change partners. Suppose you and Ross break up. You're going to have to compromise with *any* man to live in harmony. You think there's a whole army of guys out there better than what you have? Men won't give up power. And wrestling a woman for it turns them off."

Georgia could not fault her sister's argument. But it gaver her no comfort to face that fact. "Being in the business world has made me understand Ross better," she admitted. "I understand his pressures. Why can't he understand mine?"

"What are your pressures?"

"I have this terrific life force burning in me. This tremendous desire to live life to the fullest. I like what I've become. I'll be goddamned if I'm going to throw it all away."

"Give the guy a chance, huh?"

"Ross is a good salesman. He can flatter. He uses people. It's part of his corporate training. He has this tremendous knack for using people. Especially women."

Her sister smiled in agreement. "All men use women. They were brought up to use women. And they don't think it's all that terrible."

"Well, they can't. I mean Ross can't!" she cried out. Then the tears flowed. "Women like me are caught in the middle. We want the marriage and the independence."

"You can't have everything," Frannie said quietly. She did volunteer work, charities absorbed her days. And she didn't seem to mind a bit. She took her sister's hand. "Maybe . . . maybe you want too much."

"Too much! No!" Georgia protested and withdrew her hand.

"Didn't it cost you more than you gained?"

"Listen. I would have ended up a depressed woman. Or an alcoholic. Or like my mother-in-law, a Valium addict. She's been swallowing Valium for years, Miltown, Valiums, whatever."

"You take a risk, you pay the price," her sister declared.

"Let me tell you something. If Ross dropped dead, God forbid, I wouldn't be a weak Nelly. I'd survive and stand on my own two feet. That's worth everything, isn't it?"

Her sister lowered her eyes. She looked doubtful.

It is unlikely that Georgia will step back in her career to rescue her marriage. A woman with self-confidence rarely sabotages herself.

Georgia now finds in work the stroking she found in the early years of her marriage. Stage One satisfied her completely because she felt she had power. Raising their sons was a *powerful* responsibility. She did it well and her husband appreciated her. Her role in his success was equally vital and he appreciated that, too. Therefore, her sense of worth was reinforced.

Now, her career is providing her with positive feedback on many levels she had never tapped.

In Stage One, Georgia was *validated by her man.*

In Stage Three, Georgia discovered she is *validated by her work.*

In establishing Country Antiques, her creative talents grew and she stepped out onto new terrain, the exciting world of business.

She feels her new dimensions, and they both please and define her. Her days are joyful now, she is having fun. Country Antiques is flourishing. Georgia feels alive, involved, and engrossed. Charming, wealthy clients turn to her for advice, pay attention to what she says, pay money for her opinions! She makes decisions for them that run into the thousands. They flatter her and invite her to dinner in their homes.

Additionally, she finds that she stands up well against her competition. That she's good at her work. The business world makes her tingle. Her self-confidence soars.

Still, Georgia would truly like all three: her marriage, her career, and her independence. She would like to shake Ross out of his rigidity and resentments, recapture the romance of their first twenty years. But her short two-year sojourn in Stage Two has informed her that she cannot tread water. Nor can she turn back. She would be deeply disturbed and depressed to return to her old self. She cannot settle for that shallower version. Her self-respect will not allow her to throw it all away for Ross. In achieving her own independence, in making her own money, in feeling her own powers, she has gained a new personhood.

She has taken risks and now she is prepared to take one other risk: Ross. Another risk for which she will accept the consequences. She is an independent woman now, strong and self-assured. With Ross or without him she will make her life satisfying.

A sweet passion has returned to Georgia and put roses in her cheeks.

11
The Power of the Weak:
Dolly

When Dolly was six, her sister, who was supposed to be taking care of her, rammed their sled into her knees as they came down the hill at Jackson Park. The pain stung so badly, she wailed all the way home.

"Shuddup, crybaby," her sister ordered, dragging her along with all the authority of a nine-year-old. "Dontcha dare tell Daddy." They were both scared to death of Daddy, a fast-with-the-fist bus driver on the Dallas/Fort Worth line.

But Dolly, the baby in a family of four girls, knew how to get around Daddy. She was his babydoll. Her sisters might be taller, smarter, and stronger. But by six, the frightened child figured out the power of the weak. She had an edge, she could get most anything from Daddy. All she had to do was plunk onto his lap, weave her arms around his neck, and nuzzle. Magic! If she whimpered or cried, he'd cuddle her and say, "Think my babydoll can dry those tears?" And the moment she stopped, out came a Hershey, a Baby Ruth, a Milky Way. "That's my Dolly," he'd say. And the name stuck.

Now, forty years later, she wore it everywhere. Spelled out in metal across the license plate of her Alfa Romeo. Strung across her slender wrist in diamonds. Monogrammed in red silk into the lining of her Canadian lynx.

At seventeen, during her senior year in high school, Dolly took a modeling course that she followed up with a six-month course in fashion merchandising. She was ambitious. And photographers turned her all-American, blue eyes–blonde hair beauty into a classy look.

For a year she modeled for two stores in Fort Worth, and at eighteen she landed a still-photography job modeling juniorwear for a mail-order catalogue. Dolly could make a $3.98 cotton blouse look expensive. She learned to look soft and sexy, and added a Marilyn Monroe pout to her painted mouth. When she spoke, she whispered, a trick she learned from the movies. While her sisters took beauty culture, Fortran, and secretarial training, Dolly's career plans could be summed up in one word: rich. Modeling would be a start. But she'd also learn to sing and act and cut records and become a movie star.

A fortune teller once read her tea leaves. "You will be rich, very rich, and travel to exotic places."

"Yippee!" she yelped like a coyote. "I'm gonna be rich."

She resolved to get out of Joshua, Texas, population 2,004.

Modeling, she soon discovered, produced a volatile income, uncertain and undependable. As for acting and singing, there were pretty girls like her lined up for every open audition in Dallas, hanging around the phone for a callback. Getting rich was harder than she thought. When she looked around, she felt scared and vulnerable. The boys she dated were strictly run-of-the-mill locals with no education and no opportunities. Nice boys who'd turn into hard-working, dull husbands struggling for every ten-dollar raise.

At nineteen, Dolly got her lucky break at a car show in Dallas. She represented "Miss Convertible" for Pontiac, posed on the hood done up like a Persian cat in a white furry leotard and a rhinestone tiara. She wore stiletto heels and black stockings flecked with rhinestones to show off her gorgeous legs. She smiled and called everyone, "honey." A boring six-day run, but it paid well. Texans were crazy about cars.

On the fourth day, her boss introduced her to a vice president of a chain of supermarkets expanding to the Southwest. The man was young, not much over thirty, six-feet-two, with a diamond pinkie ring that demanded attention. He wore a tall Stetson tipped rakishly over his dark hair, and cowboy boots that must have set him back twice her six-day salary.

Her boss took her aside. "With a little persuasion, Dominic could place a hefty order. Be nice to him, Dolly. There's a bonus in it for you, honey."

When the vice president asked if she would have drinks with him after the show, she agreed. She liked his dark, Latin looks. She was flattered. And the word bonus was sweet music. She promised to meet him in the lobby bar. They shook hands businesslike, and he said, "Call me Dom."

At ten, he held her hand across the small cocktail table and he was caught up by her fragile beauty.

At eleven, he was eating out of her hands. "Sign me up, sweetheart." He bought a fleet of ten Pontiacs.

By midnight, Dom was hopelessly in love. He wanted Dolly so much it hurt. And Dom was used to getting what he wanted. Easily. Quickly. Without much trouble.

They met again on the fifth and sixth nights, and he told her he had been married once, that the marriage was annulled by the Church. No children. Single for six years, he messed around, played around, bought whatever he fancied. Now he wanted Dolly.

Dom had two things going for him. He knew how to please a lady. And he was rich. Those charms were not lost on Dolly, whose savvy instincts recognized a man enthralled. She sized him up and vowed she would not sleep with him until she had the band of gold. Sex was one marketable skill Dolly knew how to use.

Normally, Dom had a short attention span and he found women interchangeable. But Dolly was driving him crazy with desire. Unaccustomed to being turned down, he tried everything that had worked before. But Dolly held out. Dozens of roses, balloons, and other gifts could not tumble her into bed. What could he do?

With his hair thinning and his waistline thickening, maybe Dominic should reconsider, marry the girl. His elder Old World parents, in their seventies, wanted to hold grandchildren. Until he set eyes on Dolly, Dom resisted remarriage. But now it was clear that nothing less than marriage would get Dolly to bed. The bulge in his crotch appeared at the sight of her.

After eight additional weeks of wooing, Dolly won. They were married in a small pink church and Dom flew Dolly's family in on The Supermarket Chain's six-seater Lear Jet for the reception in Dallas.

"I feel like a pig in mud, Mama," she whispered on the reception line, a delicately beautiful bride, peppy and bubbly as a cheerleader.

Her three sisters, in pale polyester, stood by wide-eyed.

Marrying money was a lot easier than earning it. And Dom was so sweet to her. He bought Dolly a sprawling colonial on forty acres and named it Double D Ranch for Dom and Dolly. A self-made man who started with The Chain at twenty-two right out of college, Dom combined his C.P.A. with sharp retail skills and relocated twelve times in ten years. Now he was ready to settle down and be a family man.

But Dolly needed more excitement. She was spirited as a colt and playful as a kitten. And in six months, lonely, very lonely. Nineteen years old on forty acres felt strange. No one around to talk to.

She kept telling herself she was damn lucky to land Dom. He was handsome and rich and lusty. He showed her off like a prize mare, dressed her in décolletage to display her beautiful breasts. Her style was flashy, feathers and beads, and he couldn't keep his hands off her.

Obligingly, in three years, she gave him a son, Dom Junior, then a daughter, Angie. At twenty-two, with her figure back and her mind racing, Dolly was now ready to take on the world.

She missed modeling clothes, was bored hanging around Double D all day with the kids and the maid. So after she put them to bed one night, she crawled onto Dom's lap, and all kissy-poo, asked him if she could go back to work.

"A little bit. Couple of afternoons," she cooed into his ear.

"What for, honey? Don't I give you everything you want?"

"You do, sweetheart, you do." Her voice was pure syrup and she wove her arms around his neck and nuzzled against his chest. "But you're gone all day and you're traveling and I'm so lonesome I could die."

"Aw, you really miss me, huh."

"I do, I do. That's why I sure would appreciate a little activity a couple of afternoons. Okay? All right? Please?"

Dom could not refuse her.

She started with a line of inexpensive pants, skirts, and blouses, taking them to homes, making a kind of Tupperware party. It was gutsy to go into some of the poorer sections, and she had a couple of unpleasant experiences that Dom never knew about. But in one year, she was grossing $1,200 a week of which she netted 30 percent. Not bad for three afternoons work. When Dom got home at seven, she had dinner cooked, the kids bathed and fed. He had nothing to object to. He didn't ask her how much she made or to put it in the family pot. A silly diversion, he figured, like some women play bridge a couple of afternoons.

Dolly went wild with delight. She felt independent, energetic, thrilled with herself. At Double D, she felt chained and confined. Now she was itchy to make more money, a kind of security, to build up her private nest egg.

She continued to meet Dom's demands. They joined a country club. She entertained lavishly and he was easy with her. Like a daddy, he wanted to buy her lavish gifts. For the Christmas dance, he told her to go whole hog.

"Go on, honey. Spend whatever you like in the way of jewelry, gowns, accessories. Top to toes. I want you to look just right."

"Show me off, huh?" she grinned.

"You betcha."

When she walked into the fancy shops, they brought clothes out for her reluctantly. They weren't sure. Is this kid for real? Can she afford what she's asking to see?

"I want something special, real nice, around $2,000, royal blue. And I want everything to go with it." She laughed.

They thought she was a tootsie. Until she handed them Dom's American Express Gold Card. Then they tripped over each other being deferential.

When Dolly got home, she threw the packages across their king-sized bed. And after dinner, she called Dom upstairs and closed the bedroom door.

"Private show!" she giggled. And she modeled every single item as if she were strutting down the runway.

"Show them your sparkle, Dolly," Dom urged from the sidelines. He was her audience. He owned the whole show.

Over the years, Dom worked harder and earned more money. With it came more responsibility, longer hours, more time away from the ranch. He turned moody, demanding. When he was under stress, he bossed everyone around, especially the kids who grew afraid of his sarcasm and short temper. He became serious, a complete corporate officer, commanding and authoritarian. He expected instant gratification and would not tolerate frustrations. Where once he was playful with her, now he was impatient. Business pressures left him tired and irritable. All he wanted when he got home was peace. It was Dolly's job to see that everyone was quiet, that the house was nice and comfortable, that the kids stayed out of his way. Whatever Dom wanted, she said yes, sure, you bet, honey. For the sake of peace, she did what she was told.

At home under his eye, she remained the perfect corporate wife, firmly entrenched in Stage One. Meanwhile, she continued to build up her business. However, she made sure not to appear too pleased or too excited by it. She played it down. Dom took her afternoons as a trivial diversion; he showed no interest in what she was doing with her time. He didn't want to hear about it; he had bigger fish to fry. He was now, ten years into the marriage, completely immersed in The Chain. The corporation was his life and required his total attention, a seventy to eighty-hour week, his priority.

Dolly was too smart not to size up her situation. She could see where the marriage was going. "Rich" was not going to be enough for her. She was too feisty, too itchy to spend the rest of her days at kissy-poo. She felt dissatisfied, disturbed, discontented. Stage Two seized her and sent shock waves through her, reshuffling her dreams. But what could she do about it?

To complain to Dom would be fruitless. He would always be the boss—rigid, immutable, tyrannical. She could not afford to incur his wrath. She and her children needed his protection. Once or twice, when he was in a good mood, she tried to speak up candidly, very cautiously, and failing, saw that she could not make a dent. Reluctantly, she concluded that further attempts might even be dangerous.

It was hopeless to try to change the marriage.

What could she change?

To a casual observer, it would appear that Dolly skipped Stage Two altogether and went directly into Stage Three. Since she never complained, not to Dom nor to friends, she appeared to be unchanged, as devoted to her role as corporate wife as the day she married. However, Dolly had a plan. She wanted it both ways. To keep the marriage for security and to create an independent life, too. How could she maintain both?

She bifurcated her life. She created two worlds. Separate. Distinct. Like heavenly bodies, their orbits never crossed.

In Dom's presence, she remained dutiful and obedient, adjusting to whatever he required. At home, he came first and everyone tiptoed around him. The children grew increasingly alienated from him. He was rarely available, and when he was he barked orders at them as if they were his servants. As they became teenagers, he set down house rules, gave them jobs to perform which had to be carried out to the letter of his instructions. He gave short shrift to what he deemed laziness or sloppiness in performance. Allowances were cut back or withheld for failures, no excuses accepted. Toe the line or else.

"Not again, Mom," they groaned to her when he went on a rampage about some minor infraction.

Frequently, she canceled appointments with her children because Dom wanted her present at some corporate function. Her children's resentments grew, but she retained her position as peacemaker and defended Dom.

"Your father works hard for his family. If he's short-tempered, it's because he's tired, kids. Try to understand."

"He stinks," Dom Junior said and turned away.

"C'mon," she would argue. "He's a generous man. He gives you everything." And indeed he did. Clothes, cars—whatever showed and made his children look good. "Isn't he buying you a computer for Christmas?" she reminded her son, a silent message to stay in line.

Dolly, too, remained his house pet. Under Dom's surveillance, she purred like a pussycat. At corporate affairs, she continued to look smashing, to appear charming, a Southern wife who knew her place.

Who would suspect that three afternoons a week Dolly entered Stage Three? That she was now running a demanding and profitable business. That on the outside, she was independent, financially capable, ambitious.

In time, Dolly took in a wealthy woman partner whose capital helped expand the business. Lila was fifty-two, ten years older than Dolly, a woman whose incredible energy matched her own. They worked well together for two years until Lila became afflicted with arthritis. In the course of her own treatment, which included massage and physical therapy, she suggested they get out of retail and into physical therapy.

"This is the eighties, the age of therapy. Consider the advantages," she urged Dolly. "No merchandise to handle, no orders to ship, we don't go to them, they come to us."

In six months, they phased out their retail operation and began courses in massage and physical therapy. Lila had contacts in health clubs, gyms, and country clubs. She secured endorsements from physicians and psychologists. In addition to physical therapy, they expanded to facials and makeup instruction. Dolly loved the sociability and the gratitude of her clients. And she liked having ready cash available. No reporting, no billing, no paper work. Dom had gotten tightfisted with the dollar. More and more she spent her own money.

Perhaps it was the ransom threat that changed him. Or the fallout with Dom Junior. Or his poor health. Perhaps all three.

The ransom note struck fear in them. It was left under the front door threatening Dom's head and hers. *You will be machine-gunned unless . . .* They were terrified. It came at the worst possible time, during a period of hard union negotiations, problems selling stores, and two warehouses burned down, arson suspected. The note said where to drop the money and what to do.

"Call the police," Dolly begged.

"No."

"The F.B.I. Please, Dom."

"I said no! I'll handle it. No publicity!"

Dom ordered the chauffeur to drive the kids to school every day and never let them out of sight. "Never take the same route twice."

Dolly was so frantic, on Halloween night she didn't dare open the front door. The kids were allowed to drop candy out of a second floor window, nothing more.

Dom employed security guards to watch the house, a permanent bodyguard, and he wore a bulletproof vest. For six weeks they moved out of the house to a Howard Johnson's. Even when they moved back, they took precautions. The incident made him harder. He took it out on his son.

Perhaps there was always an undercurrent of bad spirit between them, a cruel competition for Dolly's affection. One pulled her this way, the other that way. The blow-up between them came when the boy decided he would not be a lawyer, his father's dream for him. There was a terrible battle, angry words spat at each other. Dom threw the boy out of the house. It broke Dolly's heart.

"Don't you dare go babying him. You hear me!"

"But he's a boy, your only son, he's . . ."

"Don't go near him. If he calls, hang up." He glared. "Understand?"

She swallowed hard. "Yes." She knew that the one with the power and the money always won.

For two months Dolly cajoled and flattered Dom. "He needs you, Dom. A boy needs a father's strong hand."

Dom took his boy back. "Okay. But on different terms. My terms." He was ferocious, even to Angie, who was daddy's little girl, and both kids, now teenagers, turned against him.

"Why don't we leave him, Mom?" Dom Junior said. "You deserve more than you get."

"No," she replied coolly. "You don't walk out and close the door. We're Catholic." Dom was pushing sixty, developing physical problems, high blood pressure, cardiac arythmias, diabetes. She knew she and the kids would be well taken care of. There was his will.

"But even if I were flat broke, I'd survive," she thought and she continued to work afternoons long after Lila left the business.

In September Dom Junior went off to college. In his sophomore year, he switched to psychology. Dom, too tired to argue, let him know he was on probation, that he would pay the bills, but there were strings.

"I pull those strings," he told his son, "and I can snap them, too. I want to see good grades, or else." There were always threats wrapped into every gift. My way. My terms.

To outsiders, Dolly's private life remained unruffled. She continued to be as ladylike as any other corporate wife. Now they never went away alone. It was always with other corporate people. She didn't ask why, she didn't care. Dom was slowing down. He had minor surgery, prostate trouble. Sex was no longer of interest. When he came home, she served him his cocktail and his dinner, and he pooped out in front of the television. At one point she was hurt, deeply pained by their lack of intimacy. She missed sex in her life. And she made a decision.

Work would be her passion. Work and friends. Every day she left the house charged up, and when she returned she felt satisfied, fulfilled.

My God, she thought, preparing Dom's cocktail, I saw a woman today who couldn't lift her arm after mastectomy. Not a doctor in Dallas or Austin could help her. And I did!

She received notes and gifts and Christmas cards from grateful clients, an outpouring of love for her. Whatever ego stroking she needed, she got from her work. In the private massage room there was only the client and the therapist, an intimate relationship where secrets were revealed and affection flowed. People waited weeks for appointments. She no longer needed Dom emotionally. Every day she received love.

What she missed was sex.

She tried to play it down. Eh, what good is sex. He uses her; she uses him. There are nicer things to look for in a marriage. She made up excuses for Dom. He's not demonstrative. He's getting older, he's ailing. Where once she longed for sex, now she no longer needed it. She made a tenuous peace with her celibacy.

To smooth over the embarrassment, she kidded Dom, laughing to let him know it didn't matter. "It's okay, honey, you got problems down there, we just put it aside." In bed she stared at his back. Going out and taking care of forty-five women a week was what counted. Those women depended on her. Loved her. Forget sex.

"You have a gift, Dolly," many people told her. "Go out and use it. Share it." Her career satisfactions grew. She went back to school for additional certifications. She made a life for herself outside Double D Ranch. She was in charge, successful. An achiever.

Yet she continued to be Dom's wife. There were satisfactions there, too. She met President Reagan and Nancy, Frank Sinatra, the Kissingers. She met powerful people at the U.N., ambassadors, celebrities. Marriage to Dom had its pleasures, too. She drove imported sportscars and lived well. She dressed in the flashiest, trendiest styles, weighted with diamonds and furs. It took so little to please Dom, a tiny slice of her energy, why make a fuss? She continued as a Stage One wife.

Her real life was spent in Stage Three. There she felt powerful handling her own career, having money she could share with her children and friends. Coming and going as she pleased. The freedom to make choices, to organize her days to please herself. She had health, energy, exuberance. She was in control of her time. Her work, her women friends, her clients—there was stroking on so many levels. She bounced out of bed at six. Back home at six. Tired. But satisfied. Not a bad life.

To improve herself, she took yoga, studied music therapy, traveled to Boston and New York for additional courses. She began to believe truly in her own psychic power to heal. She had the gift.

Dom Junior became her confidante. He, too, felt he had extraordinary gifts, that he was destined to be a giver, like his mother. He became a born-again Christian.

"You'll run rings around your father," she encouraged him. She recognized now that Dom had gone up the ladder, not because he was brilliant, but because he was a plodder and he stuck to it. The Chain rewarded such loyalty. It was Dom Junior who was truly gifted. Like herself, he was singled out to do important work.

When Dom Junior found Christ in the born-again church, he

found direction and peace. But he made the mistake of trying to sell his religion to his father. Passion, which Dolly learned to hide from Dom, pressed a finger into the boy's back and urged him to try to convert his father.

"Lay off," she warned. "You don't tell your father what to do. You don't challenge his beliefs. He challenges you. That's his makeup."

But the boy's passion could not, like Dolly's, be bottled up. He kept at it.

"He's the boss. He doesn't like being pushed. Be careful," she warned. "You don't know how to handle him. He wields all the power. Don't tell him *anything*."

"But Jesus loves him, too."

"You need him, don't step on his toes. Look, I don't have to account to him. If I want to buy something, I do. I even buy him gifts, expensive gifts. But I don't push. Understand? You still need him. Until you have your own money, you need him."

"But, Mom . . ."

"Don't! He holds a grudge. He won't talk for weeks. You want the silent treatment? Back off. Avoid an open clash."

She managed to avert another bruising battle.

To juggle between Stage One and Stage Three became second nature. She bifurcated her life with dexterity, appearing as a Stage One corporate wife on one hand, then switching to an independent woman in Stage Three. What she couldn't bury any longer was her need for sex. She missed it terribly.

She developed a teasing flirtatiousness that a lot of men responded to. Like an athlete flexing his muscles to see that everything was working, she tested her sexual powers. Yup, I can still turn on a man. She toyed with the idea of an affair. But sleeping around seemed sleazy, cheap.

But she ached to be held, taken, possessed by a man. At forty-six, Dolly was vibrant and sensual. For amusement she played games with twerps half her age to see if they would respond to her. Her tennis instructor. The vet who groomed their horses. Of course they did, with embarrassment. Waiters brushed her hand. An usher in her church choir whispered love songs to her. Men touched her arm, her shoulder, her face.

"Know what you are, Dolly? You're a tease," a lawyer at the racquetball club told her. "A real cockteaser."

She roared with pleasure. Flirting was such fun.

But sex, real sex, how she missed it! Lusty, noisy sex. The letting go, the abandonment, how sweet it was. For all the glorious achievements of Stage Three, what was lacking was sex. The one passion she required.

At night something deep inside her ached to be touched, to feel a man moving inside her, kissing her breasts, his tongue in her mouth—would she never experience that again? In bed she stared at Dom's back. Was that to be her portion?

Amazingly, the blessed dawn delivered a new day to her. By six she was out of bed, eager to enjoy being an independent woman. People were waiting for her.

Twelve hours later, back home, she turned into a lady again, soft-spoken and compliant.

Two lives. Many satisfactions. One terrible emptiness.

At eleven, Dolly slipped on her Dior nightgown and lay down beside her snoring husband. She listened to his rumbling sounds, watched his heavy torso rise and fall. She turned away.

A beam of moonlight painted a brushstroke of warm light across the blanket. Dolly smiled. She remembered Dom's will.

"I'll probably outlive him. And I look wonderful in black. If my looks hold out, there'll be plenty of sex ahead. Plenty."

Do you know women like Dolly who live in two worlds? Successful, independent women who are well respected in their work. Yet these same women turn into simpering children at a twinge of scorn in their husband's eyes.

Are these women fish in Stage One? Or birds in Stage Three? Why do strong, achieving women revert to an earlier, undeveloped version of themselves? Why do they return to Stage One every night when they demonstrate every day that they can fly freely, soar higher and higher?

Can a woman bifurcate her life in one clean slice? Can she exist on two levels? What does it cost her to take two steps back after she has gained recognition and independence?

I know such women. Perhaps you do, too.

A successful lawyer. At her office, she is forthright and spirited. She speaks with authority and skill. She stands up to her adversaries and talks back. She is a full adult. At home, she turns into a purring house pet. She talks baby talk to her husband—what Dolly calls kissy-poo. She hedges her opinions and avoids making statements.

"It's up to you, dear, but I'm wondering if we could buy a new sofa."

"Would it be all right with you if I spent a weekend with my mother?"

She does not say: "I'd like to spend a weekend with my mother." This is a clear statement. Nor does she express her own opinion: "I think we should buy a new sofa."

Another, a professor of medieval literature, head of her department, a published author who is widely quoted, makes decisions that affect curriculum studies and faculty appointments for the university. Her opinions carry weight. However, in a social situation with her husband present, she becomes a diffident wife, excessively adoring, a sickening sycophant. At parties she accepts his rudeness to her with a slight shrug or a sweet smile. She would not dare to correct him or cross him. In public she consistently defers to her man.

A hospital administrator runs a busy pediatric clinic. She has impressive credentials in several disciplines and manages twenty-four employees. She makes decisions on advertising, executes sophisticated financial maneuvers, and dictates executive policy. At work, hers is the last word. Yet in public, she folds up the moment her husband's opinion opposes hers. She backs down, corrects herself, apologizes like a clumsy servant.

Like Dolly, these women do not feel equal. Dynamic and defiant at work, they constantly defer at home and employ *the power of the weak*.

These women can cope with disgruntled employees; they can execute hard business negotiations; they can stand toe to toe with an adversary. But in the presence of their husbands, they *cannot* operate as equals, as adults, as partners. They overlook his rudeness and sarcasm. Their public stance is the plastic smile.

One may understand their reluctance to put on the boxing gloves for a public brawl. However, even in the privacy of their bedroom walls, they defer, they comply, they adjust. Many of them, deep down, feel that they are nothing without a man. Only a man can validate them. They require his protection and his approval. To lose him would mean to be erased.

Feminists have suggested that the woman who earns money has more power than the woman who stays home or does volunteer work. Often that seems to be true. Yet we all know women like Dolly who earn money and *still* fail to earn equality. How does this happen?

Perhaps these wives have an insatiable need for security. Often they squirrel away their earnings, or else they spend them on lavish gifts to buy love.

Dolly remembers her childhood poverty and she is terrified of returning to poor again. Untethered from her husband's substantial earnings, where would she be? Dolly is no fool. She will not bite the hand that feeds her. Dom is her safety net and she will not step out from under his protection. At worst, her marriage is unpleasant. But it is not intolerable. And, she reasons, it has its perks. Financially, she lives well. For status, she is Mrs. Dom, The Chain's top banana, and that confers power in itself. And most important, it takes little of her energy to play kissy-poo with Dom. Her business judgment tells her it is a small investment for a large return.

Her real life is spent in Stage Three. Her energy, her thinking, her attention are all funneled into Stage Three. There she is free, on her own, making important decisions. All day long Dolly is doing what she loves to do. She is receiving appreciation and applause. She is earning money.

But perhaps earning money is not the full answer, although wives who earn money feel good about it.

Most wives do not make anything near their husband's salaries, least of all corporate wives whose husbands are high earners. Often, like Dolly, to buy peace in the family, they hide their joy in work—he might become jealous—and even subvert their earning power. Where, then, does their security lie? In an investment portfolio? A will? Personal relationships with friends? Their own marketable skills?

For Dolly it is everywhere, anywhere she can find it. As long as she cannot support herself and her children as well as her husband can, she suffers anxiety. She feels insecure. She requires a man's protection. That is the power of the weak.

Many corporate wives suffer indignities in their marriage. They are exploited and treated badly. But, they rationalize, what's out there is not appetizing either. Even if they earn considerable money, they are too scared to be Stage Three all the time. Alone, on their own, is total risk. So they retain their safety net. A man validates them. That is the power of the weak.

Some corporate wives can and do change their husband's attitudes. They help them grow as they have grown. They succeed in negotiating a new marriage. But Dolly's situation with Dom was intractable and she quickly tallied the score. Faced with an unchangeable husband, a wife can play house pet for a few hours a day. As long as there is compelling work she can do, as long as she is free to earn money, as long as she can be an adult among adults, she transfers her passion to her work.

It is amazing how many successful women do exactly that.

Passion, once the domain of the bedroom, has moved into the workplace. There is passion in achievement, passion in success, passion in independence. I've seen the passion of the attorney when she mediated a brilliant labor-management dispute. I've witnessed the passion of the professor when she published her new book. I've watched the passion of the medical administrator when she dictated a successful new policy.

For women who live most of their lives in Stage Three, passion for work may have replaced sexual passion. Perhaps, like Dolly, sex is sublimated. Sex is secondary. Sex is stifled. Many of these women will confide to a friend that they think sex is highly overrated.

Perhaps sex is the trade-off for those who move in and out of Stage Three. When her husband holds back sexually, he is delivering the ultimate blow: You may be a hot shot out there, baby, but if you don't please me, I don't sleep with you. If your own husband doesn't desire you, who the hell do you think you are?

It is a message as caustic, as burning, as deadly as lye. Women who swallow it accept the power of the weak.

12
Turning Entrepreneur and Taking Risks: Allison

Three women lie languorously, silently, on their chaises facing into the sun. They have positioned themselves at the deep end of The Breakers' pool.

Hidden from their view are the Florentine fountain in the front of the $6 million Palm Beach Hotel, the twin belvedere towers inspired by the famous Villa Medici of Rome, and the elaborate decor of the Italian Renaissance public rooms with their fifteenth-century Flemish tapestries and painted beamed ceilings. Nothing in Palm Beach surpasses The Breakers for class and taste. Early guest lists included John D. Rockefeller, J. P. Morgan, John Jacob Astor, William Randolph Hearst, and Andrew Carnegie.

Basking under the Florida sun in mid-December, the three women daydream, inserting scenes like a slide show from other moments in their lives.

They have been here before. But this December morning they are the only three women registered into a triple room. Three wives unaccompanied by their husbands, here by choice, not the demands of a convention. They are three friends of long standing. Years ago, they met here at The Breakers, around this very same pool. In those days, they were obedient corporate wives.

They have come for a reunion. Today, although married to the same men, their lives have each taken a sharp turn. Their husbands have each left corporate life to become entrepreneurs.

Why? Why did their men, safely ensconced in the corporate structure and on their way up, leave before they reached the top of the ladder?

Allison, the slim vivacious one in the white bikini, tells her friends, "We sat down as a family and made the decision together, Phil and I. It was a financial decision. Phil was too sharp to stay corporate," she recounts with some pride.

Susan, the chubby one with the dimples, says, "I made him leave. I manipulated. I cried. I coaxed. I wheedled. Whatever it took to get him the hell out. I rescued him. I saved us."

Lorraine, the tanned blonde with the squint lines around her eyes, mutters, "That lousy corporation. They did it. Dumped us. Threw us out after twenty-five years of loyalty. Bastards! Criminals!"

Lorraine, forty-eight, is still angry and defiant.

Susan, forty-five, is content and calm.

Allie, fifty-one, is joyful and exuberant.

They are no longer corporate wives.

As she slathers more suntan lotion across her silky shoulders, Allie is thinking that it would be Christmas soon, with corporate parties so lavish they'll be hiring guards to keep the crashers out. She remembers the obscenely ostentatious affairs.

"Will you miss them? The bashes at Christmas? Jealous?" she asks the other two and lies back.

"My friend from Apple Computer," Susan reports without turning her head, "told me the company held nineteen holiday parties last year. *Nineteen*. Another friend married to a BM Communications exec attended a $45,000 gala. Picture it."

Lorraine stiffens with contempt. "My cousin in Silicon Valley went to a black tie extravaganza with a fifty-piece orchestra, a feast of chateaubriand, and a famous Hollywood crooner. That's what corporation dodos spend their money on. The stockholders should be up in arms. Jealous? Not me. They can stuff it."

They turn silent again.

Behind her dark glasses, Allie pictures her upcoming Christmas with pleasure. Free of corporate obligations, she sees her family snuggled in their ski house in Vermont, the fire warming the whole first level with a rosy glow. The three-story windows will paint a calendar picture. Snow will be smeared like white icing across the tennis courts. Phil will have our favorite tapes playing, and a few Vermont friends will stop by for eggnog.

If the weather's good, Phil will fly them up in the Cessna with the older boys. The girls will come straight from college. She sighs and slides one slender ankle over the other. Miss those torturous corporate affairs? The phoniness? The who's wearing what? Who's making out with whom? Good riddance! Glad to be out of their clutches.

At forty, Phil had faced the big decision. Stick with The Real Estate Corporation or get out? For a vice president making $50,000, it was a weighty decision. He consulted Allison whose advice he found consistently sound.

"I can make more on my own. Working for commission gives them the edge. Why work for The Corporation? I can do better myself and keep the whole pie," he explained. She appreciated that he didn't talk down to her or cut her off with paternalistic remarks like, "don't bother your little head."

"I'm all for it! You're too smart to stay corporate."

He wanted her to understand the risk. "You're not worried?" he asked. She shook her head. "It's a risk. I won't be allowed to compete in their territory for a whole year after I leave. They could sue if I invade their territory. I'll have to go out of state. It could be a lean year, Allie."

She smiled. It was scary to start from scratch. But she gave back confidence and optimism. "So we eat baloney sandwiches. We won't starve."

It was uncanny the way her upbeat personality was always there for him. The daughter of a coal miner from Pennsylvania, the baby in a family struggling with nine children, she should have been scared silly. It was difficult to explain why financial security was not the first and uppermost priority to Allie.

"I'll bet on you, Phil!" She hugged him.

"There's security in corporate life." He handed her one last out. "You sure you want to give up all that?"

"Let's do it."

Allie was twenty-six when she married Phil. In the late fifties, that was close to over the hill. But she didn't feel pressed to marry, or defensive about being single. Working for the phone company straight out of Lincoln High was okay with her. The urgency to marry struck when she met Phil. He was on his way up in an established corporation, a winner, she could tell. She liked his easygoing manner, his playfulness. He was fun. Among the workaholics in the company, Phil stood out as a maverick. Maybe Korea had put things in perspective for him.

In the early years, they laughed about the dumb family picnics that the company sponsored, with the car caravans parading down the streets honking horns. Then came the elaborate bashes where competitive women vied as acidly as their husbands for status. Who was wearing what? Who had on the most expensive jewelry? The men also flaunted status and dressed to the nines.

At home, they laughed over it. "We're all clones. Penguins." Allie grabbed Phil's hand and did a two-step with him with stiff knees and elbows. They felt secure and optimistic in those days. Invulnerable.

Allie, the extrovert, could talk to anyone. She was bubbly and outgoing and could warm up any stodgy executive. An asset to her husband.

She remembered a frantic, birdlike woman at one of the cocktail parties who wailed to her in the restroom. "What can I say, Allie? I'm terrified, I can't make small talk."

"Say anything," she instructed. "No one's going to remember it tomorrow." And she pushed the woman out the door. "Smile!" she commanded.

Fortunately Phil didn't have to travel and he was there when she needed him. They had four kids in eight years, and in those prefeminist days, he never changed a diaper. But Allie didn't expect him to. The division of labor was clear. Expectations were met. Roles were defined.

It was after Allie read Betty Friedan that the women's movement came into focus for her. It opened her eyes. She did not complain to her husband as many women did who needed to pass through Stage Two. Instead, she explained rationally how her feelings were changing.

"I want to go to college. Part-time. At night. I want to be more than your wife." She searched for hurt in his eyes.

But he only nodded. "Sure. Why not."

She was thirty-seven, a housewife with four kids, when she turned their lives around. It was not easy.

Her first fall semester class met at 6:40 P.M., and the campus was an hour's drive away. It meant getting ready to leave at five, the witching hour. Cranky kids to feed and bathe. Dinner to prepare. As she drove down her block, she imagined every kitchen oven turned to 375°, and guilt burned in the base of her throat. *I should be home. With them.*

By the second semester, the guilt lifted like a light morning fog. She was reading feminist magazines and books about the women's movement. They opened her eyes and raised her aspirations. At college, the night classes were jammed with adults, often women like herself who were going after degrees and establishing careers. She measured herself against them and felt a surge of new confidence. She felt reborn, remade, renewed. The women's movement changed her life. By May, she had three courses under her belt, two B's and an A. She reevaluated her priorities.

"I've changed," she admitted to Phil. "I see things differently. I want more for myself."

Phil did not oppose her, although she suspected that secretly he wondered if she'd ever see it through to the finish line.

"Six years is a long time, Allie. Part-time is a hard pull," he observed. "So take it easy, okay? Don't burn yourself out."

He began to help her with small household tasks. He told her to get baby-sitters and mothers' helpers. He encouraged her. It was Phil who drew the charts for her "Statistical Analysis of Trends in Sixth Grade Reading Levels," which earned her an A.

Allie changed everything. The whole family. Her husband. Her children. Herself.

"Your turn to empty the dishwasher," she told the boys. Her

Women's Consciousness-Raising (CR) Group had discussed the dumb sex stereotypes imposed on children. Now she treated the girls differently, too. She told them to cut the lawn and bag the clippings. They all grumbled, but her good-natured prodding won out.

Six years later, Phil gave her a graduation party. Ninety people congratulated her and told her she was wonderful.

"Yup, I did it!"

The awful part came when she started to work as a substitute in the middle school. It should have been a moment of triumph. It was a disaster.

"I hate it," she told Phil. "I've got to go back for my certification in library science."

"Three more years?"

"That's what I want. I'll do it in less." She didn't apologize and Phil did not admonish her.

"If that's what you want, go for it."

Perhaps they had something special that other married couples did not. Neither she nor Phil believed in fashionable "togetherness," so highly touted as marital glue. Each had interests to pursue independently. Phil had been taking flying lessons, had bought a Twin Cessna 310 that he flew on weekends for short hops. Allie didn't object. Wasn't every man entitled to a hobby? And Phil loved his toys. After the plane came a motorcycle. He bought her a neon red helmet and she rode behind him, hugging his back. They gave each other room to be themselves. Allie learned to wallpaper a room, refinish furniture, grow prize vegetables, sew, knit, crochet—she was always occupied, interested, involved.

When she wanted to take a three-week course in London at intercession, Phil said, "Go"; their oldest daughter, home from college, would pinch-hit.

"Why was it easy for you?" a woman in her CR group asked.

"Easy?" She pondered the question. "Not easy. Easier maybe because Phil was always doing offbeat things. He'd fly to Florida for a weekend, to Canada, to Maine. I gave him freedom. I didn't have to have him at my side every second. So when it came my turn, I expected the favor returned." She smiled. "Togetherness is overrated.

We didn't ask permission like other couples who feel guilty if they do something separately. Maybe," she summarized thoughtfully, "we're both individuals who need freedom."

When she and Phil talked about his leaving The Corporation, there were no histrionics, no shouting, no hysterics. They were rational people. They measured the benefits of corporate life against the rewards and risks of Phil's striking out on his own.

"We pay so much back in taxes because my salary's exposed. Financially, I can do much better working for myself," he explained. "With The Corporation I'm on commission and bonus. Why make money for them when I can do it for myself? There are writeoffs, tax advantages. If I do well, we flourish. I like that part. The challenge intrigues me." He lowered his eyes. "Maybe I'm not the corporate type, Allie. Only it took me fourteen years to find out."

She nodded. "No regrets. You paid your dues." She knew he hated looking busy when there was a lull of activities in the mortgage department or leasing was slow. "Corporations," he once told her, "attract stoical types who hide behind the file cabinets and wait for decisions to come down from the chiefs." He hated waiting around.

They used to sit back and laugh at the corporate charades that went on. If corporations attract hang-in-for-security types, they had the wrong man in Phil.

"Another point," he said. "I want more time for myself. I'm not about to grind myself down for any almighty company and wait for the president to die. It's not that I'm lazy, Allie. I'll work twice as hard for my own company. But *I'll* call the tune, not them."

She understood. The man's nature was that he liked to test himself. Challenges excited him. Corporate life was dull, structured. Loyalty counted more than ingenuity.

"And I want fun in my life."

"Of course." It was what attracted her to him at first glance. His playfulness. The sense of fun.

"The corporation wants workaholics. They own you body and soul." He looked deep into her eyes. "Our first priority should be the quality of our life."

"Sure, Phil," she teased. "If you want to put your feet up on your desk, you don't need a note from mommy."

"I can make the break now, before the college bills come rolling in."

"Sure. Let's do it."

That night they made love wildly to celebrate their decision. It was fiercely satisfying lovemaking, a sharing of passion with a strong undercurrent of playfulness. He brought her a Milky Way in bed and licked the chocolate off her fingers, then sucked on them one by one. "Delicious. Mmm."

Allie felt especially cherished. Phil loved her. They were partners. So if he wanted out of corporate life, fine. He'll be a success!

In the morning, pulling the razor across his chin, he said gleefully, "No more Tuesday morning meetings. Ah."

"You won't miss your nursery school class?" she kidded back as she made the bed.

Tuesday was the day everyone got called on the carpet to be chewed out and insulted, treated like a child, accounting for every moment and every decision. Oh, the corporate chief did it smoothly, but it was degrading. All the more so since it was common knowledge that the Tuesday tirades were conducted by a president of operations who, long married and well into his sixties, was fooling around. If he was less sarcastic than usual, the sly winks meant she must have given him a good time. His girlfriend, thirty-two, who attended conventions with him as his "consultant," brought forth secret snickers. But then conventions were the pits. No call girls—just plain old fooling around. Allie had gone to two or three, one at The Breakers, then stopped. Phil, of course, continued to attend. She didn't worry about him. Fidelity was part of their code of honor.

"When will you tell them?" she asked, plumping a pillow.

"End of the month."

"No regrets?"

"Only one. A few of the guys will see it as disloyal."

"Going on your own is disloyal?"

"You'll see."

He was right. Some corporate people dropped them. They felt

uncomfortable to continue a friendship with infidels who deserted the corporate family. Disloyalty was the unforgivable sin.

It took Phil only two years to catch up to what he had been making at The Corporation. Then his annual earnings rose and rose and rose. Working for himself led him to insiders' deals and he caught on fast.

His plane gave him great pleasure, too. Especially when Allie announced she was going to take the Pinchhitter's Course, a popular series of special instructions for women whose husbands fly.

"Phil, I used to say that if you had a heart attack, I'd want to go down with you. If your number's up, it's up. But the women's movement told me I was crazy. I'm a valuable person. So I want to learn to fly this baby and land her." She told him this as they sliced through a cloud over Chesapeake Bay. She took the course and passed.

"In an emergency, I can land now. Take her down nice and easy," she told her CR group. Every one of them stood up and applauded her.

The crunch came over money.

"You messed up the checkbook again," Phil said, hunched over the bank statement for their joint account. "I'll take over. From now on I'll do it!" He was annoyed at wasting an hour cleaning up her mistakes.

"No you won't. So I messed up two entries, big deal." It gave her an opening. "And speaking of bank accounts, I want my own checking account."

He pushed up his reading glasses. "What do you mean? You can write a check whenever you want."

"Uh-uh. It's not the same." She shook her head vigorously, prepared by her CR group, which urged every woman to take control of her own money. The group had rehearsed scenarios to instruct wives about countering their husband's objections. Their leader, an ardent feminist and twenty-six-year-old C.P.A., assured them in her calm and deliberate tone that women could and women should handle money. That it was not something only a man could do.

"That's ridiculous," he said, his blood pressure rising.

"No!" she insisted. "If I give $25 to a campaign fund, if I send a check to N.O.W., you don't have to know about it. I want my own money."

Annoyance tightened his jaw, but she was glad he didn't rush in with the standard macho arguments.

"Maybe it's ludicrous to you, Phil, but . . ."

"Don't I give you everything you want?" he interrupted.

". . . but it will make me feel in charge. Independent. I'm a grown woman, an adult. Personal growth means a lot to me."

He put $500 in to start her off. When it was gone, he put in another $500. She kept her statement accurate to the penny.

As soon as she began earning real money, she offered to put a part of her earnings into their joint account. "Now that I'm earning, we can split the bills. You pay the big bills, the mortgage, the insurance, the cars. I'll pay for my clothes and the gifts I buy."

She had never been demanding. No mink. No new car for her. She was pleased to take Phil's car every two years when he got himself a new one. Feeling wildly extravagant, she bought herself a silver bracelet at a crafts fair for $350. "I like having my own money," she said to him as she showed off her wrist.

"So where's Phil this weekend?" Susan sat up and put on her straw hat.

"He flew to Baltimore to see the new harbor."

"Expensive hobby." Lorraine sat up, too. The sun was blazing overhead.

Allie laughed and stretched. "He loves his toys. 'There's such peace up there in the sky,' he says."

"What the hell do you do up there in Vermont?" Lorraine asked.

"I run a hotel—guests almost every weekend. Phil would rather be alone. But I love the people and the conversations and we play doubles all weekend. The clay courts are great. I cook. I whip up something fast, for six, for eight. I bake. It's nothing to me."

"And Phil?"

"He reads. Listens to music. He's easy to be with. I'll say, 'Let's go to a movie, eat out,' and he's agreeable. He's laid-back up there."

"He never was the country club type," Susan commented. She had put on extra pounds again since their last reunion. Saddle bags were forming, and her thighs were slapping against each other.

"Phil bought a second motorcycle for Vermont, did I tell you?"

"Jeez! Dumping The Corporation turned his head. He's turning kinky," Lorraine said.

"No way," Allie laughed. "He's my lover, my dearest friend."

"Yeeuch!" Lorraine rose from her chaise. "You two are too much."

"Well I think it's wonderful," Susan sang. "What's the magic ingredient? Tell us, we're jealous."

"The magic ingredient?" Allie tapped her forehead. "It's *me!* It works because of me, my personality. I clear the air. If something's bothering him, I get him out of it. And now I'm a doer. I'm up early. Loads of energy since I started working."

"And she eats like a horse and never gains," Susan added, snapping her swimsuit lower over the moons of her buttocks. "What changed it for you?"

The two women awaited her answer. They stood there. Serious.

"Feminism. My frame of mind is so much better. I'm full of wants. I want more. More for myself. I want to work for at least another ten years. I'm ambitious to be more than I am, to stretch myself. So what if I got started late?"

"We all did. But what do you want for yourself?" Lorraine probed.

"Well," Allie stood up and pulled her robe around her. "Everything! Not a mink. Not diamonds. Oh, I don't know." She thought about Phil's latest dream. "Maybe we'll pick up roots and move out West. Arizona. A horse ranch. Phil could fly a charter service."

"You'd move? Go way out there?" It was what every corporate wife dreaded. Lorraine's eyes narrowed suspiciously under her sunglasses.

"Why not?"

"C'mon, that's Phil's dream. What's yours? What about you, Allie?"

"Me? Okay, I'll tell you. I want to own property. Lots of land. That's where to put money today. Invest in real estate. Watch your holdings grow. Maybe . . ." She hadn't told anybody yet, but it seemed the right time. "Maybe I'll get a real estate license. I'd be great at it. Don't you think so?"

From corporate wife to independent woman. From Stage One to Stage Three. Was it too easy for Allie? What made her fly so successfully when so many other birds flutter and smash to the ground?

For one thing, Phil was flexible and encouraging. When she increasingly asserted herself, he did not stand in her way. No blow-ups. No ugly fights. No terrible tirades. Having a supportive husband was half the battle.

Then where was the risk? What happened to the dangers in Stage Three? The turmoil?

Perhaps it was easier for Allie because she was not the standard corporate wife. From the start, she had had a strong sense of herself. She didn't hang on to Phil, she didn't expect him to provide her with personal satisfactions and self-esteem. She was open to new ideas and eager to grow. These qualities are a powerful arsenal in any woman's life, at whatever stage she is in.

Perhaps, too, the women's movement came along at precisely the right moment. Her consciousness-raising group gave her an enormous support system, and her college classes provided her with a network of women, like herself, to whom she could talk openly about her changing feelings. She didn't feel alone. Many women, reaching toward actualization, stumble and fall for lack of that kind of support. They wonder: am I crazy?

Even when Phil tried to wrest control of the checkbook from her, she stood her ground. Feminism was not merely an intellectual theory. Allie *acted* on it. Her firmness and good humor did not permit her to fold up when her husband and children balked. Allie had grit and courage.

There is always risk when one person in the family wants to change the established dynamics of family life. Guilt, one of the most pernicious factors women deal with, did not do in Allie. Allie may have driven to her college classes riddled with guilt, but she stuck it out.

There was financial risk, too. Financial security has kept many a corporate wife in chains. It has cut down too many women struggling to reach Stage Three. When Allie gave her husband encouragement to leave The Corporation, she was taking a considerable risk. Suppose Phil had been unlucky? Suppose they had lost everything? Surely it would have been easier to try to dissuade him. Security, plus four small children, could have tilted her toward safety. Yet, Allie chose risk.

Allie gave Phil freedom to be himself. When her turn came, she expected the same.

For some corporate wives, *my turn* never comes. They never insist, never put their needs first. But Allie discovered that she was a valuable person, and her self-esteem soared. When she no longer wanted to go down in the plane if Phil had a heart attack, she was doing what Stage Three requires: Taking responsibility for her own life. Refusing to place her destiny in her husband's hands. From dependence to *I can, I will* take care of myself is an enormous leap!

Respect and honor were paramount in this marriage. When Phil said *the quality of their life* was his first priority, he was paying Allie the ultimate compliment. *You come first.* Not the corporation. Allie returned the compliment when she described Phil as her lover, her dearest friend.

When asked what was the magic ingredient in her success, Allie eschewed coyness and false modesty. "The magic ingredient? I am!"

Allie made it happen.

13

Alfalfa and Affairs: Susan
Bitterness and Betrayal: Lorraine

For Susan and Lorraine, the other two former corporate wives, entrance to Stage Three had been messy and painful.

"In the old corporate days," Susan told Lorraine as they watched Allie doing laps in the pool, "we lived such different lives."

"And now?"

Susan chuckled. "We're okay now. Finally we're okay. But when Doug left The Food Corporation and we started the Country Store it was. . . ." She fell back and closed her eyes to summon the past. "It was rough! It was as scary as being back in the sixties with me struggling to put Doug through school."

Lorraine hoped Allie would continue swimming. She and Susan had a special bond of shared pain. Unlike Allie, neither one had an easy time leaving corporate life. "Miss it? The truth. Miss the corporate parties?"

"Sometimes I miss the glamour. When I'm hoisting a twenty-pound drum, I think, shee-it!" Her voice turned serious. "But there was no substance to our lives with The Corporation. Or with any corporation."

Lorraine pursed her lips. She hoped Susan wasn't going to go off on one of her political speeches. Was she still a hopeless sixties hippie?

Lorraine didn't want to hear a diatribe against the military-industrial complex or the moral decay of modern capitalism. What she really wanted to find out was the state of Susan's marriage. Did Susan have lovers? Was she having an affair?

"In the beginning Doug liked the trappings of executive life—the attaché case, the neat office, the status of the three-piece suit. But soon he was bored. He got so good at it that he could do his job in two hours and then sit around. He'd come home and talk about Jell-O. Who cares about Jell-O? Every year another product to hype. To package and design and budget and market research and advertise—a repeat performance. Where was I? Home alone, cut off, wiping noses and asses."

"Weren't you interested in his work?" Lorraine used her superior, Waspy tone.

"In the latest dog food? Come on! It was all such nonsense. I didn't share his environment. He was having three-martini lunches and couldn't concentrate for the rest of the afternoon. As a Jew, he'd never be president. So what was it all about?"

"But he was making a lot of money. So was Heywood."

"And I was going crazy. Two babies and a miscarriage in twenty months. Relocation after relocation."

Lorraine nodded sympathetically. "I know, I know. No wonder you had the breakdown." She knew how to draw Susan out.

"I was mentally and physically exhausted. In and out of the hospital for a year. The electroshock treatments wiped out some of it, Lorraine, but I remember how miserable I was. He'd run off to the office and I'd be stuck with two screaming babies, isolated, cut off. Every two years we'd move. I never even got to unpack my Lenox."

"Lucky your mother and sister helped out. Lucky you got over it." Lorraine wanted to hear about *now*, not Susan's psychiatric history, but she knew that patience paid off.

"After we moved to a new place, another depression set in. In six months I was in bad shape again and back in the hospital."

"Why didn't you complain to Doug?"

"Because I didn't have your big mouth. I *never* complained. A nice Jewish wife did her job. If I didn't get his suit from the cleaners, I was anxious all day. I hated being a housewife. It stunk! I was trapped. No way out. And Doug didn't understand," she said sadly.

"But you went back to teaching. That helped."

"Substituting is not teaching. I did it to escape." She smiled. "I had my first affair that year. Did I tell you that?"

Lorraine perked up. Here comes the good part. "Was he a hunk? Gorgeous?"

"Not really. A school teacher, married, sweet. I was a virgin bride at twenty, never knew another man. I wanted to find out what life was all about. I fell madly in love with him. Doug was such an idiot, the affair went on for three years under his nose and he never suspected. He was so involved with his Dribble Dog Food, he never saw me as a person. It never crossed his mind. His wife? No!"

"How did you . . . pull it off?" Lorraine wanted the details, every sordid one.

"Oh, I'd say I had an afterschool meeting or I was going shopping. We'd go to a motel. I felt so, so . . ." she hugged herself, ". . . wanted. I danced all the way home."

"Was he—you know—a good lover? Great in bed?" She sat up on one elbow not to miss a word.

"The sex was great because he gave me time. Time. With Doug I never had an orgasm."

"Never?"

"Never. And I love sex. He took a lot of time with me. Doug was too busy making a living to notice I didn't come. I did it but I got nothing out of it. And the affair gave me such an ego boost. It was a relief from marriage."

"Then why did you break it off?" She wanted to know more about affairs. She had toyed with the idea herself.

"I knew his wife, and my friendship with her made me feel guilty."

"Were there other lovers?"

"A few," Susan admitted. "Whenever I got angry, I had a short temporary fling. At that time my ego was rock-bottom, no self-esteem. My brother was a prominent surgeon in Boston. My sister was a hotshot real estate lawyer in Chicago. I was the family dummy, doing dishes at ten P.M., falling into bed exhausted. No time for myself. No fun." She sighed. "The affair taught me a lot."

"What?"

"My lousy sex life wasn't my fault. It was Doug. He wasn't a considerate lover. One, two, three—and goodnight, lady. I'd lie there angry, defeated, disgusted. The resentments built up, especially when he'd bring work home to prove he was a loyal Company man. I felt unimportant, left out. Although I had as much education as he, I was reduced to a drudge."

"You were jealous."

"I hated him for putting me in this box. I didn't complain; that was unthinkable. I'd collect my wounds and build up my rage. I hated him. But I never verbalized it. The way I did it," she sat up on one elbow to face Lorraine squarely, "was to get sick. It was my form of protest. *I don't like what I'm doing, so I won't do anything. I'll withdraw into illness. Drop out, the way we did in the sixties. I won't function. You take over the shit.* It was a way to punish him for his neglect."

Lorraine was impressed with the clarity of Susan's analysis. She had once suspected that Susan was a bit of a flake, a leftover sixties bleeding heart, quite unfit for corporate life. Now the explanation drew her respect. "What was it that changed you? *Really* changed you?"

"The encounter weekend. Absolutely. Doug admitted he had an affair and I owned up to mine. We made a commitment to talk openly, to vent our emotions when we felt them. We examined our motivations for fooling around. I admitted I wanted to prove I was attractive, that other men wanted me."

"The encounter weekend did all that?"

"Sure did. It made me realize I wanted the marriage more than the affairs."

"So you don't have uh . . . flings anymore?" Lorraine was slightly disappointed.

"No. We took a ten-week course to learn about ourselves. A

couples group. Remember 1972? It was a turning point. The political climate did it, too. *How can you be pushing dog food when people are dying in Vietnam?* It didn't make sense. I needled Doug. *Why don't you do something that has social significance?* 'Fido, Fido,' I mimicked his last ad, 'Is your dog food c-c-c-crunchy?' I told him what he did was bullshit. *Do something meaningful with your life.* We were people who cared about issues. *Isn't there more to life than this? Let's get out!*"

Lorraine twisted the fringe on her towel. "You sure fooled me. You were the perfect corporate wife when I first met you, here at The Breakers' pool."

Susan shrugged. "It was a sham. I just put on my plastic smile like every other woman. Phony, phony, phony."

"Is that why you went to Israel?"

Susan sighed. "We decided to make a major change. Escape the isolation of suburbia. Escape the corporate phoniness. Find satisfying work."

"Picking bananas is satisfying work?" Lorraine sniped.

Susan smiled. "Try to understand. First we investigated communes here, but most of them were Vietnam vets ten years younger than we were. The girls were nine and ten, they needed friends. Israel seemed attractive. A year out, no more. So we sold the furniture, the cars, everything, and went to a kibbutz."

"I couldn't believe it when I got your letter."

"Only we picked the wrong time. The Yom Kippur War broke out and down into underground shelters we went. I was so scared. War. Then my mother died, my aunt died, and my best friend died. I flew home for funerals. Then Watergate and Nixon. Doug was glad to be away from that filth, and corporate life seemed part of it. Remember 1974 when Jerry Rubin wrote that relationships are a bitch?"

"But you lived so much better here. How could you give it all up and . . ."

"The possessions possessed us. The trappings owned us. Weekends were: wash the car, transport the kids, paint the dining room, unpack, relocate, change companies. In Israel on the kibbutz it was Stop the

World, I Want To Get Off. No trappings, no status, no power struggle, no phoniness. It was beautiful. We lived way up north on the Lebanon border. The children were taken care of in the children's house while Doug and I worked. We were always with other people and it was nice not to be left alone all day."

"Honestly," Lorraine checked her cuticles, "I don't see how Doug could stand it."

"He wanted to get away from the scramble for power. He was picking bananas and I was in the kitchen sorting supplies."

Lorraine frowned, but held her tongue. Susan was a bit off the wall.

"We'd sit under a tree and remind ourselves how we hated the old life. The ad presentation meetings where the new product was shown on a screen and everyone was supposed to comment. What a laugh. Everyone was scared shitless, kept their mouths shut waiting for the chief honcho to say, 'I like it!' Only then did they all agree. 'Yes, sir, a fine presentation!' Yes-men. Phonies. Doug became uncomfortable with those lies."

"A square peg in a round hole."

"Exactly. He looked the part, played the part. But he was feeling lousy, laughing at them, disillusioned." Susan tilted her head to catch a memory. "My father was incensed. 'How can you do this? Are you crazy?' He didn't understand how tired and frustrated we were with the deceptions of corporate life."

"Then why did you come back?"

"Too many pioneers for us. They had a shared history. We were Americans. Funny, Doug even had an offer, an attractive offer, to come back to The Corporation, but it seemed crazy. The year in Israel gave us a new perspective. We felt a social responsibility. We had worked for civil rights, for the underdog. It underscored our social conscience."

"A case of bleeding hearts?"

"No." Susan scowled. "But if Doug could hire an ex-convict, an ex-druggie, he'd do it. He's also a businessman with a practical eye. But a humanist, too."

"I hated leaving the corporation," Lorraine said. "I went crazy when they phased out Heywood's department." She hesitated, trying to move the conversation back to Susan's marriage. "What about you and Doug?"

"In Israel I realized my marriage mattered. We took that year to work through our emotional problems. And we made a five-year plan. Stop spinning wheels. Stop the self-destructive behavior. In Israel we spent evenings reading farm catalogues, stuff about food and agriculture methods. We got to talking about the fun it would be to do something like that when we got home."

"Be farmers?" Lorraine cried incredulously.

"Not exactly. But maybe open a health food store in a small college town, Pennsylvania or Ohio. My father was so thrilled we were coming back, he let us stay with him for a year, rent free, while we worked out our plans and sold stuff in the farmers' markets."

"So that's how you got to Marietta, Ohio." She lowered her voice. "No more. . . . you know. New Yorkers call it matinees. In Los Angeles they call it nooners. What do they call it in Ohio?"

"I don't know, we're too busy for that." She brushed the remark aside and set her bare feet on the ground. "I found a building for sale in the shopping district and we converted the upstairs to an apartment, the downstairs to a natural food store. We showed the bank detailed plans, and my father helped us get a loan. We went to every farmers' market to figure out our opening inventory and projected profits. If we could survive three years, we'd be okay." Her voice rose with excitement.

"Perseverance pays off." Lorraine stifled a yawn. The sun was making her sleepy.

"It did. The store took off when we went into alfalfa sprouts. But then," her face fell, "a mall opened and emptied our little business district. Our core of customers dried up and we made the painful decision to close the store."

"But it has a happy ending. The alfalfa sprouts saved you, right?"

Susan nodded. "We're doing terrific, Lorraine. First our sprouts sold because people were curious. We opened accounts in restaurants, schools, supermarkets, small shops. Now we distribute directly, no middlemen, no brokers. Doug develops marketing strategies and

I do inventory and billing. We've got every restaurant within forty miles and we ship to six states: Ohio, West Virginia, New York, New Jersey, Connecticut, Pennsylvania. Our runs include tofu, and . . . oh!" She was pumping her hands with delight, "Lorraine, we love having a family business. *We're* the final word. *We* make the decisions. And . . ."

"The marriage?"

"It affected the quality of our marriage. We have to keep the channels of communication open. Everything's better."

"Alfalfa sprouts improve sex?"

"Our work is good for us, it's our life-style. No contradictions in philosophy and ethics. We sell nutrition. We feel spiritually satisfied."

It was not the answer Lorraine expected, but she kept quiet.

"We've gone from a silverware drawer to a cash register. And next month we're bringing in a computer."

"Alfalfa sprouts. I wish Heywood could find a magic something." She crossed her arms. "Ever think about divorce?"

Susan grinned. "Only when I get mad. But I won't do anything about it. I still threaten Doug, 'If you're too busy for me, I'll find someone else,' but I don't mean it."

"You sure?"

"My sex life is good. He takes time with me. I have power now. I make money. I make decisions. I feel good about my life. I'm not looking for trouble."

A tinge of jealousy flushed hot against the back of Lorraine's neck. "Nice."

"At forty-five, I'm flying."

"Nice."

"We love small town life. Marietta's a great town. Walk to the library, the barber shop, the hardware store. It's funny. We're Jews; they're gentiles. We're democrats; they're republicans. We're veggies; they love their roast pork. But we're accepted and successful. Trading the station wagon for two trucks was a smart move."

Lorraine rose. She stretched and reseated herself. "I'd swim, but I don't want to ruin my hair."

"Take a chance," Susan called over her shoulder and headed for the diving board at the deep end of the pool.

Left alone, Lorraine sucked on her despair. The sun slipped behind a cloud and the sky turned dark. A turning point, a solstice; she needed one, too, like Allie and Susan.

Heywood was home struggling with The Decision. To join another company? Or start up his own business? *His* decision would become *her* future. They had been agonizing for more than a year over the pros and cons of entrepreneurship. She had had it up to here! This weekend with Susan and Allie was more than a distraction from pain. Their descriptions of their new lives cleared her head.

Why hadn't Heywood left the company years ago? Like Allie's husband. Like Susan's husband. Was he too scared to give up the status and the security? Well, it was my fault, too. The more he made, the more I spent. Corporate life was seductive. It sucked you along, all the time tightening the noose.

Lorraine stretched her long sleek legs and shut her eyes against the tension headache delivering blows to her forehead. Sure, those were heady years when Heywood was second in command at The Security Company, top dog next to Max, the CEO of the privately held company.

Every year a "business trip" to Europe to meet the distributors, followed by a three-week tour of England, Wales, Ireland, Scandinavia, Germany, Spain, Portugal, or France. They'd seen them all. Always dinner at Maxims' among the glitterati of stage, business, and politics, the *sommelier* showing off the 1927 Chateau Lafite-Rothschild or the 1865 Chateau d'Yquem.

The winter vacations over Christmas and New Years with Max and Peg at Dorado in Puerto Rico where The Company was developing land parcels. The trips to the Bahamas, Florida, California with Max and Peg and all the kids. It was like family. Max was a demanding tyrant, cold and calculating, but give the man credit. He was a high roller, a big spender, and an excellent mentor who groomed Heywood and depended upon his soft-spoken diplomacy.

Hey didn't mind the long hours and being at Max's beck and call. He was building a future and he was proud to be the provider.

Lorraine was proud to be his wife. "We Do Things the Company Way" was their private theme song. If it cost kiss-ass, so what? The rewards were considerable.

Only once, right here at The Breakers' pool where she first met Allie and Susan, had she opened her big mouth and let Max have it.

"You've been talking business twenty-four hours a day for a week!" she hissed. "Are we here on vacation or not!" She stamped off. The hell with adoration. Max and Peg, the king and queen, controlled their lives at home. But not on vacation!

One of the vice presidents grabbed her roughly and pushed her into a corner. The big lug was shaking, trembling with fear.

"Fool! He'll take it out on all of us!"

"We're not his puppets," she protested, full of righteous indignation.

"Shut up! Just shut up! Don't ruin this vacation for everyone!"

Heywood, whose diplomacy could lead you to think he was singing Happy Birthday when he had just told you to drop dead, never violated the cardinal rule: *Don't offend Max.* On the racquetball courts, he pretended not to see the ball go out, afraid to call it against the boss. So both he and Lorraine took the insults, made sacrifices in their personal life, because the higher Heywood got, the more they had to lose.

They became big spenders. As Heywood rose and rose and rose, so did their fears and obligations. Risk it all? Lose it all? No way. The Caddy had been his bonus one year. The kids went to private schools. Even with his salary totally exposed to taxes, they lived well. The sable coat, the diamond necklace, the Peugeots, the Jaguars, the Ferraris, and the BMWs—they were always into a bundle in cars. It was nice to own a gorgeous Georgian home, beautifully decorated; to have a maid, a gardener, membership in a health and tennis club, and endless charge accounts. Nice to pick up a $800 pair of gold earrings on a whim. The power and status of a corporate wife was sweet. The risk of going it alone in business too scary. Off and on, over the years, they talked about leaving The Company, but Heywood never acted on it.

In the seventies, The Company's land development and condominium sales in Florida, California and the Caribbean were flourishing. Along with it, The Company's secondary business was security systems and burglar alarms. Cashing in on the political climate of the country while fears over vandalism and break-ins mounted daily, The Company developed a closed-circuit television market that outstripped their land developments.

At a moment of clear triumph, when profits were rolling in, Max dropped dead of a heart attack. Peg was left at the helm. Distraught, she asked Heywood and her oldest son to arrange the funeral. A widow at fifty, she took to her bed for a month. The reverberations were felt throughout the business community. The Company was thrust into its shakiest position.

For Lorraine and Heywood, it was a period of terror and trauma.

From her bedroom command post, Peg called a meeting of the top five executives.

"My children do not wish to enter the business." Her announcement drew an audible sigh, although it was common knowledge that the two sons hated their father and resented The Company.

"Heywood will take over as CEO and everyone will answer to him as they did to Max." The tension in Heywood's shoulders eased.

A few days later, Heywood made his move. His request to be made a partner as fair payment for his years of loyalty was met with stony silence and an icy stare.

"A partner? No! Absolutely not. My husband built this business. It is a family business, not a public company. Max wanted it that way and it will remain that way."

"But Peg, I built this company with Max. We did it together."

"And you were paid handsomely. No! What's mine is mine. My husband left it to his family. Family comes first, second, and third."

Appalled, Heywood and Lorraine talked it over. Now, *now absolutely*, was the time for Heywood to leave, to strike out on his own. Bitter disappointment made them furious.

"The hell with her. The hell with The Company," Lorraine cried.

"If we're going to do it, now's the time," Heywood agreed.

"After all the shit we took, you'd think she'd be grateful," Lorraine raged.

Heywood smiled knowingly. "Grateful? Grateful companies don't exist."

Within a week, Heywood changed his mind. Maybe he didn't have the guts to make the change. Maybe his responsibility to his family, the upcoming college bills, his security at The Company watered down his fury. The Company meant known rewards. To leave would risk everything he'd worked for for twenty-five years.

He came up with another position: a new contract.

"Let's see what she says to it. Then we'll decide."

Peg agreed. "Your terms are acceptable, Heywood. Fair. I need you. The Company needs you. I want you to continue to run this company."

So it was settled. The five-year contract buried their dreams of entrepreneurship. It gave Heywood assurances that he was fully in charge and added a small percentage of the profits. Peg urged him to take control, to reshuffle the company during this period of enormous strain. She promised him absolutely that no family member would be brought in to replace him.

Despite power struggles, Heywood flourished. Normally shy, he had always taken a back seat to avoid upstaging Max's flamboyant personality. Now, free of the tyrannical boss, he made leaps in his personal growth. His leadership qualities, formerly under wraps, now blossomed. At conventions, he addressed audiences of a thousand without a note. He developed new policies, built new territories, added franchises and dealerships throughout Europe, the Caribbean, and the United States. No longer hiding his capabilities, he moved the company into a position of enormous growth. And he felt the power of being kingpin.

Peg stayed out of his hair. She spent two years recovering from Max's death in her villa in California. However, unknown to Heywood or to anyone else, including her two sons, she was busy renewing an affair with a former lover, now married, with whom she trysted outside San Diego for two years while he got a divorce. At her annual Christmas party, she announced her forthcoming remarriage. Every guest was shocked.

She slid her arm through Heywood's and took him aside. "Walter's a stockbroker. Wall Street's where he's headed." She took pains to assure him that her new husband had no designs on The Company.

Within three months, Walter was enshrined as Heywood's boss. There was only one year left to fulfill the five-year contract. Heywood, furious beyond rationality, and Lorraine, out of her mind with rage, reviewed their options. There was a lucrative bonus of $150,000 due at the end of the five years. They had to see it to the end. Collect.

His last year at The Company saw a personality change in Heywood. He and Lorraine became obsessed with their situation. Where could they go? He was over fifty and fired—whatever euphemisms they used. Every dinner was now a glum rehashing of corporate betrayal. They talked it to death. It was a year of torment.

For distraction from her hideous predicament, Lorraine took a part-time job at an ad agency. With no college, but armed with a gutsy attitude, she went from not earning a cent to folding a small paycheck into her Fendi bag. She liked getting up and getting dressed three days a week. The old days of contrived busyness now seemed boring.

Then she met the women's movement.

It made her feel unhappy and guilty. *I could have done more. I didn't do enough with my life.* She listened to women in her consciousness-raising group express her own secret fears. It released her. It also placed a heavy burden of responsibility on her. She took a course that explored career opportunities. She took aptitude tests to advise her about options.

Heywood remained kind, even supportive, during this torturous year. Both were searching to understand their personal situation, the binds they were in. Separately and together, they considered the quality of their lives.

"We were too materialistic," Lorraine said to the bathroom mirror. "It was nothing for us to blow $300 on a Broadway show and dinner at Lutece. Heywood's watches ran into five figures, his suits and shirts were custom made. My last Anne Klein was $1,200. And the kids, nice decent suburban children used to the best, turned down summer jobs that didn't meet their qualifications of 'clean' and 'not too taxing.' " She shook her head. "We lost sight of something. What?" she asked her image.

Heywood took to mumbling to himself as he looked down at the spectacular view from his penthouse office in the steel and glass Company building. "Soon I'll be unemployed. No place to go. Fired. Me! The one who did the firing." He became depressed, his thoughts morose. He moaned in his sleep, "I let my family down," then awakened with a start to stare at the ceiling. Deprived of the role of provider, who was he? Suddenly he, who had control of multinational companies and decisions running into the millions, had *no control*. He felt ashamed to announce his departure to family and friends. His ego hit rock bottom. He was too shaky to make the decision: *Strike out on your own or go to another corporation?* It hung in the air like vapors from a volcano.

His five-year contract had a year to go. It also had a two-year restrictive clause that closed him out of certain possibilities. And Peg made it clear that she wanted him out the day the contract expired. He conducted a half-hearted search, talked to headhunters, toyed with the idea of starting up a financial consultation company with a friend who offered him office space. Although he had a year to prepare, he was no closer to the decision on his last day with The Company.

"Give yourself six months to make your move," a friend advised him. But in six weeks he was grieving, feeling it, hurting badly.

Suddenly, the sun came out and burned across Lorraine's cheeks. She felt sticky tears. Was I crying? Quickly, she wiped them off with the back of her hand. She sat up. In the distance she could make out Allie and Susan sitting along the edge of the pool, splashing their feet and chatting.

She remembered meeting them here during the glorious days of the Young Presidents Organization, that elitist group of winners, all presidents of a million-dollar company by the age of forty. By fifty they had to leave YPO. But, oh, the phenomenal experiences, the fascinating people, the trips to China, Singapore, and Hawaii. The seminars where she met President and Mrs. Carter, President Ford,

Philip Habib, Robert Strauss, Mary Cunningham, and generals whose names and analyses of geopolitics she no longer remembered.

Oh God! Poor Heywood. The company betrayed him. Turned him into a defeated man.

She was furious at The Company. Furious at Heywood. Furious at herself.

He should have left five years ago when Max died. He should have taken the risk and gone on his own. We would have been happy now like Allie and Susan. She felt ashamed of herself. My fault, too. I'm not a risk taker. I played it safe. Why haven't I used my capabilities? Why have I transferred responsibility for my life to Heywood? I never developed my own powers. Never grew. Never accomplished anything on my own. I should have made more of myself. Like Allie. Like Susan.

Maybe, just maybe, it's not too late. Forty-eight is *young* middle age. I still have my looks.

She swung around and planted her bare feet firmly on the ground. Opportunities don't fall into your lap. You can't wait for someone to light a firecracker under you.

She stood up and waved to Allie and Susan who beckoned her to join them.

"In a minute," she yelled back and held up one index finger. "Have to make a call."

From the outdoor pay booth, she phoned Heywood. His hello was listless.

"Hi. Did you give that corporation your answer?" she asked straight off. He had had three interviews at a company in Connecticut, a two-hour commute away.

"Not yet. I'm thinking about it. Did you buy out Worth Avenue?" he teased. "Do they still call it Net Worth?"

"Listen!" her voice rang out and intensity italicized her words. "I don't want you to work for someone else. Make less, I don't care. But be your own boss. We can spend less, we can take our knocks. *Corporations stink!* Let's make the break now."

There was dead silence at the other end.

"Hey, *Woody*." It was her pet name for him. "You there?"

"How many glasses of wine you had?"

"No wine, I'm thinking clearly. Very clearly. I never want to be in their clutches again. I want to work, too. For us. I can! Please. Are you listening to me?"

"When will you be home?" His voice became stronger.

"Tomorrow morning. First plane out. Arrives 9:15."

"I'll meet the plane. We have a lot to talk about. A lot to do. I've been thinking . . ." he trailed off for a moment. "I'm thinking the same way you do. I'm glad you feel that way."

"I do, I do! You're too damn terrific to go corporate again."

When she plunked herself down at the pool's edge between Allie and Susan, she was grinning, feeling the eagerness of the first days when she and Heywood were a team: two against the world. It would be risky. It would be tough going. But they could do it.

Like Allie and Susan, Lorraine dipped her toes into the waters of Stage Three. With one quick move, the other two gave her a shove.

"Ooooh," she wailed as she bobbed up from the deep end. "I ruined my hair."

"You'll survive," she heard as she swam off.

14

Dancing Between the Sun
and the Moon

===

Women who enter Stage Three—no matter what their background
or personal needs may be—bump into similar fears, strategies, and
experiences. Like travelers in a foreign country, they must alter their
language, perhaps even learn a new one. The climate, the food, the
water, the landscape are all different. This is new terrain. Another
country. An unfamiliar environment. They are aliens here and Stage
Three is dangerous.

Many wives, especially younger ones under forty, come prepared.
They have read the travel folders and studied them well. Dependence
and compliance are not for them. They are the new eighties women
who seem to have been born into Stage Two. Magazines, books,
films, and television have told them about who they are or ought to
be. The women's movement has helped them define their options.

Even older women, reluctant to be called feminists, are not un-
touched. Even if they avert their gaze they cannot help admiring
younger wives. They see that their own daughters have different
marriages and perhaps this helps them make small changes. Some

alter themselves to appear modern, but they don't stray far, and they still clutch the familiar—their husbands—for security.

Women in Stage Two, lucky enough to have supportive friends or consciousness-raising groups where they can share their concerns, enter Stage Three with less discomfort. But it is the rare woman, regardless of her past, who jumps headfirst into Stage Three with no trepidation. Even if her husband is a sweetheart, society mitigates against her independence. The struggle for equality and personhood is *hers* every step of the way. If she goes from homemaker to paid employee, she must fight to be taken seriously, and no amount of assertiveness training can inure her against the slings and arrows. It is not a fight every woman can handle. So some, having taken two steps up, move one step back.

Even if she has packed for this new territory with proper garments and realistic expectations, even if she is well armed with good information and smart tactics, Stage Three is no piece of cake. Once she arrives, there is the jolt when the plane touches down. *I'm really here! This is it! A new country.*

What does it mean to enter Stage Three?

Every woman is surprised when she arrives. There are no preparations thorough enough to prepare her.

Even flexible and feisty women who expect Stage Three to be easy are astonished by the difficulties they encounter. "I expected the flak and the unfairness at work," a woman married to a Department Store Chain executive explained. "I figured I could handle those Neanderthals. And my husband is a nice man so I expected him to understand my gripes and be sympathetic. But he didn't see my side at all, and my new attitudes confused him. I was happy. What was he so damn mad about?"

Other women, quiet and conservative by nature, think Stage Three will be too dreadful, too hard for them to tackle. They hang back and make excuses. Yet once they've made the first small step, they find themselves pleasantly bemused, even thrilled, to feel their new powers.

"Why didn't I grow up ten years ago? Look at me," a museum assistant married to a television executive said. "All the time I wasted. I'm a real person now and I love it. Why was I scared for so long? What held me back?"

What holds women back from taking the necessary steps? What fears imprison them? Are they afraid of failure?

STAGE ONE: THE POWER OF THE SUN

"I'm no women's libber. I *like* to depend on a man," many corporate wives declare.

In talking with more than 200 corporate wives, I became aware of common threads that distinguish Stage One, Stage Two, and Stage Three. In Stage One, there is a childlike dependence, the feeling that life will remain pleasant, safe, and comfortable forever. As long as their husbands remain heroic figures, wives bask in their status and security.

"I like being taken care of," the wife of an insurance executive declared. "I want him to be the boss, the provider, the star. My job is making his home comfortable. That's a woman's first responsibility. I take care of his home and he takes care of me."

This is the simple tradeoff of Stage One wives who like being taken care of. They do not recognize themselves as childlike.

Certainly there is a part of every woman and man that enjoys being taken care of. If all goes well and the Stage One wife continues to have a husband who is her protector, if her romantic notions are never dashed, if she is never flung into the world to survive on her own, a corporate wife may never need to move out of Stage One. Never tested, she will remain cushioned from adulthood, viewing her position as safe and secure.

Journey to another country? What for? These women will not even board the plane. They want the status quo.

But what life, what marriage, remains the same? Few. If we accept the divorce figures, marriages have a fifty-fifty chance of success. And of the fifty percent of marriages that remain legal contracts, how many are alive and well?

The woman who remains in Stage One—and there are still many—

is taking an enormous risk. She is depending totally on her husband's largesse. Dependency costs, but she doesn't appear to care. She is not a risk taker, not one who can deal with failure. She will not bet on herself.

Instead, she bets on her husband's success. Through him she believes she becomes invulnerable. He is her lifetime guarantee. If it occurs to her, as it must from time to time, that all is not well in Camelot, she dares not complain. The plastic smile is her armor. Her husband's growing salary is her power.

When I talked with women in Stage One, I found a consistent theme: Their conversations were about their husbands, not themselves. *His* work, *his* achievements, *his* success. They told me what *he* said, what *he* thought, how *he* felt. These women were not unhappy to be dependent. They smiled and nodded politely. They were agreeable and cooperative. They liked where they were and felt safe and secure. They regarded themselves as successful women. They regarded their husbands as the Sun, about whom they revolved. Like the Sun, HE was the source of their strength.

STAGE TWO: THE LUNAR INFLUENCE

Women in Stage Two are not *visibly* so different from women in Stage One. They fear change, they fear risk. They fear alienation from the man who is their source of life.

But something invisible has shaken these women. They have heard about another land that promises wonderful possibilities. They look around and see a changing world of power shifts, achieving women, and a variety of life-styles. Perhaps a friend, long married, has been dumped for a younger woman. Perhaps her personal sacrifices made for her husband so that he could move up have become demeaning for her. The dutiful wife discovers that her successful corporate husband has feet of clay. She begins to feel vulnerable, because she has placed her faith in a flawed idol.

Is the lifetime guarantee running out? Suppose he loses his position? His power? Suppose he loses interest in me? What would happen? Where would that leave me?

In Stage Two, wives allow new feelings to emerge. That's a big step.

Wives permit themselves to express negative feelings. That's another big step.

They ask questions they were afraid to voice before. Another big step.

Sometimes, they compare themselves with their friends. Some have husbands who are fooling around,. "Not my husband. My husband doesn't fool around. He's faithful. I have nothing to be worried about," a corporate wife told me. To prove it, she added, "My husband gave me my own IRA."

But the business trips become more frequent. He's too tired to make love to her. He's tense. He expects to be waited on hand and foot. Find this, do that, he orders her about. She resents his demands. She wants more respect. She sees a truer picture of where she is.

In Stage Two, the Sun no longer blazes.

At night, alone, she stares at the Moon. The cool intelligent Moon, unattached to the Sun, traces a different orbit from the Sun's. It seems closer, almost reachable. Unlike the powerful Sun, its light is cleaner, not rose-hued. She is drawn to its magnetic pull. It invites her to look at herself. She sees a truer picture of where she is.

Although the differences between Stage One and Stage Two are not visible, they are considerable. An analytical subversiveness has entered the consciousness of Stage Two women. They are reassessing and facing new possibilities. Why haven't they seen it before? Opened their eyes? Are they really secure? They observe that some wives have power and influence and money and respect independent of their husbands. What do they really have? They face their dissatisfactions. That's a giant step.

They are frightened, and complain they must. Because now they feel justified. They feel entitled to more. They want fairness and equitable solutions to their problems. They are uncomfortable with patronage and patriarchy. Maybe daddy doesn't know best. Another giant step.

"I thought it was cute when my husband said, 'Don't bother your pretty head, I'll take care of it.' Now I hate it and I let him know. Oh, I'm polite. No sense getting his dander up. But I ask him to explain why the cars and the boats and the houses are all in his name. Sometimes I'm a pest."

The Sun, once her provider is now oppressive. She can't stand the heat. She looks to the cool Moon for relief.

What strikes Stage Two wives is that everything has changed: their husband, their marriage, their family position. Remaining compliant becomes impossible. As he becomes more successful, there are more tradeoffs. He is home less and less. She must raise the children alone, relocate on demand, do what the company wants.

Stage One wives want little for themselves; Stage Two wives want more. They have to speak up.

Stage One wives keep their mouth shut and smile; Stage Two wives voice their dissatisfactions.

However, in Stage Two, wives are still afraid to risk his disfavor. Their welfare depends entirely on his pleasure, his largesse, and his good will. They have no real power yet. So they speak softly, deferentially on first entry to Stage Two. *But they speak up.* Afraid to upset the apple cart, they speak the language of Stage Two. It is another step forward.

"Could I please . . . ?" "Should I . . . ?" "Do you think I . . .?" is how they begin. They make mild requests, ask for small favors in dulcet tones designed not to offend the King of the Roost, The Authority.

But another authority is beckoning: The Moon. The Moon becomes a metaphor for independence, its light becomes the light of Reason.

It is a teetering, wobbly see-saw for wives in Stage Two. At first they try out small complaints and make hurried withdrawals if rebuffed. Not to damage the relationship. They retract their requests if their husband scowls or indicates his displeasure.

" 'Oh, I didn't mean it that way,' I told him when I saw his neck get red. I could tell he was mad when I asked him to explain our IRS form. 'Just sign,' he said, and I did."

Stage Two wives are soft-spoken and tactful at first. They back off when the lion roars. They are not yet strong enough to make major changes. That comes in Stage Three. But they see themselves in a cool new light which tells them that their feelings are valid. They can now give themselves permission to feel annoyed because their perception of their situation has changed. This is what distinguishes them from Stage One wives.

Stage One wives hold opinions that revolve around their husband.

Stage Two wives explore different attitudes—their own.

Soon, like adolescents, they test their authority. Do they have any power? Can they get what they want without a fight? Will he let them take a course, a job, a weekend trip with their sister?

A consistent theme I heard from wives in Stage Two was the way in which they defended what they judged as their failures. Often they blamed their husbands for their lost opportunities. They were not ready to take responsibility for their own actions.

"He wouldn't *let* me," an older woman explained when she described how dearly she wanted to study art history. "What could I do?" She saw herself without any options. Powerless.

In Stage Two, wives still have little power, little money, and little self-esteem. But they now know that they have to move on or slide back. This is what makes Stage Two a nervous, edgy time. One step up, one step back. Two steps up, one step back. Am I making any headway?

Timid ones are easily cowed and slide right back into Stage One. Stronger ones take heart and step into Stage Three. A few remain stuck in Stage Two, arguing, bickering, complaining, undermining their husbands out of rage and fear. They feel powerless and out of control. They don't know what to do about it. And like adolescents, they throw tantrums that serve no purpose except to embitter the adversaries and prolong the battle of wills.

A few wives appear to skip Stage Two altogether. To go from Stage One to Stage Three in one mighty jump. To leap from powerless to powerful without that confusing period of Stage Two.

Perhaps it appears that way, but I doubt it. The time spent in Stage Two may have been so short that it was imperceptible. The wife may have flown through Stage Two on the Concorde, moving so fast from complaints to action that her new forceful and forthright behavior erases recollections of her earlier stabs at personal growth.

Nevertheless, however fast and furious the trip through Stage Two, almost every woman in Stage Three has been there. Stage Two cannot be missed any more than a child can miss puberty. Some kids sail through; others are painfully self-destructive. But no one arrives at full adulthood without some experience with puberty. Stage Two, short or long, explosive or easy, is a necessary period of growth. A rite of passage few women can miss.

Although Stage Two wives want more, they don't know how to get it. This is why their steps go up and back, back and forth, as they stumble. The security of the Sun is seductive. The independence of the Moon is seductive. Which one?

Torn between dependence and independence, safety and risk, the status quo and personal growth, they hobble and stumble through Stage Two. They are dancing between the heat of the Sun and the light of the Moon. Little steps, because they don't know how to proceed.

STAGE THREE: A TIME FOR ACTION

The journey into Stage Three is remarkably similar to the journey corporate executives make when they leave their company to become entrepreneurs. Corporate executives, like Allie's husband and Susan's and Lorraine's, expressed feelings very much like women who enter Stage Three.

What do entrepreneurs and Stage Three wives share? The recognition that the time for action has arrived. Both know it will be a time of risk, one that calls for boldness. It will be a period of danger, a period of upheaval. To win, they must alter their behavior.

It is interesting that entrepreneurs and Stage Three wives both express dissatisfaction with a position they once regarded as grand and glorious. Where once they were delighted, now they are disillusioned. Both reassess their future and find it lacking. Both take significant steps to change the quality of their lives. Both view these actions as positive steps that will free them from outside authority. Both have arrived at the point where they want to cut loose, make their own decisions, and develop their own powers. Both make a contract with themselves to rely on themselves.

For both it is a frightening period.

Corporate executives who strike out on their own must leave the protection of their company, must give up the security and status it conferred, must invest their own money. Corporate wives must give up dependence on their husband's security and status, must invest in their own talents, and must rely on their own decisions.

Many corporate wives who have not worked and have no money of their own feel that a job will help them gain power. In Stage Three, they leave the protection of their home and go to work. Within months, they learn that a paycheck, however minimal, gives them more than a financial base. It confirms that they are valuable, that they have marketable skills. It confers status. It nourishes their ego. It commands respect, and it gives them the authority to decide how they will spend their money.

Once she goes to work, the corporate wife has taken a giant step.

In Stage Three, wives change their direction—invent a new orbit. Their daily lives no longer revolve around the pleasures and convenience of their husband. They no longer adjust or sacrifice according to the decision he passes down. In seeking independence and autonomy, they say exactly what executives say when they quit the organization. "I want to do it my way. I think I can do it better."

Entrepreneurs are sometimes regarded as renegades or fools by company loyalists. "Left the company after all those years? Must have gone crazy. A mid-life crisis maybe."

So are Stage Three wives whose friends have remained loyal corporate wives.

"Are you nuts? Why rush out every morning, give up bridge and lunches for a job? You don't need the money."

Is there a tinge of jealousy folded into those remarks?

Their husbands don't dance a jig either when they go off to work. Accepting their wife's decision is a slap in the face, so they give grudging consent or express sharp dissapproval.

"Don't I give you everything?" They feel that a working wife reflects poorly on their provider role.

"You're going to cost me taxes," they complain. They growl and grouse and scowl and scold. But the Stage Three wife will no longer accept the paternalistic structure of her family. She wants to implement a power shift, and in Stage Three she takes the necessary steps.

Of course, no one gives up power easily. There is bound to be friction, hard feelings, tugs of war. Anger, rage, blow-ups—even bang-up fights. There are recriminations, struggles with guilt, and tearing at old wounds. It's not an easy time. And some marriages don't make it through the stormy period. It's a risk that Stage Three wives take when they try to change the balance of power.

Additionally, Stage Three means developing new skills, establishing a career, and taking steps for personal growth. It might mean becoming savvy in areas once established as male. It could mean redressing the inequities of the traditional male dominance–female acquiescence agreement with which the marriage began. A tough task. It means *earning* respect, not *accepting* respect through attachment to a husband or his corporation.

Are Stage Three wives fools? In daring to opt for the risky path, will they regret their decisions? Will they look back with nostalgia and wonder if it was all worth it? It's hard work and it's dangerous to proceed through Stage Three. Will the cost turn out to be too high?

Corporate executives turned entrepreneurs might supply some answers. Those who left the corporation for shorter, saner hours discover that the boss works longer and harder than anyone else. His money and his reputation are on the line. If he makes a mistake inside the corporation, another department might cover and take up the slack. The corporation would not go under. But entrepreneurs can't pass the buck. They fail or succeed on the basis of their own decisions. Yet few entrepreneurs, despite the risks and dangers, ever return to corporate life.

Wives in Stage Three come to the same conclusion.

Although it is probably even *more* dangerous, risky, and painful to make drastic changes in their life, they rarely regret it. Although they have little or no experience with power, once they taste it they prefer powerful to powerless. To be leaders, not followers, to be full adults, not children or adolescents. It is a heady estate. Few turn back.

Unfortunately, society still does not support them. It says the right things and pays lip service to women achievers. But there is the wink and the nudge along with it. Entrepreneurs are applauded for their guts when they become successful and powerful. Wives who take the same journey and travel to the same alien country are put down as aggressive, unfeminine, ballsy—even that hideous epithet *rotten mothers*.

It is ironic that ambitious and achieving women who become entrepreneurs themselves are often derided the most. Guilt and contempt are heaped on them. They are told their children will suffer from neglect, that they are power-hungry, controlling, and selfish bitches.

To be powerful and in charge of one's life should be regarded as an honorable goal. Yet women in Stage Three rarely hear the feeble applause. Acquiescence to male dominance is reinforced every day, and to reverse or challenge it is an ongoing battle. So the fainthearted stumble and fall; they back down and retreat. They listen to what others tell them, not the authority of their own hearts.

The staunch and gutsy women win through perseverance. They do not give up. Each small step reinforces them. I can do it, they say. It is the same one-step-at-a-time procedure that entrepreneurs use to turn a small tender business into a successful one. They refuse to fold up over failure. They go on.

Stage Three wives become changed persons. If they value the marriage, they try to bring their husband along. They work hard at it and many succeed.

When they do, Stage Three becomes the most thrilling adventure of their lives. Like the entrepreneur, the wife now establishes herself in a richer experience. She tastes more, extends her horizons, enlarges her orbit. Like Escher's birds, *she flies.*

Once she feels powerful as a person, her voice turns from diffident to strong. Her physical and emotional posture improves. Her appreciation becomes keener, more sharply tuned. Her perspectives and priorities are reordered.

Independence and personal growth taste sweet.

What entrepreneurs found offensive in corporate life was "the phoniness" and "the fearful atmosphere." The same words come from Stage Three wives when they look back on their old positions. They now seek "a better quality of life," an arrangement that "values me as a person."

They do not apologize or coyly downplay their success. When asked, "What do you do?" they answer: "I publish a magazine," or "I'm a tax lawyer," or "I'm a scriptwriter." Like entrepreneurs, they are done with kiss-ass and bowing to authority. No more!

Stage Three wives no longer "know their place." They break free. They are like entrepreneurs who shuck off their fears and restraints. Something has entered them like a dybbuk, changing their behavior. *They act on their opinions. They seek power from within themselves.*

Corporations, built on established patterns of male dominance–female submissiveness, use the language of male sports and military operations: "The killer instinct" wins. The Old Boy networks operate like high school fraternities to blackball those who "won't play ball." Successful guys "fight to win" and are good "team players."

Stage Three women reject that atmosphere. When their corporate husbands bring it home with them, some wives are too fainthearted or too ambivalent or too anxious to break through those hard lines. The work of changing it is too gruelling and too tough to handle emotionally. So they lose by default.

On the other hand, some Stage Three wives are poised to do battle at the drop of a bobby pin. They scrutinize every innocent statement for evidence of macho. A thoughtless gesture by their husband becomes the opening round of a go-to-the-mat fight.

"What do you mean by that remark?" draws pistols.

Like the corporate executive making six trips to the coast, attending thirty office meetings, and twenty business-related meals in a brutal period, they suffer burn-out in Stage Three.

What else do entrepreneurs share with Stage Three wives? Being in a corporation can be comfortable. So can being taken care of by daddy. Both provide protection from harm. Both are highly seductive. Why move from comfortable to dangerous?

Yet more and more people are getting fed up with corporations, saying No! I won't relocate. No! I won't travel two weeks out of every four. No! I won't play your game.

Stage Three wives are saying no, too.

"I won't be spoken to with disrespect."

"I won't accept your decision."

"I won't agree to what you want."

Like entrepreneurs, Stage Three wives express criticism freely, not fearfully.

Like entrepreneurs, they advance themselves and their talents. They operate on guts and brains.

Like entrepreneurs, they regard the quality of their life as their first priority over and above financial success. They consider personal growth more exciting than portfolio growth.

Like entrepreneurs, when asked what is the magic ingredient, Stage Three wives answer, "*I* am! I'm terrific. I changed my life."

Like entrepreneurs, Stage Three wives turn their backs on passivity and become passionate. They become self-challenging and resourceful. Willing to risk for a higher reward. For them, self-made success is far more satisfying than riding someone else's coattails.

This is sexy business. Far more sexy than a black lace nightgown bought to seduce her burnt-out corporate husband.

Power creates energy. Women in Stage Three are more energetic and sexier because they feel good about themselves. The more they do, the more they can do.

Although they may dance between the Sun and the Moon for a little while, Stage Three women finally become luminous. They produce their own light and it shines forth from inside them.

Although they may repeatedly take two steps forward, one step back, they recognize the forward motion. They find that independence tastes far sweeter than dependence. That personal growth is exhilarating. That responsibility, money, power, and success are delicious.

They can be aphrodisiacs.

They can even be sexier than sex.

15

Money Without Power: Margaret

Some corporate wives like Jane, Patty, and Mary never venture outside Stage One. They remain content with compliance and dependence. They feel they have it all—safety, security, status. Even if their sole source of self-esteem is their husband—*his* job, *his* accomplishments, *his power*—they feel entitled to take it as their own. They work hard at being corporate wives. Whatever they get is their due.

But there are other corporate wives, *many of them older women, who have remained in Stage One for many years,* who suddenly feel they've had it. They leap into Stage Two yelling their heads off, spitting out complaints at their confounded husbands.

What's going on? Is she having a breakdown? Is it menopause? The husband is confused, more than a little annoyed. At this point in his life he is way up the ladder, in a position of stress and responsibility. He doesn't need trouble at home. He sits tight and hopes it will pass like a fever, and all will return to normal.

It doesn't. Not yet, anyhow.

On the contrary, these wives go wild.

From angry complaints, they jump straight into Stage Three. Without strategy, without preparation, without support systems, they snarl demands they've bottled up for years. They make mad threats and they flay about in Stage Three until their first failure hurls them straight back into Stage One, a cage from which they never escape again.

Once defeated, they return to Stage One depressed and depleted, devoid of energy, goals, even minimal expectations. They are spent. They become caged birds too frightened to ever flutter again. Even if their cage door were flung open, they could not fly out.

Perhaps because they are older women, too tired to flutter their wings. Perhaps because they are ill-fit by temperament to turn feisty. Perhaps because a small taste of freedom scares them. Perhaps because they have no support and no role models. Perhaps because the odds are simply against them, these dedicated corporate wives do not succeed in Stage Three. Very quickly, they return to their former position. Only now that exalted role has turned sour. Stage One now becomes a barren salt flat called loneliness where they reside for the rest of their lives.

They will tell you that they tried. That they did what they could to change things. That it was a case of too little and too late.

Margaret

When Margaret put her foot down, she said it loud and clear. Mousy Margaret. Where did the fire come from?

"I won't! No! I'm not going with you. And I'm never moving again. Never, never, never."

"What's the matter? Why not?" Clark asked.

"The day after you're made chairman you go to Venezuela. You come home on a Saturday night. And Sunday morning you go to Holland. Home one week, and now Iran. No!" she shouted.

"But you always used to . . . "

"No!"

"I've got a private plane and an expense account that the stockholders can't believe . . . " he trailed off, confused. "You never complained before, Margaret. What's the matter?"

"The matter?! Thirty-one moves in thirty-eight years," she hissed, "*that's* the matter! Must be some kind of world record."

"You loved it," he insisted. "You saw the world. Italy, Singapore, Nova Scotia, Hong Kong, Japan, Nigeria, Venezuela, Hawaii, California, Jakarta, Beirut, Mexico City. How many women . . . " He stood up and patted his favorite piece of sculpture, the baby elephant they brought back from Thailand, an exact replica, four feet high, carved in rich teak.

"I hated it. Did it for you, for the company. I loathed Saudi. Women are absolutely nothing to them. Hated it. All the maids, men. The shops, all men. Nothing to see but desert. No hairdressers, no beauty salons."

"Oh, come on, you loved Holland. Remember the five hundred tulip bulbs they sent us?" He was feeling impatient. Maybe he could jolly her out of it.

"We had to give them away, get rid of them," she reminded him. "Even if you're home, you're no company. It's work and golf, work and golf. You're never here. Out at 6:30, home at 8. You eat, go upstairs, and work till midnight."

"I like to work."

"You're a workaholic. They write books about you. You're Type A. It's dangerous to work so hard." Maybe she could scare him.

"Ridiculous. I'm strong as a horse."

Reluctantly, she had to admit he was in superb condition. Fit and trim, he bounded out of bed every morning at 5:30 to do his Canadian Air Force exercises, the pushups and running in place. Then three miles on the bicycle before he even took his shower. Everything timed to the minute, two steps to the frig, five steps to the stove.

"I'm alone all the time, I have no one to talk to. The highlight of my day is to go to the supermarket." She put her head down, trying not to cry, a handsome woman of sixty-three, still slim, with the high cheekbones of a young Gene Tierney and her shiny dark hair held, 1940s style, in a simple barrette. "You only come home to get clean underwear." Saying it brought back the pain of the last stockholders meeting.

She loved to go to them. Every year she looked forward to it.

Seeing the other corporate wives whose husbands came up together through the ranks, catching up on their families, the socializing and the shopping, the dinners and theaters and museums. New York was a whirl of activities, of dressing up and going out every night. She prepared for it for a month. And she lived off those juices for another month.

But Oh, God! The last meeting. That's what woke her up. Made her see her position for what it was.

He was introducing her and his secretary to someone. He pointed to his secretary and said, "Here's my right hand." Then he pointed to her. "And here's my washerwoman." He laughed. It was only a joke.

Her throat had tightened, but she didn't lose her composure. "That's right," she said to show her good humor. "I'm the highest paid washerwoman in the world."

She thought about it all week, steaming. His washerwoman. Also, the girl who put him through engineering school. Who raised his two daughters. Who moved and relocated thirty-one times and *smiled* through every emergency.

After they had moved fifteen times in eleven years of marriage, shy, little Chrissy, in and out of private schools, looked up and asked her, "Do we still have a daddy?" It broke the girls' spirits to move and move and move, start school in Nova Scotia and graduate in England. No friends, no time to adjust. What did he care? It was The Corporation first, last, and always. Building cities, industrial complexes, and fuel plants was big business. Crises at home? He wasn't around for any of them. She learned to cope.

"No! I refuse to move again. You can live wherever you want. I'm staying here. I refuse to go." She could hardly believe her own words. Refusing him. Making her own demands. Oh, it felt so good. Scared, but good.

"Suit yourself," he said with the velvet authority of a man comfortable with power. He viewed it as a tantrum. But he was not a patient man and he did not suffer fools lightly.

He had been quiet during her complaints of the last month, expecting them to pass. But he wasn't going to be ordered around.

"Refuse to move? Okay. Stay here with your crossword puzzles." He turned his back on her and walked out of the room.

In the morning, she did not hear the chauffeur slam the car door or the limo pull out of the driveway punctually at 6:00. But as she lay in bed, regrets flooded her. I came down too hard, I was nasty. I have what I want. I can go anywhere. It's a good life. I can buy anything. The trouble is there isn't anything I want.

He was home a week later, but they fought again.

He had bought her another Gucci bag with another Gucci wallet folded inside.

"I have enough Gucci bags to open a store," she told him, still sizzling from last week. He bought them, she knew, because he felt guilty. Coming home one day and going out another. Leaving her home all day while he played eighteen holes at the country club. Canceling plans at the last minute.

"But I wanted to go to this thing. You said . . . "

"Look, go ahead, I'll get you a driver. It's five couples, they won't miss me. You'll enjoy it."

"No, I'm not going by myself. I'd feel funny about it." She stayed home and sulked.

Now with the twentieth Gucci bag staring her in the face, her anger resurfaced. I have all the money I need and I don't enjoy it. Why? All the travel, private planes, and limos and I sit home alone. Time to put my foot down. Demand more. Will he listen? Or will I be talking to the lamp?

Through the years, she'd obeyed because she felt that the wife who refused to move would hold back her husband. She went along—a good sport. Not like the young wives today who are balking. Oh no. "Good ole Margaret, she helped Clark move up." They all said that about her. Well what did it get me? A kick in the face. He doesn't respect me. Doesn't spend time with me. I'm just his god-damn washerwoman.

Did other women her age feel the same way? Maybe they resented it now, too. But not in those days. Then The Corporation was "a happy Company." The women didn't talk among themselves. They were all in the same boat. Pioneers. What good would it do to vent their feelings? They joked and kidded, but it was all shallow, an acceptance born of dependence.

They knew that moving to another country was not a significant adjustment for the men who spent their days in luxurious offices with other engineers and executives. It was the wife who had to cope with finding a shoemaker, a butcher, a laundry; who had to learn the customs and the new language.

Despite her anger, Margaret suddenly laughed out loud, remembering the Oreo cookies. They couldn't get them in Venezuela, so her mother-in-law mailed them cartons of Oreos and they hid them in the wall safe behind the picture. It was the only thing they kept in the wall safe. Boxes and boxes of Oreo cookies. A sweet comfort from home that made living in other peoples' countries with other peoples' furniture a little more bearable. *You make-do* was the corporate attitude in those days. She wound up buying fourteen make-do lamps and twelve make-do ironing boards along the way, sticking it out through those years.

Too young to say no the first time they moved to Italy, she had listened carefully to Clark's instructions. "Now you know we take nothing. Nothing." Even then his tone was commanding and explicit.

"Well, I can't go without this pan, I'm taking this pan." She held up the small fry pan that made perfect eggs.

"No. We're going on an ocean liner. Just pack our clothes in the suitcases."

She packed. But the last thing she stuffed in was the pan. At night, on board, Clark opened his suitcase, pulled out his pajamas, and the pan hit his foot.

"What's this? I told you no pan."

She remembered it with devilish glee.

But now what did it all add up to? The years in between raising two children—both married now with children of their own—living such different lives. Her daughters working, the babies in day-care centers. In those days The Corporate message was clear to wives: take care of your husband and we'll take care of you.

Who will take care of me if Clark dies?

Her brother-in-law's death last month, coming on top of the "washerwoman" incident, was the second blow that made her re-evaluate her position. Watching her sister-in-law turn into a helpless child made her take a look at herself. What she saw frightened her. I have financial security. But no training, no capabilities, no skills. Money, but no power. What good is it?

She didn't even enjoy her money. It was Clark who was after her all the time to buy this and buy that.

"What do you want for your birthday?" he asked.

"Nothing. I have everything I want. Really." It was a replay of a hundred conversations.

If they were out somewhere and she saw something and said, "Isn't that nice," he'd go out and buy it.

"Now Clark," she'd scold, "I didn't say I wanted those earrings, I just said they were nice."

"But if you liked them, you must have wanted them."

"No. I didn't want them," she answered and dropped them back in their velvet box. "You buy me things because you feel guilty about working all the time."

He gave her a scathing look. He was a man ill-suited to reproach. No one questioned his decisions, least of all an ungrateful wife.

Why couldn't he understand that it was Clark she wanted? His attention, his interest, his time. Not his damn presents. She could buy her own earrings. She had plenty of money.

She remembered the poverty in Nova Scotia where they lived for sixteen months. The young couple with the five kids and the big boxer "Rudy" in the back, back woods. No paved streets. The people so poor. Every night she'd cook a bit extra and take it over and say, "We had these leftovers, here, give it to Rudy." It was for them! And the next day the kids would say, "Boy that was good." A poor family, but nice. A close family, rich in ways she could not be.

She didn't talk about it to anyone, but she wondered if other lonely wives had love affairs. She could see where it could happen to a younger woman, but she couldn't picture it for herself. Who would want her, anyhow? Her own husband had no time, no interest in her. She thought of the lost opportunities, of attractive men who had made passes when she was younger and had sex appeal. No, she wasn't the type for an affair. What about Clark? If it happened while he was away, it was because it was available.

It wasn't the sex she missed. It was the companionship. Having someone there paying attention to you.

"Even when you're here, you're not here," she yelled at him. "I could be talking to the wall, you're too busy to listen."

He sat up and folded *The Wall Street Journal.* He didn't answer.

"When you're away, I make up a list. But by the time you come home, it's stale, so I tear it up." She was screaming at him, demanding that he listen.

But his eyes glazed over. How could he take her seriously? Her lists and her demands.

"*Will you listen to me!*" It was a scream he never thought her capable of.

His jaw hardened. "Go on."

"Are you listening?"

"Go on."

"Never mind. It's all so trivial to you. I could say two words and your mind is off somewhere else, on another two million-dollar nuclear base in Transylvania."

"Well maybe," he shot back, "it's because in those two words I can tell it's not going to be interesting."

"Is that so?" her eyes blazed. He had gotten her to the point where nothing seemed worth telling. Why bother? She felt brainwashed. "Everything I say or do is trivial. Not important enough for your ears."

Complaints first. Didn't work.

Then attacks. Demands. Didn't work.

Nothing worked.

She had failed.

Broken and defeated, she withdrew into a cocoon of loneliness. What power did she have, anyhow? Only the power to deny him the pleasure of buying her a gift. The power to prevent him from assuaging his guilt. Small satisfactions.

In the old days, she had loved to go to museums. The Tate, the

National Gallery, the Prado. In the old days, she loved to go to the opera. In Milan, they went to La Scala, in England to Covent Gardens. Now there was no place she wanted to go. Nothing she wanted to buy. That made him angry. Good!

"What do you want?" he shouted back, a man who rarely raised his voice.

"From you? Not a thing in the world I want."

"For Christmas," he said, moderating his tone. "I'd like to buy you a new fur coat."

"What for? We go by limo to a restaurant and I take it off. No, I don't need it." She watched the cords in his neck stand out and it gave her a certain satisfaction.

"Earrings," he suggested.

"No. I'm not a jewelry person, my hair covers it."

"A bracelet."

"Bracelets get in the way."

"Here." He tossed her the Gucci catalogue. "What do you want?"

She gave him her old smile.

Silence.

Three weeks later, from Norway, he sent her twenty-five pounds of chocolate. She ate it, every ounce, for breakfast, lunch, and dinner. Alone, in silence. She was now a chocoholic, rarely cooking, living on junk food and vitamin pills. Angry, bitter, and lonely.

I let him do this to me. Let him put The Corporation first. He has no respect for me.

She licked an old wound and, remembering it, sucked on the humiliation: Three years ago we had tickets to *Chorus Line.* It was a weekday and he said he'd pick me up at four. We were going to meet some people, have cocktails, and go to the show. I was thrilled, dressed to the nines and waiting by 3:15. At 3:30, I took out my coat. At 4:00, I put it on to dash out to the limo. At 4:15 I took off my coat . . . 4:45 . . . 5:00 . . . I was mad as hell. I phoned. I kept calling and getting no answer. Then fear struck. Suppose he was in an accident, dead at the side of the road. I panicked. I could feel the sweat staining the underarms of my silk chemise. At 6:30 the phone rang.

"I forgot."

"*For-got? You forgot?*" She put the phone down and wept, trembling with fury.

"That's why you keep buying me things," she accused him when he got home. "It's guilt, not love."

No. No more screaming. No more yelling. Might as well accept it. I'm totally dependent on him. I know absolutely nothing. I'd be lost without him. I'm helpless when it comes to money matters, stocks and bonds and income tax. He takes care of that. He takes care of *me*. I don't have a life of my own. I just have to sit here and wait. For thirty-eight years I've been waiting. It's not going to change.

In the next month, Margaret retreated, and they talked amiably about his upcoming retirement. He never referred to her strange periods: the period of the complaints and the period of the demands. They were back to status quo and he liked it.

They took a trip together to see their grandchildren in North Dakota and Iowa. But she begged off the other trips.

"I don't have the energy to travel. I've been all over, I've seen everything. I'll just stay put, Clark. Okay?"

"You sure now, hon? Don't want you to be lonely."

"Well, I've got my crossword puzzles. And I'll watch the Yankee games. I'll be all right."

She didn't mind anymore that he left her alone. When he went away, she slept the clock away. Stayed in bed for days, eating sandwiches and junk food. Take a bite and go back to sleep.

Friday. I've got one more day. He'll be home tomorrow. One whole day ahead. Do another puzzle. Eat another chocolate bar.

What else is left?

Margaret was unable to go the distance.

Why did she fail when other women in the eighties are succeeding? Was it a case of too little and too late? Yet sixty-three is hardly the end; nor does age mitigate against succeeding in Stage Three, although it is a factor. Many will insist that sixty-three is no time to restructure a marriage. Yet changing the balance of power *often* comes in the sixties when retirement shifts life goals, and couples redistribute the male/female tasks that they used to perform.

In the sixties, creative energy, which was snuffed out by tough career demands during their thirties and forties, can now be released. Hard-driving men may soften; and women, who were devoted wives and mothers, may look toward doing other things. Both can relax now and explore whatever they postponed as wage earners and family nurturers. In their sixties—if health and money allow—they can become useful and productive in different ways.

For Margaret, however, whose usefulness ended with her child-raising years, there was no incubation period to make and revise plans. No adequate time spent in Stage Two to ruminate and reexamine her goals. No preparation for growth. Like many women who let their husbands make their decisions, she was passive to the turns in the road.

The dormancy many wives experience after children grow up and leave can become a period to cultivate a new sense of themselves. To establish their worth. To pursue personal goals. To establish themselves on the basis of their talent, brains, or skills. *Margaret did none of that necessary work.*

It is ironic that Margaret, who had money, health, and beauty, made no strides toward personal growth in her forties or fifties. Yet at sixty-three, without preparation, she broke out like a rash into welts of anger and demands, breaking the long-standing contract between herself and Clark.

"No, I won't!" and "No, you can't make me," are statements of defiance. But they are not sufficient to support successful demands. They do not carry the strength of well-thought-out, realistic plans. "No, I won't, but this is what I'm going to do," carries more weight.

At sixty-three or fifty-three or forty-three, one cannot grow roses without doing some spade work first to prepare the soil. To go from Mommy to Miracle Worker means paying dues. Athletic ability, artistic talent, even brain power must be exercised along the way to go the distance. Achieving strong self-esteem and productive life goals means doing hard work well in advance of plunging into Stage Three.

Women *who do not do the hard work, who do not perform the necessary tasks to effect changes,* accomplish nothing. They are perceived as bellyachers. They command no respect. They earn no credibility. Their husbands are irritated, even amused. But never do they take these wives seriously.

Margaret's attempts to scare Clark about the dangers of his work were weak tea. He was fit and trim, vigorous, powerful at work, and an eighteen-hole golfer at play. He was in charge of his life. Contrary to the finger waggers who predict that CEO's will drop dead from stress, new evidence suggests that people at the top deal well with stress because they are in control. It is the middle management employees, without power, who keel over from stress. "I don't get ulcers, I *give* them," the top bananas boast.

Clark held all the cards. Margaret didn't have any. He paid no attention to her. He was a man whose daily life was spent in real power wars. He knew his wife had no power. No self-worth, no goals, no plans. He knew Margaret would return to her cage, imprisoned by the lock she had fashioned. His estimate proved correct.

What kept Margaret from self-growth? Was it laziness? Fear? Weakness? In Stage Two, she realized that the wife who relies on her husband's largesse places herself in a dangerous situation. She remains powerless. She commands no respect. Without respect there can be no love, no companionship.

Margaret needed to feel important. As long as she believed her own description of herself as "the highest paid washerwoman in the world," she could be squashed like a bug. Her attitudes defeated her. Yet actions can change attitudes as effectively as attitudes can change actions. Failure to do either results in paralysis.

Personal achievement is what confers power. Respect must be earned. Self-esteem must be won. It is accomplished only through the tough, grueling day-by-day buildup of personal growth. Those who hold back—out of laziness, weakness, confusion, scattered goals, poor self-esteem, age—are likely to return to the old patterns that once gave them pleasure.

Stage Three requires effective action. Useful activity. New behavior. Success, when it arrives in Stage Three, comes as a result of the thinking-through process of Stage Two, that useful itchy reassessment period that is necessary for growth.

To change behavior, one must first feel the force of conviction.

Margaret paid lip service to Stage Three, but there was no conviction to prod her to action. Tears and tantrums do not cut the mustard. It's the old saw: actions speak louder than words.

To change directions, one needs the fire of purpose. New goals to pursue. A mountain to climb. A task to achieve. A sense of urgency and need. A willfulness. Passivity does not produce action. In Stage Two, Margaret did not find that purpose. Therefore she remained too passive, too weak, and too helpless to take action in Stage Three.

Change occurs when there is the sense of usefulness. Even people in their eighties and nineties have a spring in their step and an eagerness in their eyes if they perform useful work. "I did that. Take a look," they say with pride—whether they mastered a Chopin cadenza on the piano or transplanted a zinnia. Useful work establishes their personhood. They gain pride from accomplishments. Margaret's work ended when her children left home.

In the eighties, many women say that raising children is not enough to feel purposeful and useful. In 1900, when the life expectancy was about thirty-seven, it *was* enough; indeed it was a splendid accomplishment. But women today have been granted another whole life to live because their life expectancy has doubled. Additionally, their options have multiplied many times.

What to do with this extra time is a troubling question for some wives. Having outlived their child-raising usefulness, how can they still remain important doers in society? Going to work is the answer for some. Returning to college, taking on volunteer work, polishing a musical or artistic talent are answers for others. Growing roses, becoming a collector of coins, an expert in antique paperweights— whatever goal they establish roots them into a new turf, provides them with purpose.

Self-fulfilling work rejuvenates a woman far more dramatically than the cosmetic creams that promise to return her to youth. Far more than a surgical facelift, personal growth performs the miracle. It infuses her with vitality, sexuality, and a spirit that energizes her. It tastes sweet, too, because it carries a splendid seasoning of wisdom.

Women in their fifties and sixties who *do* more, *can* do more.

They go the distance because they paid their dues.

16

Power Without Money: Buffy

At fifty-three, Brenda enjoys her power. Never has she felt so on top of the world.

She is the first to admit that a portion of her power is *derived*. Her husband Wayne is a corporate chief at one of America's top ten advertising agencies, a corporation with annual billings reported close to $700 million.

Yet the major source of Brenda's power is herself.

Brenda—even the corporate moguls call her Buffy, her old Mount Holyoke name—has no personal portfolio. She has no accumulated wealth, no private holdings, no inherited funds. Indeed, her ability to borrow money from a bank (without her husband's co-signature) is zilch. In fact, the checking account she writes from is their *joint* account; she has none in her own name. Nor is she an entrepreneur whose wealthy husband has set her up in a business of her own. She does not hold down a paid job; she earns no salary. She is, unlike Margaret, a woman without money.

Yet in spite of these facts, Buffy wields considerable power: power without money. It is power she has earned. Power she commands on her own. What is the wellspring of the respect she commands?

Her beginnings were hardly auspicious. Nor were Wayne's, for that matter, a boy who grew up in a Massachusetts mill town, son of an illiterate father who worked in construction. Wayne disliked his father. To escape, he served four years in the Navy, then used his G.I. Bill to get a solid education at Columbia. Now president of the Communications Division at The Agency, executive vice-president, and member of the board of directors, his salary exceeds $200,000. And the perks are delicious. Buffy and Wayne have traveled extensively: South America, Brazil, Italy, France, England, Belgium, Holland, and many places in the United States. All at company expense.

In the beginning when he traveled, Buffy stayed home because the girls were small. Right then and there, she set their ship on the course it would follow throughout their marriage. She would not play the compliant wife, and she made her complaints known. No beating around the bush, no coyness, just straightforwardness. With her Wasp cool, she let Wayne know he couldn't push her around.

When he came home on Friday nights, he expected the house to be perfect and he held her accountable.

"Hold it." She stopped him in his tracks. "This is not a hotel, Wayne, and I am not room service." Her no-nonsense voice had the same edge she used to discipline the children. "I'm not your housemaid. Take care of your own clothes."

"But you had all week. Why didn't you see to it that my suits and shirts were . . . "

"Wayne," she warned. "I won't have this. Better shape up."

Maybe it was her old college training, that Mount Holyoke spirit of self-confidence. Although she was a person to whom many things came easily—the basic math, horseback riding, swimming—she stretched herself, did a lot of things well. Well enough that the other girls would say admiringly, "Hey, Buffy, you're good at that."

She liked to be good at things. But she wasn't driven to be the best, the expert, the perfectionist. Nor was she a dilettante. It was enough for her to be a generalist, to do what she had to do well. And when she failed, she didn't panic or fall apart. The old Mount Holyoke spirit bolstered her up: do what you have to do.

Maybe it was the Wasp background, too. She thought of herself as a low-key Wasp. A person who keeps a lid on things. As an only child, she was encouraged to be independent, and she grew up among adults. Like Wayne's parents, hers were not intellectuals and they had no pretensions to grandeur. Just solid middle-class Wasp values. They told her that she could tackle a job, that she was a capable person, that she could see things through. A Wasp household in a Wasp town. Her friends were all Wasps, too; everyone was the same. She was accepted, approved of, she never felt the pressures of being an outsider or an underdog.

It gave her a confidence that she carried through life.

Neither Wayne nor his corporate position could cow her.

In the early years when he traveled, the Mount Holyoke–Wasp values sustained her. She looked up on his schedule—away Monday through Friday—not as abandonment, but as freedom to be independent. She admired people who could talk about ideas, she sought friends who were good talkers, informed conversationalists, and careful readers.

It was Wayne who felt deprived, who apologized for his absences. He hated being away.

"I'm missing out on the best years with the kids," he'd say.

And she'd bolster him up. "C'mon. Let's enjoy the weekend." There was so much to do, so much to talk about as a family.

The crunch came early in his career with The Agency.

"They want me to head up the Dallas office. What do you think?"

She couldn't sleep for nights thinking about moving. Leave her friends and family? Start all over? Take the girls out of school, make them leave their friends? But if she said no, Wayne's career could be stymied. The Agency was a powerful corporation, and Wayne loved both the creative and management side of it. Would she ruin his career?

One night, unable to sleep, she went down to the kitchen for a cup of tea. Wayne found her there, brooding, her hands under her chin. "You don't want to go, do you?"

"Oh, Wayne, that's the last place in the world I want to go." It released her tears. "No. I can't go."

He held her and rocked her in his arms. "Okay, okay, we won't go. You hold the power of the veto." For Wayne there was never any doubt about it. Family was his first priority.

He continued to travel and she continued to do what had to be done. Why encourage *Sturm und Drang*? She was a practical person.

It helped that Wayne admired her independence, that he backed up her opinions and encouraged her to make decisions on her own. If she said, "The washer broke down while you were away," his reply was a matter-of-fact, "How did you handle it?"

It helped that Wayne never brought work home, that the company never competed for his affections. It was family first. He refused to make sacrifices to the corporation. Refused to accept a commitment in California the day their daughter graduated from grade school. It was understood, not even verbalized, that it was more important to be a family than to go for the bigger title.

It helped, too, that she and Wayne enjoyed a life of the mind. He read voraciously outside his field. Not business journals, but literature, novels and biography. They both gobbled up newspapers, current titles, loved theater, ballet, music, and dance. They shared a lot.

He even bounced his corporate ideas against her. Her degree in art and architecture had prepared her to listen to a creative mind at work, to nurture ideas. He respected her remarks, sought her opinions. Additionally, she had a good business sense which he came to rely on.

"You're the practical one with the business head," he'd say.

"And you're the creative genius." She'd return the compliment.

The children gave him enormous pleasure. He was interested in everything they did while he was gone.

"I missed my two pumpkins," he'd tell the girls as he balanced them both on his lap. "What did you do while Daddy was away?" And he ate up every word they said, the school fair, the lost sneaker, the dog that chased them.

"Having a husband who travels all week has its compensations," she told her scowling mother.

"Oh? And what are they?"

"I like pulling the boat by myself, doing things my own way at my own pace. I have extra time for myself and the children," she replied. An honest answer.

"Do you have time to practice?" her mother asked as she leaned against the polished Mason and Hamlin grand piano. "You used to be good, Brenda dear. Accepted to Juilliard. A pity you didn't go," she sighed.

Yes, she had turned down Juilliard to go to Mount Holyoke. A mistake? She preferred not to look back. Too much introspection only made for regrets. She could hear her mother's voice way back then: You could be a piano teacher in your declining years. A hideous proposal. Concert pianist didn't appeal to her either. Maybe she should have pursued a career in art or architecture. Worked for an architectural firm or a museum. The truth is she hadn't wanted it that badly. There was enough to do, enough excitement in her life.

Wayne's schedule, helped her grow. She learned to think independently, to make choices and act on them. She didn't have a husband to lean on or to provide her with an interesting life. She made her own.

Joining the League of Women Voters, gave her an intellectual outlet. She had women friends whom she respected. She liked those women, enjoyed their company. Their brain power excited her. They discussed issues, political events, economic and social trends. They argued points and assigned research jobs. It was stimulating and she thrived on that.

The corporate wives she met appalled her.

They had no personal goals, they were content to be appendages of their husbands, and they played the politics of corporate advancement. Their husbands were so devoted to The Agency that they had no time for family or intellectual stimulation.

The women were content with their lot and obsessed with their homes. Their conversations were about sofas. Decorating and redecorating, they talked constantly of wallpapers and fabric samples, their hands incessantly doing their needlepoint.

She tried to be one of them; she could not. She understood their positions, but she could not get in their line. Their mothers had told them to marry successful men and have a beautiful home. Their expectations were easily met. A favorite pastime was to flaunt evidence of their success: their jewelry, fur coats, and cars.

"Van Cleef and Arpels," Alice told her, waving her wrist during the corporate meeting in New York. The new sculptured gold Piaget watch adorned it.

"Lovely," she smiled, noting all the women look-alikes in their Castleberry knits.

These were wives who depended on their husbands to provide them with the entertainment and excitement their own shallow lives lacked. They went to their husbands for everything. He controlled everything: their activities, their purse strings, and the quality of their lives. They did not perceive themselves as independent persons.

She observed their tactics. They were content to be given things, and they used their feminine wiles to get more and more. They used artifice, cunning, even coquettishness to control their husbands. They had little or no power other than manipulating their husbands.

On a corporate level, she remained friendly with them. But she chose her real friends from among the interesting women from the League who shared her enthusiasm for intellectual subjects.

No, she thought, listening to the corporate wives speaking to their husbands, I can't use their little-girl voice and purr "Hon-eee," when I want something. It just makes me want to throw up.

Early on she made the decision. Become a typical corporate wife? Not for her. She let Wayne know that she would not fall in with them, that he couldn't pressure her to play their game. Conspicuous consumption was anathema to them both. Oh, they lived well enough. But if Tiffany came out with something new, they didn't feel compelled to dash to New York and buy it.

Many corporate men feel their wife's appearance reflects directly on them. To dress her in sable affirms that they are powerful providers.

Buffy refused a mink coat for years. Then one day, seeing one at Bendel that pleased her, she bought it. No fanfare. No permission. No hoopla.

"Look," she told him. "I finally bought it." She tried it on for him.

"You look wonderful. What took you so long?" he teased her.

Buffy and Wayne enjoyed many perks of corporate life. They went to the ballet, the opera, the Philharmonic on the company expense account. They had a corporate box at the Metropolitan and one at Avery Fisher Hall. Corporate people first, but if they couldn't fill it up, they'd take friends. There was also the car and driver to take them there, to drop them off, and pick them up when the performance ended. There was the box at the U.S. Open tennis matches. The five-acre estate in Connecticut. The second house in Vermont they built in 1970, and the clay courts they added the next summer.

Money? She had none of her own. But it pleased her to manage a sizable family income. Every penny of Wayne's salary was in her hands. She dispensed it the way she saw fit. The purchases, the method of payment, the priorities, they were all her decisions.

It had begun when Wayne first started traveling. Maybe it was laziness on his part that he gave the job to her. Balancing the checkbook and paying the bills was the last thing he wanted to do on his weekend at home. Later he simply let her take over. She was good at math, good at business. He was on cloud nine, the artist, the dreamer.

"Then you want me to handle the joint account? Everything?"

"Why not? You're better at it than I am."

She remembered telling two divorced friends of hers, wives with long marriages who were dumped for younger women, that she didn't even have a bank account of her own. They issued dire warnings.

"Are you crazy, Buffy? Where's your self-respect? Where's your sense of worth? Where's your self-interest?" one argued.

"What happens, God forbid, if Wayne ups and leaves you?" one proposed. "Where would you be financially? You have to protect yourself."

"It doesn't bother me. I don't need to establish my own separate account," she insisted.

"Money is power." The first one wagged a finger at her.

"There are other kinds of power," she replied.

Strange. She considered herself a feminist. She considered Wayne a feminist, too. Hadn't she spent years educating him along the way?

Stopping him short when he displayed a streak of macho chauvinism. Refusing the sex stereotypes that divided labor into male work and female work. Hadn't they had a few stormy years after he read Simone de Beauvoir's *The Second Sex* which opened his eyes to women's plight?

Basically, she had a lot to work with. Wayne had a strong mother whom he admired, and he liked women. He was supportive of women in independent roles, admired women achievers. When advertising agencies were bastions of male authority, he spoke up for promoting women to top positions. And he encouraged their daughters' efforts to be emotionally and financially independent.

"Who's going to be the first Supreme Court judge?" he teased the girls throughout high school. It was his way to tempt them to become lawyers.

If he reverted to me-Tarzan, you-Jane, she had it out with him. Another go-around. Unpleasant, but necessary work. She didn't get angry. She didn't burst out and accuse him. She didn't lose her Wasp cool.

She had always regarded Wayne as much more emotional. Therefore, she had to be the cool negotiator. At work, he had the reputation of being quick-tempered, impatient, and intolerant of inefficiency. When those attitudes spilled over to his family, she let him know they were unacceptable.

With quiet authority, she taught him to be less demanding at home. He expected the house to be operating well at all times. The right liquor in the cabinets. A proper dinner if they were eating at home. Fine. But when things didn't fall into place and he threw his weight around, she let him have it.

"They tell me you're a hard manager at the office," she told him. "Your clients say you're brilliant. They say you're a straight-shooter, too, that they know where they stand and they admire that. Well, Wayne," she spoke softly, confronting him as an ally, not an adversary. "I admire those qualities. And I want to behave the same way. But understand this clearly. You can't demand perfection. This is a home, not an ad campaign."

She knew Wayne to be basically a fair person. Reasonable and intelligent, he would respond to a rational approach, not a screaming bout. She was direct. She complimented him and avoided insults.

She knew that anyone who worked for The Agency was not a typical corporate executive because The Agency was not a typical corporation. It was an idea factory, a place that deals with creative people, a special breed of highstrung types whose creative ideas need nurturing and whose psyches and egos need to be handled with special attention.

She knew also that commuting to New York from Connecticut took its toll in stress. Wayne came home tired. So she carefully chose her moments for confrontation. Let him unwind before she tackled their negotiations. Get him comfortable. Then she dug in. Appealing to justice, she stated her case. No gamesmanship. No guile. No deceit. Just cool negotiations.

Wayne's serious health problems came like earthquakes, turning their lives around. For two years it was one crisis after another.

First he became diabetic. A change of diet, a change of life-style. Monitoring his sugar imbalance seemed to him a harbinger of diminishing physical powers.

Then his balance problems required a series of frightening neurological tests. The specialists detected a brain tumor. Brain surgery left him with a long recovery period. Although he was grateful that the tumor was non-malignant, it imposed months and months of idle time. For a man in the thick of creative activity, convalescence was unbearable. Too much time to think. Time to confront his mortality. An emotional man, he became deeply depressed.

Then an infection forced him to be circumcised—a psychological trauma for any man approaching fifty. It seemed to reflect on his male potency. Was he losing all his powers? Sexual power? Physical power? Creative power? For him, the prospect of surgery was particularly complicated because he was a diabetic. All of these, coming one after another, he saw as plagues visited upon his house.

Because he was an emotional person, he expressed his unhappiness and discontent in long sad soliloquies.

"I'm falling apart. How much time do I have left?" He sat in bed staring at the ceiling, feeling the fates were out to destroy him. He was frightened. He contemplated the end. "Where am I going? Where have I come from?" He asked himself the unanswerable metaphysical questions. He assessed his life. It didn't add up.

For Buffy, it was a painful and wrenching period. Less contemplative and more practical than he, she gave Wayne tasks to perform. She tried to engage him in activity to avoid his morbid introspection. But she knew that creative men like Wayne were all peaks and valleys. His highs soared; his lows plunged. His days were measured out in tremendous mood swings. Wild, fantastic recovery plans were swept away by worsening and deepening depressions.

He had had a record of depression. But this time there were physical complications: the diabetes, the brain surgery, and the circumcision.

"I'm leaving for Vermont," she told him when it got unbearable. "Be back in a few days." Let him work it out, I have to escape.

Their daughters blamed it on corporate life. "Daddy's burnout." They swore they would never become nine to fivers.

Maybe they're right Buffy thought. If we get through this, she decided, we're going to sell the house in Connecticut and rent an apartment in New York. Life in Manhattan would be easier and pleasanter. It would eliminate that arduous three-hour commute.

She put the estate in Connecticut up for sale. As soon as he recovered, they moved to New York.

It changed their lives.

They rented an apartment on the fashionable East Side. When it went co-op, they bought it at a marvelous insider's price. Their spirits rose. New York was a festival of activities, a movable feast. Their daughters were on their own. And Buffy, now forty-seven, had time to develop her own interests. Museums, theaters, ballets—they were all in her backyard now. Wayne was back at The Agency, his depression lifted, operating at full tilt.

When she was asked to work on her co-op's board, she jumped at the opportunity. No pay, but what high-powered minds she rubbed against. She spent three years learning to run a business that controlled a $1,400,000 budget. She sat next to powerful people. An investment banker. President of a prestigious New York accounting firm. Two financial planners. A Wall Street attorney. She listened and observed their brilliant minds at work. They asked her opinion, sought her vote, respected her positions. She could reach out to important people, phone them for a favor. She stood toe to toe with them.

She felt powerful. In charge.

When they elected her president, her ego soared.

This was heady and exciting. It confirmed her growing power. Her position took her into housing courts. With a staff of twelve, she organized litigation proceedings against a tenant on non-payment of maintenance fees for which they were taking depositions. The more decisions she made, the more she enjoyed the power she wielded.

Wayne was proud of her growing abilities, and he turned out to be a marvelous sounding board. He was interested in her problems of running a business and she was interested in his. They talked back and forth, offering advice, consolation, and support. Life was busy, exciting, full of stimulating people.

In preparation for a stormy stockholders meeting that she was going to chair, a business executive on the board offered to put her through the public speaking workshops his company ran. They were designed for executives who would make public appearances on television and give interviews.

"Really? I'd love to go," she told him. The opportunity to improve her skills excited her.

She learned, over the six-week course, how to speak more effectively, how to present her ideas more cogently, how to fend off hostile questions. Her original speech was edited and suggestions made. She rehearsed it on videotape. They appraised her presentation and gave her advice on performance techniques.

"It was an extraordinary experience!" she told Wayne. To learn to speak well in public added another skill. She felt more powerful than ever.

"It did a lot for you," Wayne observed with admiration. "Bet you could go on Donahue now and no one could rattle you."

Cool Buffy. There was passion and purpose in her life now. Moving to New York was like starting over. In her early fifties, she was growing, learning new skills, making decisions, controlling millions of dollars. People of stature respected her. It felt good. Damn good.

At the stockholders meeting, she got a real high from running the show.

"I have to come down off the wall after this meeting," she told Wayne. "It was so great." She felt energized, willing to try her talents in other areas.

"What do you think, Wayne, about me starting a business in Vermont? I can use my skills to do some consulting work. I've already seen a tax man about working up a cash crop on our land. What do you think, huh?"

"You'd be terrific in business. But let's not go crazy. Vermont is for weekends."

"We'll see," she replied. Actually, they were pretty busy out there socializing, entertaining, and skiing. Wayne was a down hill skier and she was cross-country. Could she run a business, too? Whoever thought fifty-three would be so good?

What she regretted—if she had to pinpoint a disappointment— was the loss of sexual passion. In the early days, Wayne was an ardent lover; his sex drive far exceeded hers. But since his illnesses, he had become impotent—probably due to the diabetes. She tried not to think about it, they shared so much else together.

Perhaps in their fifties they had mellowed out. Sex was no longer so urgent for Wayne and he was happy to have cooled off. They still enjoyed sex. Once or twice a month seemed to satisfy them. Buffy's sexual needs had peaked in her early forties, then declined. In a way, it was not a bad adjustment because now they were more in sync. Yet she remembered the ardent days.

Having an affair—though she was certainly attracted to other men— never appealed to her. It was a moral decision. How about Wayne?

"Do you see other women?" she asked once.

He appeared amused and contemplated his answer. "I don't know why, but I haven't, Buffy. No." She believed him. "You?"

"No. I wouldn't feel free to do that."

If sexual passion had diminished, passion for personal achievement had soared. She focused her energy in other areas. Her position on the board. The house in Vermont. The excitement of New York. Moving to Manhattan was a symbol of change. They had established a new life together. They had started over.

In New York, she took on a new identity. With her ego stimulated and her self-esteem stroked, she became a person of personal power.

"Do you like it?" she handed him the box of new gray and silver stationery from Tiffany. It said Brenda T. Harrington. "I'm no longer Mrs. Wayne Harrington. I sign checks this way. I have charge accounts this way. I introduce myself this way." It was a symbol of change as surely as the move to New York divested them of the suburban image.

"Nice." Wayne had no problem with that. They had their own identities. In addition, they shared most things.

Except for the riding.

"No, Wayne, I don't want you to learn. I want that for myself. That's my big emotional release. Learn something else. It would spoil it for me."

"Why?"

"When I go riding, I want to do it alone. You do other things alone. I want this for myself and I don't want you to have any part of it."

"Okay. Okay." He wasn't angry.

They had become more comfortable with each other. They could dish out criticism and take it better, too. They knew who they were.

"While we're at it," her gray eyes turned serious, "I have an idea. You have mandatory retirement at sixty, right? Only three years away. How about subleasing Vermont for two months a year and moving to another great city?"

"Europe?" They had toyed with the idea once before.

"Paris. Rome. London. What do you think?" she asked.

Passion sent a silver glint to her eyes and brought a glow to her cheeks.

There are winners and losers among corporate wives playing for high stakes. Margaret lost. Buffy won. They demonstrate how power is lost and won. How self-esteem is gained. How identity is established. Like Buffy, wives who spend sufficient time in Stage Two and do the hard work of Stage Three increase their chances of winning.

Many people believe money constitutes power. They argue that without money, there is no power. Feminists (myself included) feel that without paid work or personal money, women lose a substantial measure of power. Yet for some women, even without money, achievements can establish power. There are powerful women in government, journalism, and media who are not financial heavyweights. They command respect and they hold positions of authority. They earn admiration through achievement. Their work, not their income, identifies them.

Power resides on many levels: athletic, intellectual, artistic. The poet, the composer, and the artist are powerful figures who instruct and inform our lives. Sex appeal, beauty, and charm have power, creating mythic dreams since Paris set sail for Helen of Troy. Political and religious power have altered governments, rewritten legislation, and brought on bloody wars. Power is everywhere.

Personal power, distinct from money, resides in the ability to wield influence. To make decisions. To be in charge. To command respect. To gain authority. To produce action. Power-hungry corporate executives frequently eschew the grand title for the position that confers the most power.

Corporate wives, unfamiliar with power, have little experience to draw from. Margaret accepted her own estimate of herself as "the highest paid washerwoman in the world." A weak negotiator with few skills, her ability to win in Stage Three was minimal. Margaret was doomed to fail.

Buffy, however, early in the marriage did the necessary spadework to acquire power. When she told Wayne, "I am not room service, I am not your housemaid," she rejected his estimate of her. Many women have similarly cried, "Damn it, I'm not your slave," only to return to their former positions of servitude. But Buffy held fast.

It may appear that Buffy had an edge. An intelligent feminist husband improved her chances for success. But by refusing to move to Dallas, by invoking the power of her veto, she established their family-first priority. Even a macho husband, whose culture does not allow his wife to contradict him, may secretly admire that grit. It may earn his respect. More important, it earns her *self-respect*.

Many wives suffer when their husbands travel. They feel abandoned and they gather resentments against their mate and his evil company. Buffy took the opposite attitude. She used the time to develop her interests. She made decisions on her own, accepting responsibility if she failed. This was a training ground for developing independence. Instead of making Wayne feel guilty, she flexed her intellectual and business muscles, handled the family income, and weathered the children's crises. Instead of waiting until Daddy came home, she used Wayne's absence as an opportunity to grow. She built a life of her own. Women who never risk cannot succeed in Stage Three.

There is an extra dividend to this. Women who enrich their own lives enrich their husbands' as well. They become more exciting, more attractive partners. They bring another dimension to the marriage. Their husbands appreciate their sparkle. Buffy did that for Wayne.

Women who fail in Stage Three are often those who did not develop skills along the way. Like Margaret, they screamed and raged with no sensible plan for attaining their goals. They didn't do the necessary work of Stage Two of reexamining their goals. Reassessing their priorities. Reevaluating their options. Stage Two is the launching pad to success in Stage Three.

Risking is the hardest part of Stage Three. Buffy was not lazy. She did not avoid go-arounds with Wayne. She educated him, a job every successful corporate wife must do who is playing for high stakes. Buffy stated her position clearly, appealing to reason and fairness. She increased the odds by remaining cool and rational.

Go-arounds, unpleasant as they are, can become opportunities for wives to gain power. Buffy understood this. She demanded her rights as a person. Whenever Wayne displayed an obnoxious corporate attitude, Buffy—without screaming—let him know macho was unacceptable. "This is a home, not an ad campaign."

It is a risk to flout a powerful man. It is frightening for many women to stand up to the husband who brings home the bacon or the Beluga caviar. Yet sometimes it must be done. Avoiding go-arounds is safer, perhaps, but it seldom reaps rewards.

Buffy played for high stakes and won. Throughout the crises of Wayne's illnesses, she did not give up her fight. At that point, it would have been easy to shift back to her mothering role, to lose ground, and to sacrifice herself to her recovering spouse. She did not. When Wayne's depression became unbearable, she didn't play martyr, either. To save herself, she escaped to Vermont. To leave took strength.

The payoff came when they moved to New York. Buffy seized the opportunity the city offered. Her work as president of her co-op board was an extraordinary boost to her self-esteem. It established her as a powerful person.

Buffy survived aloneness while Wayne traveled, survived his bouts with depression and physical illness, and survived their clashes of will. With the tenacity of a terrier and the skills of a negotiator, she succeeded in Stage Three.

Her power came from personal growth.

Margaret had money, but no power.

Buffy had power, but no money.

One can live either way.

Perhaps when the two are joined, the combination of *money and power* is like the combination of *sex and love*. When the two come together, one celebrates. It is a rare and heady experience.

17

Strong Women and Bitchy Broads: Joan

It was their first whambang fight and Joan, a new mother at twenty-six, could feel the heat flush her face.

"Italy? Oh, no." It was frightening.

"If I'm told to go somewhere on assignment," Coleman said in that stoical New England voice, "I go. I am the wage earner and that comes first."

She felt diminished, angry, and frightened. Worse, she felt ashamed for feeling that way. A good wife in the fifties didn't feel resentment, didn't complain. They had been married only ten months when their first daughter was born—hardly enough time to establish a relationship. Move to Italy? Now? With a toddler?

"Okay, okay." She didn't have the power to say no. Negotiate? It never occurred to her.

It was a plum for Coleman to have landed a place at The Publishing Corporation. His background was pure conservative Maine. An ordinary business degree and short stints at two communications companies. The word was out that The Corporation, already acquiring magazines, would be the major force in books, films, and records. They viewed his climbing aboard from the business side as evidence of conservative economics, okay as long as he could write punchy prose in The Corporate style. Coleman demonstrated that he could. Over the years his salary and assignments grew. In a competitive corporation, the quiet style of the guy from Maine was recognized and he moved up, up, up.

Italy was Joan's first trip out of the country and she learned something about herself. She looked at the other wives bitching and moaning about the yucky Italians. Arrogant, ugly Americans upset because their darling Akitas and Shar Pei dogs could not get the right cuts of meat. She heard their contempt in their whines to shopkeepers, their provincialism in dealing with maids. They were women stuck in a puddle of self-pity and she vowed not to become one of them. Bitchy broads.

Rome for six months was a problem to be solved. Her liberal arts education at Wellesley—like her mother's before her—had taught her to be curious about the world. The bitchy broads who complained about bouts with diarrhea and allergies were exhibiting a primitive negative attitude that aroused her contempt. She would rise above all that. Be brave. Competent. Make Coleman proud of her.

At thirty-three, with two daughters now, they were sent on their second foreign assignment to Holland, to the Hague where political-financial news was breaking. The assignment was a step up for Coleman. But it came at the wrong time. Joan had postponed graduate school with each child's birth. Now a third postponement? Her involvement in the children's schools, her activities with the League of Women Voters, and her volunteer work as a teacher's aide in the Montessori schools were all satisfying, even rewarding. But something was stirring, unsettled and needful in her. An itch that only graduate school would address. She put it off again.

Although Coleman's promotions and salary were soaring, it left her feeling depressed.

In Holland, the pieces came together.

I have a choice. Join the bitchy broads for their luncheons and early cocktails. Become bombed at noon on martinis. Or . . . ? Instead she bought a bicycle and learned to speak Dutch. She had domestic help, of course, ostensibly a good life. But still there were days of depression. Something was not right. Coleman, insulated against tradespeople and shopkeepers, didn't bother to learn Dutch. Yet his position grew. She resented the disparity. She was treading water, he was flying. I am his wife, the girls' mother. Is that all I am? She watched the other women drinking, a kind of self-medication against the loneliness and anxiety. Would she wear down and become one of them?

Holland was a pivotal experience. It was there that she began to change.

"You used to be a sweet kid, full of quiet charm," Coleman observed with steely eyes as he hung up his slacks and got into his pajamas. They were quarreling again—this time over her behavior at the van Steen's dinner party. In front of the others, she had corrected him about the painting in the Royal Picture Academy. He had bristled. What made her do it? She had, up to then, assumed a deferential posture, letting him control the conversation. But tonight, she showed a will of her own. She spoke up, talked freely, and expressed her opinions.

"It was a Ruisdael. I remember because it was hung next to the Hals and across from the Vermeer." She wanted to avoid another argument before bed, but it was important to claim her rightness.

"You're quite a little authority these days," he replied in acid tones.

"I go to museums, I learn, I study." She wouldn't back down.

"A regular smart-ass." He turned his back, hogged the covers, and flicked off his lamp.

Good God. Am I turning into a bitchy broad? She felt the conflict. Coleman's moving ahead. Where am I going? Stuck. I have no separate identity. Who am I?

She had developed this idealized self-image: she had to be perfect. And if she wasn't perfect, she was a failure. Without a separate identity, she had no self-esteem. Stuck, trapped—what could she do?

She went into the kitchen, put her head down on the hard oak table, and wept into her arms. She felt so angry that she wanted to wake him up and bang her fists against his chest. But she could not do that. Her impotence bred rage, a rage that was internalized. She became more depressed. For months after the incident, her depression lingered, clung to her, and worsened. *If I can't rage at you because you're my powerful husband who supports me, I am nothing.* She worked herself into deeper depression. *What's left for me?*

It was a turning point. A salient experience.

She had arrived in Holland compliant and dutiful. She left, angry and depressed. Which paved the way for her to come finally to a new sense of her possibilities.

Perhaps the Italian trip laid the groundwork. Because her Italian maid spoke no English, she had to learn Italian. Coleman did not. In Holland, for the first time in her life, she had dependable household help, children in school, time to explore her needs. She wasn't on call twenty-four hours a day and she allowed herself to be released from the unspoken wife-mother burden—that sinking feeling that there is no beginning, middle, and end—that everyone needs so much from her.

She tried to express it to Coleman. He was not tyrannical; neither was he tuned in. He expected to set the rules, and he made the New England assumption that his wife would go along.

"Stop complaining, Joan. Stop bitching. I make a good living that provides you with the niceties. If I'm not available, I expect you to cooperate."

Rule 1: Wives cooperate. She gave him a baleful look.

A Corporate wife she barely knew rang her up. "Do you or Coleman know where my husband is? I haven't seen him for five days. But I know he was home because he left three wet towels on the bathroom floor." Another uncooperative wife. How many were there?

To inoculate herself against becoming a bitchy broad, she seized Holland as an opportunity to immerse herself in sightseeing, learning fluent Dutch, and becoming a museum buff. Eat up the widest variety of experiences, she instructed herself. She made a list of lofty distractions.

Their eight-year-old daughter, upset at changing schools, was now at the International School. Thirteen nationalities. The headmaster was beset with arguments among the parents. The simple solution occurred to Joan.

"I've started a P.T.A.," she told Coleman with some pride. "It's an innovation to them. The Indians, the Far Easterners, the Europeans." She felt useful. Another lofty distraction.

When their daughter experienced difficulty with several teachers, she transferred her to the American School which was quite military and structured. The child suffered.

"She's not learning, she's not conforming," the school complained. It was a problem she solved with no help from Coleman.

When they returned to the States, her daughter's four best friends had moved and she did so poorly in the public schools, that she was designated "learning impaired."

"The girls must go to private school," Joan told Coleman, and he agreed. It taught her that there were options. Problems could be solved. Why not options for her?

In her mid-thirties, Joan reexamined her relationship with Coleman.

Shall I get rid of him and have a career? Or should I stay put and remain a corporate wife? Shall I be a nice mouse at home? Or a full woman and leave him? I could make sure he doesn't get into my life. I could have affairs—she had had a brief one after Italy—start a career, return to graduate school, and show him. She felt a destructive and erosive hostility. These were extreme choices.

On the other hand, Coleman was no ogre. Taciturn and stubborn and conservative, he had his warts, sure. Maybe a solution would be that I don't have to look at them. We could spend a limited time together. At the dinner table. In bed. Vacations in Maine. Balancing the checkbook. No more than that to avoid strain. We could have a working relationship, a peaceful coexistence. Far better than a cold war. Still, she felt so many needs.

So began a ten-year period—a whole decade—of enormous changes. Jarring and uncomfortable. Frustrating and futile. Eruptions neither one of them could avoid.

"You've changed," he reprimanded her, charging her with the crime. He was not unaware of the distance between them.

"Of course. Change is healthy. I was happy raising the girls in those early years. I played that role lovingly."

"They still need you. Teenagers have rough times ahead."

"I have needs, too."

He was silent. Clammed up.

She thought about divorce. Another affair. But she did not act on either. Would an affair be fulfilling? Or would it take energy? And once it lost its glow, would it become another job? To keep it secret. Make arrangements. Stay sexy. More and more tasks to perform.

Coleman sulked. He shut up, kept his feelings to himself. Found respite in a sullen Yankee resentment. Funny, she thought, everyone sees him as the nicest guy in the world. Except me. The shit he dishes up, he doesn't even know he's giving to me. Financially, he's a responsible provider. But he can't express love verbally.

The girls felt it, too.

"Daddy, if you love me, why can't you say it?" the oldest demanded.

"I show you. Isn't it enough what I do for you?" He snapped his portfolio and left the room. Was it his Yankee background? Or his Corporate training? Be calm and cool, not passionate. Women are emotional. A sign of weakness to use emotional words like I love you. His lovemaking was silent as a stone.

The third trip to England, another two-year-assignment, brought it all to a head.

In London, Coleman withdrew. Conflicts tore them further and further apart. However she tried to avoid it, he turned her into a bitchy broad.

On returning to the States, Joan took stock of herself.

Her five-foot-ten body was still boyishly trim, sensual, and serviceable. Her long thin throat gave her an elegant aristocratic air. Her blonde hair, darkened to brown, should be streaked with golden highlights. And her green eyes should not be hidden behind tinted eyeglasses. Buy contacts. Also a new wardrobe. A workout program at a local gym. Along with the list came the determination of an iron butterfly.

The first week home, she laid down some rules.

"Cole," she told him over second cups of coffee, "if this marriage is going to continue, we have to get to a marriage counselor."

He hardly raised his head when he nodded. "Okay."

"I'm forty-three, and I'm going back to grad school. Now. This fall. I want to become a psychotherapist. And I want to begin my own analysis." She waited for his reply.

He avoided eye contact, fiddled with his spoon. Another quick nod. "Okay."

Something ugly hung in the air. He had agreed too readily.

He cleared his throat, his attention glued to the spoon. "There's a woman I've been seeing."

"A woman? Another woman?"

He would not tell her the name. "An old flame," is all he said. They had been having a torrid affair for three years. Mentally, he had divorced her. Had decided she was too difficult to deal with.

"Were you seeing her in London?"

He nodded.

So that accounted for the period of estrangement. The cold war. The bouts of impotency. He had resented the changes in her, which were uneven, full of emotional ups and downs. The flashes of anger and tears. Had sought solace in the arms of an old flame.

"Bastard! Damn you!" She flung their coffees off the table, the crash to the linoleum releasing her feelings. While I was fighting a battle for our emotional tightness, he was having an affair. "Bastard! Bastard! Bastard!" Her fists banged his shoulders, his back. With his head lowered, he did not move in the chair.

She followed through on graduate school. He followed through on marital counseling, his affair ostensibly over.

"Why didn't you ask me for a divorce?"

"I thought you were going through an early menopause, that it would pass."

Their oldest daughter, now sixteen, seeing her mother's unhappiness, told her, "Daddy's never going to satisfy your needs. You should get a divorce."

Four years later, with the scar tissue a hard thickening over her wound, Joan graduated as a psychotherapist. At forty-seven, she was ready to pursue a new life. With marital counseling and her own analysis, she had moved from bitchy broad to strong woman. It was hard, hard work. It took ten years.

When Coleman's next foreign assignment came up, in Hong Kong, he asked her, "You want to go along?" It was an offhand offer. She rejected it.

"I've just established my private practice. I can't possibly leave now." It was an enormous risk to refuse. Would she propel him straight back to his old flame? What kind of fool would take such a chance? Only a strong woman.

What it amounted to was a two-year separation.

"Let's make a contract," Joan suggested in a shaky voice. "We don't know what's going to happen to us, do we? I'm feeling very threatened now. But I also feel confident enough to stay here and spend two years seeing if I can live alone."

"Alone? But I'll come home three or four times a year. And you can fly out whenever . . . well whenever it's convenient."

"Okay. No strings. You see whoever you want. I will, too. Then we'll decide. Agreed?" She could not control the quiver in her voice.

He nodded.

"When you return, Cole, we'll renegotiate our relationship."

"Renegotiate?" It was not a word he felt a wife should use.

After he left, the impact hit her. She rattled around the house mumbling to herself. "I'm alone. On my own. Starting a new life, a new profession. I've taken a terrible gamble. I could lose the marriage, too." But Joan realized that hanging tough was now the only way to go. Strong women do not back off, fold up, or retreat.

While Coleman was in Hong Kong, she took a lover, a man fifteen years younger than herself.

"A mistake," a confidante told her with tight-lipped disapproval.

"No. We have a sexual-emotional tightness I've never experienced."

"How long can it last?"

"It will end when it ends—we both know that. But for now, I've never felt such an intimacy. A wholeness. He's my dearest, closest friend."

"You're dreaming, it can't last."

"Even when the sex part is over, I want him to stay part of my life."

It lasted about a year and Joan had no regrets.

The amazing thing was that during the affair, she uncovered new virtues in Coleman. Each time he flew home, he was laden with gifts for her and the girls. Yves Saint Laurent outfits, Cartier watches from Lane Crawford, silk kimonos from China—bargains he got along the Golden Mile. They got along better, and there was much to talk about, perhaps because she was less needful, less the bitchy broad crying out and sabotaging herself.

In the past her rage had flung arrows of accusations at him.

"It's all your fault for not being expressive. Your fault for not responding to my growth. Your fault, your fault." He'd back off from her. Now she saw clearly that lovesick wives were like rebellious teenagers crying, "Love me more," no matter how unlovable they were. She began to see his side, too. That his inability to understand what she was going through was rooted in resistance. Many husbands enjoy their wife's dependency. Indeed her autonomy threatened his very manhood.

Instead of wailing that he should change, she changed herself.

With a flourishing clinical practice, her self-esteem grew. The affair, however, short-lived, told her she was sexy and desirable. Having a lover was a step toward loving herself. She felt powerful and strong. She developed a new perspective on her marriage. For years she had been the needful bitchy broad trying to find out *who am I?* Trying this and trying that, an extreme form of rebellion. Now what she expected from Coleman was different. The taciturn New Englander in his fifties was not going to flip over and become a voluble expressive conversationalist. She came to accept that few women can say: all my needs are met in one man. A ridiculous dream.

"What do you want?" she asked Coleman after his two-year stint in Hong Kong.

"I was thinking about a divorce when I left."

"Oh?" She'd been incredibly naive; of course it crossed his mind. "And now?"

"My visits have been very good. I feel stronger about you, Joan. I really care about our marriage."

"I thought about divorce, too," she admitted. "It would be a loss of a whole network of mutual friends. A loss of our life in Maine. A loss of our family assets. I began to think of all the good things we have together." She did not add that it could be bloody awful out there for her, that the financial scramble would be an added stress. That divorce would drain energy from her work. She'd have to focus on a financial settlement, lawyers, dispositions, a new apartment, moving. If I were my own patient, I'd ask: Will this, in the long run, serve you? And the answer would be no. It was easier, nicer to stay married.

"Our agreement would have to be clear," she said, secretly relieved and enormously pleased that he felt their marriage mattered. "It's important for us to have friends and interests of substance that are not together. Do you agree?"

He nodded.

"See, I'm absolutely spinning at this point, Cole. Feeling good about myself. The practice is growing, and I like working fifty to sixty hours a week. Will this be a problem for you when you retire in a few years?"

"We'll manage to work it out."

"I feel powerful, Cole. I can say to you: 'I want this.' Or 'I will not have that.' I know I may not get what I want, but I have the power to ask. See?"

He nodded.

"I had to change. I couldn't stay in that niche—the nurturer mommy-wife—because I outgrew it. That's why I became hostile." She smiled at him and took his hand, that hairy paw she knew so well. "I'm a full adult woman."

"I never doubted it." Then his eyes grew concerned. "Are you just making peace?"

"No. I'm saying I don't need as much stroking. I'm getting so much satisfaction from my practice, from friends, from other levels, that I don't need you to do all that for me." Their sex life had improved, too. She felt freer.

"Well, that's a relief!" he teased. "Maybe now we can have some fun."

She laughed. "Giving up the maid for a secretary was a big step for me. My paper work is in better order than the house."

"You're telling me!"

"I can let it pile up catch-as-catch-can. I can look the other way. Does it bother you?"

"No. I make a terrific Szechuan omelette, and I clean up after me."

"Look," she warned, "I expect to continue to grow. I'm not there yet."

"Does that mean dinner with your weird friends who tell me I'm emotionally constipated?" He chuckled. Actually he accepted their fatuous claims with a good deal of grace.

"We've learned to fight better. To have an honest argument with a beginning, a middle, and an end."

Could the halcyon days return?

After a decade of turmoil, Joan found that Coleman did hear her. Did admire the strong woman she'd become. If her choices sometimes confounded him, he respected and admired her.

"You were awful hard to get along with. But you're more interesting and exciting. You're magnificent!"

In rare tender moments, he even said the magic words: "I love you."

Joan's ten-year struggle is not unlike the journey many women took who were mother-wives in the fifties and outgrew their roles. College-educated women, their aspirations were high. As their husband's salary and prestige rose, their personal dilemmas worsened. Their identity crisis echoed an adolescent shrieking in revolt against authority. Who am I? they cried out. Do I have any worth outside of being Mrs. Success?

Like Joan, many struggled through Stage Two, that painful reassessing period, unable to focus, complaining about their empty lot, feeling outraged, impotent, and frequently depressed. Trying out this behavior and that, they were sometimes destructive, sabotaging their own efforts. Often you hear these women, over bridge tables and under hair dryers, blaming their husbands who wouldn't *let them* do this or that. Like Coleman, many men who married in the fifties were standard fifties' models, insensitive and resistant to their wife's changing needs.

"You used to be a sweet kid," is how Coleman put it. Which suggests what many husbands still continue to deny: they enjoy and encourage their wife's dependency. Why? Because her helplessness emphasizes his manhood, a shaky manhood, at that. These men, like Coleman, view the expression of emotions as a weakness reserved for women whom they regard as weak Nellies. Strength is the province of males.

When these same frustrated women turn into bitchy broads, their husbands become furious. And so the battle rages. For months, even years, sometimes never to be resolved.

On the other hand, these women turn into bitchy broads because they are conflicted. To remain in their once-favored position is no longer acceptable. They have long outgrown that role. If they encounter resistance from their husband, their hostility grows. What such a wife needs is encouragement, guidance, attention. Lacking these, her anger swells to rage. You can't push me around anymore, one wife says. If you don't take me seriously, I'll find a man who does, another threatens. All along, husbands like Coleman deny the problem. Or try to fix it with a Band-Aid treatment: an expensive gift; a vacation; anything to distract and avoid a confrontation.

The crunch comes when the wife asserts her independence and wants some degree of autonomy. Does this diminish him? If he thinks so, the bitchy broad period is bound to be volatile. If he feels threatened, she may be pushed to rebel. There are enormous changes of perception along the way.

But if he *hears* her, truly translates her cries into sensible and solvable points, they can move ahead together. Many wives struggle to change their husbands. Some succeed. That the task also involves changing themselves, as Joan did, may be the difference between failure and success. Both partners must change.

"I want a separate identity" does not mean *without* a love relationship or *without* the marriage. It means a sense of achievement, personal recognition self-worth not contingent or a relationship with a husband or child. *In addition to* the marriage, not *instead of*.

The double whammy is that for some couples it becomes an either/or deal. Either you change or I'll become a drunk, a druggie, a basket case, have affairs, or spend, spend, spend. For wives who throw that at their husbands, the game can turn to war. To suicide. To divorce.

Joan, to her credit, did not go to those extremes. She was successful in Stage Three for many reasons. She got support through her own analysis. Her return to graduate school supplied a goal. Establishing her profession as a psychotherapist put her on track. She changed the circumstances and environment of her life as surely as an Escher fish leaves the water or a bird leaves the earth. She enlarged her experiences, stretched herself, explored new roads, met new people, and encountered new ideas. Opening an office, Joan went into business for herself.

As her power grew, the feelings of love and affection for Coleman returned. Like most of us, when we're feeling insecure and frightened, we don't see the other person as a whole—only his warts. Our hypersensitivity increases our hostility. Joan gave up that dog-chasing-tail behavior. As she felt her value grow, she didn't need as much stroking from Coleman. She had her work, colleagues, patients, meetings, professional activities.

Often wives who have no work to reinforce them, and cold husbands who don't understand them, suffer depression. Often they sublimate through clothes, entertaining, redecorating, shopping, socializing—anything to use up their energy. If they can't bitch about their real problems, they bitch about their decorator, their caterer, their seamstress, their hairdresser. Women who feel trapped, who feel without options, feel powerless. Intellectually, they may argue that they love what they are doing. At a gut level, they know they are helpless. Their gut and their head are in conflict.

It takes emotional health and psychological sophistication to escape this trap. To establish power over your own destiny even without your husband's support is a formidable task. To risk the end of the marriage—as Joan did—was to stand firmly in Stage Three. A strong woman.

To continue the lifelong task of maturing is the work of every woman in Stage Three.

Joan did not strike out on the two points that wipe out many women. First, she did not allow her affairs or her husband's to end the marriage. Although she was grievously hurt and Coleman was too, she slowly reestablished feelings of trust and integrity. Many spouses consider penis-into-vagina as the ultimate betrayal. Others put less stress on the anatomical coupling and more on the emotional intimacy. If they can reestablish that with their spouse, they can get past the pain. Joan saw this as her task and addressed herself to the healing process.

Second, after a long run of futile battles, during which she continued to "educate" Coleman, she changed her tactics. Although she didn't swerve from the lessons to be taught, she became a better teacher, more persuasive, less maddening. She made choices that were healthy for both of them. She no longer felt wounded if Coleman didn't give her what she wanted on her terms. She enlarged her life experiences to include stroking from many sources, which took the burden off Coleman. She did not expect her husband to change easily and quickly. She didn't sulk when he was slow or stupid. She was not arrogant, she was helpful. And she continued to pull him along.

Hard work? Of course. A terrible gamble? Absolutely. Was it worth it? Joan says yes, yes, yes.

As Joan became more powerful, she freed herself to discover what she really cared about. Her marriage, her profession, and her own self-growth made the top of the list. In Stage Three she was rewarded with love and work, that invincible combination Freud established for true adulthood.

Now Coleman beams at his wife and brags, "You're more interesting and exciting than ever. You're magnificent. I love you."

At fifty-seven, Joan became a bird. Soaring, leaping, flying high. She felt she deserved every inch, every mile of it.

18

Second Wives and
Second Thoughts:
Melinda and Ariel

From the balcony of her raspberry suite, Melinda watched the white ships sailing to Capri and Naples. She had been a spa *habitué* for years, but the Hotel Regina Isabella on the Italian island of Ischia was her favorite. The setting was extravagantly luxurious. The *haute cuisine* of diet meals was stylishly disguised. And the service was courtly and impeccable. So she returned for the third year to her raspberry suite, with the smell of jasmine wafting from the gardens below.

The guests were always a Who's Who of the rich and beautiful. She leaned against the railing surveying the newcomers as they arrived.

Why not enjoy the *dolce vita*? At home there was nothing but arguments. Sterling was in a perpetually bad mood since the mergers had fallen through. What she had envisioned as the second wife of the president of The Tobacco Company was fun, fun, fun. Well, it was no fun at all.

A breeze fluttered her Hermés scarf. In a sense they both had traded up. He had left his first wife of twenty-eight years and two grown sons for a new life with her. And she had left a promising career as a fashion model to become a corporate wife.

"Almost a Grace Kelly story," she teased him. She was twenty-nine. He was fifty-three.

They had met two years before in Palm Springs while New York was hunkering down against February's freezing slush. They had begun their affair in a perfect hideout where money buys fantasies. He rented a private villa with a pool, a chef, and tennis courts hidden behind a high brick wall.

"I want you," he told her straight out. He said that he was in a marriage he wanted out of, that he was saddled with a wife he'd long outgrown. "You won't be a homewrecker."

Sterling was a powerful man, a Papa Hemingway look-alike, whose corporate acquisitions had led to amazing profits. And she, with that mane of blonde hair, was a middle-aged man's fantasy: she was tall, sleek, satiny, with a model's bones and legs.

He wooed her with I. Magnin, Cartier, Saint Laurent and Louis Vuitton. Under a desert sky, she discarded her custom-made, hand-crocheted bikini along with any coyness. He was a charming ne-gotiator and he had swept her off her feet. After his quickie divorce in Haiti, they married, and Melinda entered the world of corporate wives.

Sterling was a big spender. The Excalibur and the silver Rolls were his—she couldn't touch them— but he bought her a red Ferrari 308 GTB. All were barometers of his power, as conclusively as the gold water-thermos placed daily on a clean linen towel on his desk. He had a reputation to maintain as a high roller and he wanted to show off his beautiful new wife.

Sterling was an attentive mentor. He taught her about fine wines, race horses, and antique auctions. The race horses were his passion. The antiques became hers. She was a fast study.

Corporate wifedom amused her for about a year, until the pleasures wore thin. About the same time, Sterling's ulcers kicked up and he was hospitalized twice. Then his colitis returned and his arthritis set in. Was she going to become a nurse to an ailing, older man? It was not at all what she had planned—not what Sterling had planned either.

He considered ill health a waste of time; it infuriated him. At the least provocation, his temper flared and, like a California forest fire, it turned everything in its path to ashes. As his blood pressure rose, Melinda doubted that she had made a wise choice. There were younger men after her. Two years before, she had thought she'd be pleasure bound when she married a wealthy and worldly powerhouse. Now she was tied to a bad-tempered, sickly patient.

All of which she might have weathered if only his guilt at leaving his family hadn't eaten him up. He spoiled his "boys," ages twenty-five and twenty-three, with expensive "toys." A white BMW for one, a safari to Kenya for the other, plus luxury apartments near him on Central Park West. He phoned them almost daily with intrusive and manipulative advice, which ended in a series of outbreaks and re-criminations. The older son blamed Melinda and sided with his mother. A twenty-nine-year-old stepmother, only four years older than he, was an embarrassment!

Melinda resented the money and time Sterling lavished on them, his attitude that she couldn't understand a father's ties to his children. They fought continuously over his sons, long raging battles that ended in her sleeping in the guest room. Did other second wives suffer the way she did? Were the children of a first marriage intent on destroying the second wife?

She felt cheated. Was this marriage a fiasco?

Melinda's whole stock-in-trade was her body, her looks, her al-luring image. She was also a creature with a high sex drive. The passionate lover Sterling had been in Palm Springs evaporated after six months of marriage. Now everyone else needed his attention first. The corporation needed his full attention. His sons required his attention. Even his race horses took precedence over her.

At first she pretended interest in the horsey crowd at Saratoga's August season. In South Carolina, she smiled through the black-tie dinners after the Aiken Hunt Meet where the oysters florentine, the duck a l'orange, and the marinated loins of venison had kicked off Sterling's ulcers. She even endured the entire six days of the Madison Square Garden Horse Show, where she took pictures of Sterling's gelding "Silky Sultan," when his bridle was pinned with a blue ribbon. But finally, it all seemed boring, worth one long yawn.

She felt restless. She missed the fast-paced work of a model, the checking in, the agency calls, the appointments, the crazy photographer jokes, the laughs. The corporate wives she met were a bunch of dowdy, dopey bubbleheads, and she had nothing to say to them about needlepoint patterns and chintz fabrics. Being on display for Sterling gave her little pleasure now. She missed her spirited friends, gals in their twenties and thirties. She missed her own checkbook.

She missed good sex. She was on fire. Her breasts ached to be fondled and her body needed loving. Sterling was now a hurried lover, and impotency—perhaps caused by the medication to lower his blood pressure—was striking more and more.

To escape her problems, she had come to Ischia to enjoy a week of pampered indolence.

This morning, in an incredible stroke of luck, she recognized her old friend Ariel arriving with luggage. As Ariel stepped out of her taxi, Melinda leaned over the railing and shouted down like a fishwife.

"Ariel? Ariel! Is that you? It's Melinda. Stay there, I'll be right down." Ariel? Here in Ischia? She felt suddenly cheerful.

Melinda and Ariel spent three days together. They talked and talked and talked, analyzing and appraising their marriages and their positions.

They had met four years earlier when Melinda, a sought after model, did the cover for a women's health magazine for which Ariel wrote a three-part series. Ariel was thirty-five then, a freelance journalist, and every once in a while they'd run into each other or meet for a drink in a noisy New York bar. It was an acquaintanceship, not a deep friendship. But here in Ischia, they fastened on to each other like long-lost friends.

Perhaps they were drawn together because each was on a cusp, teetering and uncertain about their relationships with their husbands. Melinda, more volatile than Ariel, put it in typical no-nonsense New Yorkese.

"Either he tells his kids, his horses, and his Corporation to take a flying leap or I leave. I could go back to modeling that easy." She snapped her fingers.

"Why either or? Why not both?" Ariel still had a tinge of Texas twang in her voice, which neither abrasive New York nor her seventeen-year marriage to a Yankee corporate lawyer could erase. Her disarming manner was soft as a magnolia petal, a point of considerable pride to Ken, a patent attorney and their two daughters, thirteen and eleven. Of course they also knew her other side. The feisty Ariel, a determined and practical woman. "Keep the marriage *and* the career. Corporate wives aren't slaves anymore. I do my work and The Corporation doesn't impinge on my life. Never did. I take any assignment I want."

"No entertaining? No relocations? What kind of corporate wife are you?" Melinda teased. She handed her the suntan lotion to do her back.

"We got that corporate stuff out of the way first off. When they asked Ken to go to Indianapolis, I said, 'No. Absolutely no to anywhere in the Midwest.' I worked full tilt until the babies came, and it was important for me to keep working. But when they came, it was important for me to be a mother, too. Oh, we had such good times. We bought a boat and took the kids on trips. I even wrangled a few assignments in the travel magazines. A twenty-hour week gave me enough ego stroking." She put the lotion down. "You could do that, too, Melinda. Work part-time or as much as you liked. You don't have kids to worry about."

Melinda sat up and hugged her knees. "I've been thinking about kids. I'm thirty-two, only seven years younger than you. If I'm gonna do it, I better get going. But Sterling has grown children, men. He's too busy to start over, and I'd want my kids to have a father."

"Oh, Ken was a wonderful father. He gave the girls a lot of attention. Gave them rocketship rides on his knees, played games, lots of hugging. Went to tennis camp with them. TV was a no-no in our house. If you were watching TV, you must be wasting your life. He took a day off to show them the stock exchange. I don't think all fathers do that. He did a lot of parenting and I appreciated it because my father was very distant: a C.P.A we never saw from January through tax season. Ken was great," she glowed. "We had family dinners together every night. And he supported me one hundred percent in my work. He and the girls would take over different household jobs. We assigned tasks."

Melinda was listening intently. "It's not the work of raising kids that I worry about. Would Sterling have time for us? The Company is his life. And he's fifty-three. Already raised a family. No," she shook her head sadly, "he has no patience for infants." She smiled ruefully. "Your Ken is not a typical corporate man."

Ariel nodded in agreement. As a patent attorney making just under $100,000, Ken worked in a rarified atmosphere. Ten lawyers under him, researchers of talent with brilliant minds; bright innovators who were well rounded, socially sophisticated, and family-oriented. "Right. Definitely not a typical corporate man. He doesn't have the stress and responsibility Sterling has either. Nor the salary." She laughed.

"The money, what good is it."

Ken could have done better if he had played corporate politics, Ariel thought. It's not his game. His engineering degree taught him the research values. And his law degree geared him toward a policy of contributing to society. "He has a strong social conscience, an ethical outlook that prohibits him from working for anyone producing fusion material or bombs."

"And he never asked you to play corporate wife? Never?" Melinda asked incredulously.

"No. He respected my work, Melinda. Above all, our family came first. Remember, Ken's ten years older than me, so he was thrilled to be a daddy, and he wanted one of us to be there for every special event in our children's lives."

"Saint Kenneth." Melinda rolled her eyes to heaven.

"Just practical. We decided we didn't want to turn our kids' child-rearing over to strangers. Material success wasn't that important." Ariel was thinking of the corporate scandal that broke when one of the wives literally drank herself to death. Passed out in the bathtub and drowned. Ariel used to talk to her on the phone. She had a maid and a nanny for her twins. What good did it do her?

"I work part-time, free lance. Why can't you?" she challenged. Not an accusation, but Melinda had to field it.

"You're right, you're right. I've been lazy. Maybe the soft life seduced me. All I see ahead now is boredom. There's no excitement without work."

"I learned that the hard way." She sipped her herbal iced tea through a straw.

"Is this confession time? You and Ken aren't Camelot?"

"Oh sure, he'd go shopping when other men balked. He's been sympathetic to my writing. Came out as a feminist before it was fashionable to be anti-chauvinist. He baby-sat, cooked, washed, and never felt compromised."

"Okay. So what's the problem?" She leaned forward, eager for the details. "I know," she guessed. "He was mad because you wouldn't go to Indianapolis."

"No. We got past Indianapolis. I told him, 'Take it if you want. Commute. If you really like it, we'll review our decision after a year.' Ken's flexible. He thought the patent work might have an historical place. But his first priority was us. He even thought about private practice. But the Wall Street firms—he knows some of those people—they're emotionally stunted. They have no other interests but work. We had a lot of fun together."

"Had? You're talking past tense."

Ariel didn't hear her. She was chuckling, caught up in a replay of the good times when the girls were in elementary school. " 'Look, here's how you make your lunch,' I told them. 'If you don't make it or you forget it, you don't eat.' We gave them responsibility from the start. No spoiled brats. It's a question of where your values lie. They never went to sleep-away camp because we took them on family trips. Six weeks in California. A month in Peru."

Melinda interrupted. "When did the trouble start?"

"Trouble?"

"You and Saint Ken?"

"While he commuted to Washington, D.C." Ariel stood up. "I'll tell you about it later. Time for our mud facials, let's go," she said, fluffing her dark springy curls with her fingers.

They walked across the lawn. Two attractive young women, under forty, eager to lie back and have mud smeared on their faces.

"Funny about mud. When you wash it off, you come out cleaner," Ariel commented.

After dinner, they sat on the balcony of Melinda's raspberry suite gazing at the moon and sipping Perrier with lime.

"He commuted to D.C. for two years," Ariel continued. "It was like being a single parent. The whole load was mine. Ken was in court every day. There were thousands of documents and witnesses and intense public interest in the outcome of the trial. Was The Corporation engaged in anti-trust tampering? There were technical implications and the trial lawyers needed Ken's staff to identify points because the patent information was overwhelming. He kept an apartment in D.C., coming and going, four days there, three days here. If he caught the flight out of National, he could be home in an hour and a half. Or we'd go down there because the trial was stretching out endlessly. He was preoccupied. It took all his time and energy.

"He told me, 'This must be what it's like in a private law firm,' because I was grousing at him. I hated it, hated seeing him under such stress. And I felt like an appendage, not his partner anymore. We saw marriages fold under that stress. One lawyer in his forties went on to his third wife. Another in his sixties took on his fifth. Hard to keep score. Ken groused, too. He hadn't jogged or played tennis in months. What could I do? I felt I owed him my support for refusing the Midwest assignment. I also learned something essential about myself."

"What?"

"That I was a person who had to have a separate identity. That my work was important."

"Uh-huh."

"Look, women who don't work are absolutely dependent on their husband. My mother was that way. Her interest was not in developing her own life. She was a decorative Southern lady, decorated her home and her children, a lovely hostess. Growing up and seeing her friends, I thought it was terrible. If you rely on somebody else and don't develop yourself, your real connection to the world withers. And you're very likely to be disappointed."

"Mmm, it's a big price to pay." Melinda put her glass down and spoke thoughtfully. "Are you issuing a warning? Is there a message in that?"

"There was for me, Melinda. I saw options I hadn't explored. I really loved my work and I needed to make realistic plans. Once the kids went off to college, I'd need more work, more challenge. You have to grow or you're doomed to be miserable."

"So you're saying don't turn your life over to a man."

"Never!"

Melinda looked sullen. "I guess you're right. I was doing well, modeling. Two covers in a year, not bad. Then I quit when I married Sterling. You're right, Ariel! There's no reason to return to dependency. I let Sterling turn me back into a child. Entertain me, amuse me, protect me, support me. Buy me things, Daddy! I let him . . ."

"*Let* him? It takes two to tango. Quit blaming Sterling and The Company. What did you do for yourself?"

"You're right. You're right."

"Oh, it's easy to talk it. But it's tough to live it. You wind up trying to be Superwoman. Wife, mother, work, home. It's a balancing act."

"But you do it all. How?"

"I couldn't do it if I weren't organized. I can juggle and I'm a high-energy person. But," she wrung her hands, "something goes, something gives out."

"Like what?"

Ariel avoided the answer on her mind: sex. "I rejected my mother's role model because I knew myself. Knew that work was essential to my well-being. I can't imagine the emptiness of a woman who doesn't have work that matters to her. To be distinguished," she explained, "from a job for a paycheck. Work that matters. D.C. made it click for me."

"How?"

"Maybe it all came together. That my mother and her friends had empty lives. That my child-raising work would soon be over. That a woman must have something to support herself." She tilted her head with amusement. "My mother's aspirations for me were to be a secretary. 'Something to fall back on,' she advised. 'Look at those older women who wind up shop girls in the Dallas stores. They have no skills. A pity.' "

Ariel took another sip of Perrier. "They change," she sighed. "Ken went through a cataclysmic personality change after D.C. In his mid-forties. I wondered if he would survive it. He decided to take a six-month, unpaid leave of absence from The Corporation."

Melinda rested her chin on her hand. "A nervous breakdown?"

"No. He said he needed time away. A period of reassessment. We went to live in Italy, a little town outside Florence."

"I guess I met you right after Italy. Four years ago." She was putting the story in sequence.

"Right. It was six months of hell. A lot of fighting. All that to-getherness was more than I could bear. He would go mountain climbing while I stayed with the kids. Along the way our sex life deteriorated. I saw a lot of marriages cracking when the husband hit mid-forties. I wondered if we'd make it. It was a critical time. No one's immune."

"So you thought about splitting. I have, too."

"It would have been easy to split. When you're feeling bad you fantasize about all the wonderful men out there who are more worthy of you. Endless sexual adventures. An idealized lover. Ken made me feel put upon. He was cranky and critical, doing uprooting things to us. He wasn't the Ken I knew. I saw other couples getting divorced. I lived with the hope that it was a phase."

"So you hung in."

"I'm an optimist, it's my strongest suit." She stood up and leaned against the railing. "Does divorce solve anything? It only adds a lot more economic and emotional stress."

"But you're a feminist." Melinda tweaked her.

"Of course. I used my maiden name for seven years after I was married. Now I use his name because it's easier for the kids. But I prefer personist to feminist. Some feminists aren't willing to give an equal shake to men. They've been so harassed by them, they see men as the enemy. I think men have their own set of strengths. What's wrong is, we expect too much of marriage. We let it limit us."

"Well, I expected good sex. I expected to be faithful. Now I'm having second thoughts."

"Second thoughts? About fidelity?" Melinda nodded. "Fidelity is not on my list of qualifications for a happy marriage."

"No?" Melinda was wide-eyed.

"If I found out Ken was having an affair, I wouldn't divorce him. We talked about it before he left for D.C. He'd had a lot of affairs before we were married and he was candid about them. Before he left I said something to him that I still stand by. I said, 'I've changed my mind about fidelity. Second thoughts. I'm not sure I'll remain faithful the way I have in the past.' "

"You said that to him?" Ariel nodded. "Then you had the affair. Was he furious?"

Ariel neither confirmed nor denied it. Telling Melinda was tantamount to an announcement in the *Times*. "Ken said, 'That's your private decision. What people do with their bodies is their own business. Just do me one favor, okay? In a misguided moment of candor, don't tell me about it.' "

"He said that? Sterling would kill me."

"I liked that he said that. It made me feel that our relationship was not proprietary on his part. You're talking about a sexually sophisticated man. A man who thought it was stupid that I was a virgin at twenty-two. My Southern roots denied it then. But I'm having second thoughts about a lot of things."

"You mean . . . ?"

"If someone came along whom I found sexually attractive and I admired him, I'd feel free to sleep with him."

Melinda blinked. "You would?" Most wives wouldn't admit it.

"At my age you think about getting old. If you feel unappreciated, it could become an attractive option."

"I've thought about it. Plenty."

"I no longer feel that sexual exclusivity is necessary for my marriage."

"But you wouldn't tell him, would you?" Melinda asked.

"Of course not. Discussing an affair could only have a negative impact."

"Then what really matters in a marriage? If fidelity is kaput, what's left?"

"Commitment. Commitment to the other person's well-being is what establishes the underpinnings of a good marriage."

Melinda snorted. "And commitment to the corporation dooms it."

"Ken's zest for living returned. He went back to The Corporation. His interest in learning and his attitudes toward life still excite me. He's a wonderful father, Melinda, my best friend, a fundamentally decent person. He has a set of Boy Scout rules I admire. He's vital and vibrant."

"And sex is good now?"

"Most of the time. He's rarely impotent and it's no big deal. Know something?" She put her hand on Melinda's shoulder like a big sister about to dispense truth. "After D.C. and Italy, I changed my mind about a lot of those carefully packaged assumptions about marriage."

"What did you do?" Melinda expected a juicy confession.

"I put my money where my mouth was. Went into business. Those two lousy periods strengthened my resolve that I really needed a life of my own. Starting this business was a practical solution."

A business? Not an affair? She was disappointed. "What kind of business?"

"Public relations. It seemed like a low capital investment. And it combined our skills—writing, advertising, and sales."

"You had partners?"

"Four. We were five women who had worked well together in the League of Women Voters to change the charter system from commission to community executive. We didn't have a proper background." She chuckled. "We were confident and energetic, raring to go. So we each kicked in $1,000 to get it rolling."

Melinda was impressed. "How did Ken react?"

"He loved the idea. Gave me a lot of support. So did the girls. They're very good about marketing and doing dinners during the week if I have a late meeting. We share the work."

"Some people have all the luck."

"C'mon. You make your own luck. We had awful setbacks the first year. Two of the women quit because their husbands balked. We kept getting turned down by the people we went after. We limped along for a while with a few local accounts." She counted them out on her fingers. "A car dealer, two retail stores, a chiropractic group, and a dance studio. Five. But last year we expanded to special events and fund-raising. And this year we're running a political campaign," she added joyfully. "When we go to parties now, I bask in the limelight. People want to know my opinions, they want my approval. What I say counts." She gave a wry smile. "Ken gets a little jealous. But I eat it up. I've even made some financial investments."

"Wild! Like what?" Melinda was intrigued.

"Sound investments. I got curious. Started reading *The Wall Street Journal*. I talked to a financial planner who helped me find high-income bonds where my principal is safe. Next I'm going for growth real estate." She laughed with pleasure. "I'm going to need a tax shelter. I really like money!"

"Your business must be terrifically successful."

"At the four-year mark, we just rented new space in a snazzy professional building. We have a full-time secretary, a graphic artist, a bookkeeper, and a staff. Phasing out of child-rearing and establishing myself in full-time work was the smartest thing I ever did. A smooth transition."

"Weren't you scared?"

"Sure. I'm still scared. Maybe I'll end up owing a lot of money. Maybe the business will fail. But I had to risk it." She took a deep breath and sighed. "The reason I made it is because I recognized the risks and avoided the land mines. I planned it. Then I did it. You have to act on your convictions. Or you get torn up inside."

"Right."

"I can't exist without real work. I have no identity without work. Without work, who am I?"

Melinda folded her hands thoughtfully. "Maybe that's it. I've got hobbies now, like the horses, but no real work. Maybe work, not sex, is my problem."

The phone rang and Melinda stepped inside to get it. "Sterling?"

Ariel heard genuine pleasure in her voice which dropped its New York tough. "I miss you, too," she cooed, "and we have a lot to talk about." This was going to be a long private conversation. Melinda's voice was glowing with enthusiasm. "Next week? To Ischia? Wonderful!"

Ariel waved good-bye as she crossed Melinda's suite.

Seen in chiaroscuro, Melinda looked innocent, not urbane. All anger drained from her, she looked as rosy as any woman in love.

Ariel closed the door softly.

Most women in Stage Three do work they care about. It is through their work that they develop a separate identity. Therefore, they value their work beyond its ability to make them money. Work is something that defines them. It is an important priority in their lives, not an extra. Their work validates them and establishes them as independent persons. Through their work they gain a sense of themselves, a status based on personal achievement.

Their work creates for them what Ariel calls "a real connection to the world." Often that is accompanied by a state of emotional healthiness and an abiding optimism that snuffs out defeat.

Even while they work part-time and combine work with child-rearing, Stage Three wives retain a sense of themselves as real persons. Many successfully find a combination of family and work that is right for them. They do not agonize over *either-ors*. They prefer to look for *ands*, ways to get the most from their work life and their family relationships. Not an easy feat.

Some wind up obsessive Superwomen who wear themselves out trying to do everything well. Their standards are nothing less than perfection. The perfect wife-mother-careerist. However, less demanding hyphenates can suffer burn-out too. Because when push comes to shove, the major responsibility for the household and children remains the woman's.

Successful Stage Three wives set up a balance that is realistic, that avoids burn-out and still provides a sense of accomplishment. They don't indulge in all-or-nothing-at-all.

When Melinda married, she turned her life over to her husband. She gave up her career to be taken care of. She also lost her identity. Even if her husband's illnesses had not occurred, she was bound to be disappointed. Women who have tasted success and independence do not easily give up adulthood to return to childhood.

Melinda was not realistic. She was swept away by the old myth that a man would rescue her and forever be her Prince Charming and her Daddy.

Ariel, tougher and more realistic, made plans for her future. Once child-rearing responsibilities diminished, she would move from part-time to full-time, following a sensible transition that balanced her family responsibilities against her need for autonomy. Self-growth was clearly her goal. "You have to grow or you're doomed to be miserable," she told Melinda.

And she acted on her plans.

Stage Three is no guarantee of success.

Many women in Stage Three pay lip service. They say the right words, affect the correct feminist postures, espouse the proper attitudes. But they do not take action. Like Melinda, they may have established an identity—even attained some success—before marriage. But once Prince Charming comes along, they let their husbands return them to childlike dependency.

It can destroy them. They feel one way. But they simply cannot act on their feelings.

Stage Three wives are generally high-energy persons. Bottling up that energy or siphoning it off into tasks that really do not interest them makes them angry. They blame their husband. The corporation. Bad luck. Their stepchildren. Ill health. Anything to avoid accepting responsibility for their own behavior. This induces a state of perennial anger and paralyzing conflicts.

Stage Three is all options and opportunities. It is a feast of possibilities for the woman who sees them. Work, sex, love, family, accomplishment, identity, commitment, success. Each beckons, calling: *taste me, try me.* For risk takers like Ariel, it is a movable feast.

Stage Three releases a flood of opportunities. But any opportunity carries risks. The woman in Stage Three who establishes realistic goals and has the ability to set priorities is more likely to succeed. Like Ariel, she plans for a transition period, then carries it out smoothly.

Other wives in Stage Three lose their heads and behave like greedy children in a candy factory. So much is available. So many options to pick from. They gorge themselves. The result? Pain as palpable as the cramps of a stomachache.

Ariel's need for freedom came after two changes: Washington, D.C. and Italy. She saw Stage Three as a vast unexplored galaxy. What she chose was the opportunity to grow through work. For her and for many young Stage Three wives, work and identity are one. These women raising children are eager to return to the world of competition and achievement. To be full adults.

In Stage Three, the struggle for personal growth is not won like a medal. It goes on, continuing through each new success. Failures are setbacks, but not the end. Sometimes they even offer a new start.

Stage Three is fire and ice. Setbacks and startups. Second thoughts and risks.

Stage Three offers rewards too glorious to pass up.

Why couldn't Melinda—younger than Ariel—see that a return to dependency often produces a new set of conflicts? Perhaps, like many women in Stage Three, her head knew it. But her heart denied it. Unresolved conflicts can tie a woman to a self she no longer likes. Can immobilize her and prevent her from taking action. Once Melinda resolves her conflicts, like Ariel she may feel a new freedom and move toward independence and growth.

Stage Three is both grave and joyous, fearful and optimistic, characterized by a sprightliness and even an irreverence toward established pieties. Second thoughts turn into action. Stage Three is a period of zippy energy, plausible plans, and stunning successes.

In Stage Three a woman can become more than she believes she is. More, perhaps, than she ever dreamed.

19

What About The Men?
The Husband's Point of View

A book based on hundreds of interviews with corporate wives clearly is dealing with a particular point of view: *the woman's.* Her words describe the events of her life, a picture filtered through the lens of her own sensibilities. Each journey through Stages One, Two, and Three is told from the wife's point of view.

Some of the women were hurt and angry. They expected better treatment and more understanding. Others were satisfied and content. They reported strong support and heartfelt good will from their husbands.

Furthermore, since each interview reflects that wife's state of mind at a particular moment, our picture represents a click of the shutter, capturing that woman in what film producers call a freeze-frame. If we were to return to these same women one year, five years, ten years from now, we would get another picture, hear a different interview, and capture another truth.

While science must duplicate each experiment to prove itself, human beings never duplicate the same experience. Truth changes. Or perhaps there are many truths. What these corporate wives felt at the time of their interview is one of these truths. Their words and feelings as they reported them were real feelings. Truths deeply felt, providing us with a wide range of truths we can accept.

But what about the men?

Are corporate husbands really such oafs? Bores? Clods? Are they as insensitive and unfeeling as their wives reported? Is there another truth? The husband's point of view?

I think so.

This book did not set out "to get" corporations. And this chapter is neither a defense of corporate men nor a whitewash to vindicate corporations. Let's be fair-minded. Let's make sure we know who the enemy is.

Is it corporate men?

Is it corporations themselves?

Is it our male and female cultures that fail to support us?

Is it all of the above? And more?

Let's try to get a clear picture of the corporate executive.

Wives in every stage, from compliant to competitive, described their husbands as men who were not risk takers. Hard workers. Loyal company men. Ambitious, eager-to-please employees, yes. But, with the exception of those men who left the corporation to become entrepreneurs, most corporate husbands seemed to value security above all. They were men whose power was derived from their association with a mighty corporation: the giants with the power to change our lives. Mighty corporations that cast a long shadow.

Do they attract a particular type?

Many corporate men spoke of their corporation as "us." In conversations they said "we" believe and "we" maintain. It is the language of the executive on the way up. His identification with corporate goals is strong. His ability to survive is based on gamesmanship, and he gets the rules of his corporation down pat.

Initiative and imagination are not often rewarded by corporations that attract bland types rather than show stealers. Suggestions for innovations move at a snail's pace through a web of corporate bureaucracy. Because no one wants to be wrong, it's easier to turn down new ideas than to say yes. Yes—if it doesn't work—can place your head on the chopping block.

Perhaps the reason the corporate man rises is that he never acts the rebel, never flouts the system, never pursues his own ideas if it means running the risk of alienating a corporate chief. The list of *nevers* is comprehensive. As specific as, never wear white shoes. It includes matters of personal taste that have nothing to do with performance.

Every corporation has a culture of its own. The corporate man observes its rituals. Wears the right clothes. Joins the right club. Eats the right food. Knows the passwords and speaks the code language.

This is a heavy burden. Wives who stay home—and many corporate wives do—may not fully appreciate what it means to be on the firing line every minute of the day. Of course, they are wrestling with their own domestic pressures. Very different pressures. The children. The car pools. The plumber. The problem may be that corporate husbands and wives are living on different planets, observing different male and female cultures.

The corporate man, as he moves to the top, has invested heavily in his corporation. It is more than a job. More than time ticked off in years. More than a salary. It is his ego, his status, his security. His corporation's name—wraps him in prestige. Gives him power. He carries cards with his corporation's name. Writes letters on corporate stationery.

"The corporation is his life," wives say.

Many corporate husbands do not deny it. They are the first to admit that the corporation is their primary concern. They become workaholics. Loyal and compliant. Obedient as wives in Stage One. The corporation tells them who they are. What constitutes success and failure. How they score.

What does this do to a man to have his manhood so narrowly defined? Does this stretch him or reduce him?

To measure one's manhood against corporate goals, to be forced to play by corporate rules, is a limiting experience for some men. They feel stifled and diminished. A few choose to leave corporate life altogether. They recognize that they are round pegs in square holes.

If the corporate husband is feeling constricted at the same time that he sees his wife stretching and growing, nearly bursting her seams, there is bound to be marital conflict. He has to pull back and be cautious just when she is feeling exuberant. He has to obey authority. She is establishing her own authority. He is bound. She is free. He is making more money, but finding his wings clipped. She is testing new powers. She is flying.

"I'm thinking about going back to college for my graduate degree," one wife says.

"I'm enrolling in art courses at the museum. I won't be home for dinner on Mondays and Wednesdays," another announces.

"I borrowed $5,000 from my mother and I'm buying into Fran's business," a third declares.

They are in Stage Three and flexing their muscles. Free.

Or maybe they are in Stage Two—uncertain and shaky, critical and restless. Just when he has to toe the line and play the game harder, there's no comfort for him at home. He hears her complaints as bitching, and he can't deal with it. The closer he is to the top, the more costly an error can be. He's worried. His future is at stake. Did he say too little or too much at the last meeting? Are his wingtips shiny enough? Will his strategy win him a step up? Or will his tactics be shot down by a Young Turk eager to squash him? The higher he gets, the more he has to lose. Corporate politics and status symbols take on more, not less, importance. One false move, one bad decision, and his corporate rise is over, finished.

Doesn't she understand his pressures? She used to. He has come to depend on her. He needs her emotional support and she isn't there for him. Instead, she's complaining, bitching, talking about how *she* feels, what *she* wants. He's confused. Irritated. Pretty damn mad.

All this is playing out against a background that can stretch through months, perhaps years, while his wife is coming into her own. He can't fathom this journey she's taking through Stages Two and Three. He doesn't even recognize her. And he can't take the time to find out. "I've got my own pressures," he shouts back.

But he doesn't like what he sees.

In Stage Three she is becoming feisty and playful. She's having fun while his nose is to the grindstone. She's sexually demanding. His quiet virgin bride is speaking up, telling him how to make love to her and what she wants. He's tired, uninterested in her consciousness-raising pundits. Perhaps even impotent now and then and it frightens him. Is he losing it?

She's energetic, he's beat. He drags home with his briefcase full of paperwork, stares glassy-eyed at the TV, and falls asleep with a drink in his hand. She bops out for her aerobics class in her electric blue leotard, calling instructions for popping a TV dinner into the microwave.

He feels resentful. He feels short-changed.

She's free, exploring new options. He's locked in, trapped. She can play any wild card in the deck, take a chance on a new business, a new career, a new hobby. What can he do?

He feels jealous. It's not fair, damn it!

Some men deal with this by criticizing their wives. Turning sour, angry, even vengeful. They regard their wives' growth as a threat. They argue, they resist, they refuse to make adjustments. They will not take on the simplest household tasks which are "women's work." They even place serious stumbling blocks in her path. They do not give up comfort and power easily.

Even men of good will can feel this way.

Liberated, feminist men can feel this way.

Honorable, decent men can feel this way.

Caring and devoted husbands can feel this way.

Intellectually they know what is right. In their head they know what is fair. They really do want their wives to flourish. They announce it bravely at parties. "I'm so proud of her. Do you know she's up for a judgeship?" They brag about her all over the place.

But in their heart of hearts there is a small whimper. Hey, not at my expense. There is a huge leap between what they know and what they feel.

They feel torn. (But they want to be reasonable.)

They feel cheated. (But they want to be fair.)

They feel resistant. (But they don't want to give up the services she provided.)

Ariel's husband Ken, a feminist, may have felt this way when he underwent a cataclysmic personality change and took a six-month, unpaid leave. In Italy, he reassessed his goals, backed off from the corporate world, and took time out to play. The convenient media label for this is male mid-life crisis. Ariel observed that at the forty mark a man trades in his wife or his job. It is a shaky period for men. Perhaps not unlike Stage Two for women. Corporate men may find it even harder than men not governed by a mighty corporation.

Some corporate husbands weigh it out and come to realize that in the corporate world promotions have less to do with achievement than with gamesmanship. There is the crushing blow, that moment of truth, when someone else gets the promotion. When corporate loyalty fades. When a corporate man, like Ken, takes the measure of his manhood and examines himself on different terms. *Wonderful father* counts for a lot. *Good husband* does, too. There are other rulers that measure more accurately, more deeply, than corporate success. *Family comes first* is a value that younger husbands are declaring without apology.

"Sorry, we can't relocate because my wife's just started her own business," is not unheard of today. More and more younger men are giving equal concern to their wives' careers. The corporation doesn't come before all other gods.

Yet there remains a core of husbands who still equate corporate success with personal self-worth. Their ego and self-esteem are totally tied up in the corporation. The company tells them whether they are a success as a man or a failure. Whether they're worth an office without a window or a glass wall with a view, a parking space for their station wagon or a private limo. The trappings define them. Because money and power are the lifeblood of the corporation, these men believe they are what they earn. They become tangled in a web of corporate customs, traditions, and signposts they must obey. They accept the corporation's right to issue their report card. Once they accept it, their maleness, their manhood, and their personhood are severely limited. Their focus is narrowly defined. It serves the corporation, not the man or his family.

Whenever self-worth is established by an outside force, that person is diminished.

However, the corporation is not the only force that limits men's definition of manhood. The male culture reinforces the corporation's narrowness.

Along with other myths that diminish men—myths about the male role as providers, men's proprietary relationship to women, and male sexual dominance—the male culture gives husbands little to enlarge themselves, little to draw from, little to extend their personhood and become more human. It does not encourage growth, inner strength, or maturity.

The male culture carries myths about manhood like environmental poisons in the air. If the corporations belch the smoke from their chimneys, the male culture disseminates the lethal gases. If corporations are antagonistic to family life, the male culture, which tells men how to behave toward women, reinforces those life-reducing myths.

What does the male culture tell a husband he must be?

First and foremost, a good provider.

That means make money. The more he makes the more man he is. The gifted sculptor who ekes out a mere $5,000 year is considerably less a man than the prize fighter who collects his million-dollar purse in one night.

Women's pre-feminist culture propogated the same myths. It told girls to marry up, to marry money, to find a good provider.

Young corporate wives in Stage One depend on their husband's earning power. They begin as submissive, non-assertive types just like their corporate men. Dependency keeps them loyal. Just as the corporation is the source of money and power to men, husbands are the source of money and power to corporate wives. Just as the corporation is the authority that must be pleased, so the husband becomes the authority and he must be pleased. One does not spit in the face of authority. Dependency knows its place even while it denies the reality; denies the depression; denies the choking strangulation. Denial ends with Stage Two.

The myth of the good provider limits growth for both men and women. It puts a premium on one aspect, *money*, and reduces the human qualities to second place. Families give up time together, caring, and intimacy so that the provider can make more money. The myth makes them become less than they can be. It limits their freedom and squelches their dreams.

Men's proprietary relationship to women is another myth that the male culture continues to perpetuate and the corporations continue to support.

"The company owns him," wives complain in Stage Two.

Later in Stage Three, we hear the echo when the wife declares her freedom. "You don't own me! You can't tell me what to do anymore. I'm a person!"

How far does power extend? A corporation can own and operate its business, true. Can establish rules and expect excellence in performance. But can a modern husband expect to operate his marriage unilaterally? Many do. Despite feminism's enormous contribution to the consciousness of women and men, most men are still boss in their homes. If they are also the sole wage earner, it seems to follow that they make the decisions.

Therefore, it comes as an enormous shock to them when their wives in Stage Three make decisions without consulting them.

"You what? You bought a sofa and didn't even ask me?"

It is not merely the wresting of power that sticks in their craw—not only that they expect her to ask for approval. More than that, they regard her acting without consulting him with a certain sadness, a melancholy based on earlier, sweeter days when she asked for his advice every inch of the way. Now, strong and forthright in her opinions, she takes action by herself. He can admire that. But another side of him wistfully longs for the good old days when she didn't make a move without him.

Younger husbands brought up to have a more nearly equal relationship with their spouses say they want to be partners in decision making; domestic or financial. They don't want to be left out. Intellectually, they applaud their wife's independence and spirit. But emotionally her new strengths may appear to threaten a loss of intimacy.

"Why didn't we talk about this?" They feel shut out. Hurt.

"You always used to come to me and ask my opinion. Now you decide what you want and you go for it."

"Of course," she smiles, pleased, "I'm an adult."

His proprietary rights are invaded.

Many husbands want to have an equal relationship with women. But their cultures have so long told them they are Number One that they have been socially trained to take first place and hold the line. They are socialized to expect deference and compliance from women.

When their wives enter Stage Three and also become Number One, they are astounded. It's hard to rethink basic assumptions, to change habits of thinking. Can there be *two* Number Ones? Equality is intellectually acceptable, even admirable. But once the burdens of freedom emerge, men balk. They must make adjustments. Divest themselves of proprietary behavior. Evolve a whole new way of reacting.

This requires a new maturity that many men cannot rise to. If they've believed all their lives that males are special, the sudden discovery that it no longer holds true requires an abrupt redefinition.

This is especially difficult for corporate husbands.

Corporations are built on male power. Until recently women were incidental aides to corporations. They constituted a secondary lineup of secretaries and other "girls" who carried out orders and decisions made by men. The recent influx of executive women—a small percentage despite the media hoopla—put corporate men off. Competitive, ambitious women out to run the distance against them? They could compete against men, negotiate with men, take rejection from men. But from a woman? Hey, c'mon, you can't push me around, I'm a man. It went against their grain. Their male culture. Their corporate culture. Their socialization.

If at home his Stage Three wife is also acting up, his fury is fanned. Women don't know their place anymore. Where once he could be benevolent dictator, a nice boss, a sweet daddy, now he is faced with a strong, opinionated woman whom he regards as his adversary. To compete against a powerful woman in corporate life is ego-shattering to some men. To lose is devastating. To deal with the same forthright adult woman at home is to wage battle.

To make sure they don't lose, some men resort to humiliation and abuse. They use dirty tricks against women in the corporation. At home they remain rigid and unbending. They will not transfer power or proprietary rights. They will not negotiate. They will not deal with women.

Another myth, the myth of male sexual dominance, has been flaunted since the beginning of time. Men are the sexual aggressors, women merely passive. Corporations encourage the myth of aggressive behavior. In men, not women. They talk about "scoring." Secretaries fawn over their male bosses and service their needs. The Boss attitude spills over to sex with their wives. Men initiate or withhold sex. It is in their power to demand sex. To get it as often as they like and on their terms.

In Stage One, wives often consider that giving sex is an obligation for being supported. They want to please their husband, not court his disfavor. If he is traveling, they may wonder if he has affairs. Does he meet attractive working women and spend the night? On the weekend when he comes home, sex is often hurried, something fit in after everything else is taken care of. Please him. Or someone else will.

It is not until Stage Two that wives complain.

It is not until Stage Three that they actually speak up and ask for what they want from sex.

Some men are turned on by a woman aroused and eager for sex. They acknowledge that women are sexual creatures just like themselves, that they have appetites and fantasies and they want to give and receive pleasure. A wife who tells him how to please her is a delight.

Other men, unable to divest themselves of the myths of male dominance, feel it as pressure and they are turned off. Where is she learning this experimental stuff? She wants to go to a porno movie, talks about multiple orgasms, and demands oral sex. He becomes suspicious, jealous. This is not the little girl he married—as soft and as pink as a nursery. Has his wife become a scarlet woman? She makes sexual demands he can't meet. She expects sexual satisfaction as if he were a sexual athlete. And she is no longer deferential, reticent, and passive.

For the husband whose male culture has established him as Number One, this is heresy. To lose his place as the sexual aggressor goes against everything the culture has taught him.

Myths about sex, money, and power still float in the air, their noxious poisons inhaled by men and women. The non-feminist women's culture spews them out with the same virulence as male and corporate cultures. Wives who talk baby talk to manipulate their feared husband are the evidence. Corporate wives like Dolly, for example, employ the power of the weak. To stay married to rigid husbands they cannot deal with, they act out the myths while they live in fear. Their husband is the Boss. He can fire his wife—divorce her—with the same ease the corporation terminates an employee. To stay in favor, she plays weak and passive. A nice house pet who never shows her claws.

This option is unacceptable to women in Stage Three who have become whole and healthy persons.

Finally, despite the difficulties, there is a deep well of good will between husbands and wives today. A commitment to each other's well-being that helps both of them through Stage Two and Stage Three. This good will, when transformed into good deeds, can make the difference between success and failure. Wives who develop good negotiating skills are teaching their husbands lovingly, so that both can tap a bounty of rich rewards.

Husbands who are open-minded and flexible want to nourish and support their wives through their perilous journey toward self-growth. They believe that they, too, will be the richer for it. They say, 'Yes! I want an adult partner and I want to help her get there."

"My wife has a good career in publishing. She's smart and I love to hear her talk about a new book she's acquired. It adds drama to my life. She's interesting. She pulls her weight. She's what I call a real partner."

Instead of turning her journey through Stages Two and Three into a tragedy in which no one wins the battle of wills, these husbands recognize that the first tug is not a call to war, but a plea for help. His help is vital. His encouragement is the boost she needs.

Nevertheless, many men of good will admit they feel a sense of loss, even a deep despondency, as their wives reach Stage Three. It is a bittersweet experience for husbands, not unlike a parent seeing his child grow into an independent adult. There is genuine pride when she emerges as a successful person in her own right. But along with it comes a twinge of existential pain, a nostalgia for the days of her early dependency.

It is no surprise then that husbands, malnourished by the myths of their male and corporate cultures, find the adjustment difficult. For some it is pure hell. Culture shock. They know that helping their wives to become fully mature and self-actualized is the morally correct stance. But it hurts to give up the myths. Wisdom and happiness are not the same.

Additionally, with her new strengths come obligations on his part. They now face each other as two equal adults. It is not an easy transition, even for the kindest of men.

A smart woman is sensitive to this melancholia. Observing his struggle, she often feels badly for him. She does not judge him, she sympathizes and helps him along the way. She understands how threatening it is for a man educated by the male and corporate cultures to accept the adult person she has become.

Until the seventies, the protocol between men and women was structured as strictly as a minuet. Women curtsied. Men bowed. Now, husbands are perplexed.

"Women have turned it topsy-turvy. They order the wine. They whip out their Visas to pay the check. They whistle for a cab. They phone their broker. They give orders to their secretary," a film executive griped to a colleague over cocktails.

"Shit! Her secretary is a man!"

The final humiliation is to take orders from a woman.

Georgia was sensitive to what Ross was going through. She called it "the loss of the wife he married." She understood his side. "He may admire me, but I've cost him some difficult adjustments." True. Ross was beset with contrary impulses. At times he wanted to deliver a karate chop to her. On the other hand, he knew she was right, damn it!

"Poor David," a wife confides to her sister over lunch. "He needs my attention. He's trying, really trying. But I have to fly to London for the negotiations. Be gone a week."

"I know, I know," her sister commiserates with her. "My working full-time has Hank's nose out of joint. It knocks him out and sets up stresses that are unavoidable. Husbands! It's the big topic of our

CR group." She shrugs and flashes an optimistic smile. "But he's a good guy. When he gets there, he's going to be terrific."

"Guess I have to be more patient, just repeat and repeat. Look, he's no dummy. But his whole life has been one way. Now it's another. It's hard for him to let go of *tough*." She tilts her head sympathetically like a mommy watching her kid struggle to tie her shoelaces.

Women have something going for them that men do not. Friendships.

Women talk to each other. Privately or in consciousness-raising groups, they reveal their pain and discuss their struggles. They share experiences and laugh over their mistakes. As they move through Stage Two and Stage Three, they draw strength from other women.

Men do not have that crucial protective layering of male friendships. Limited by the narrowness of their cultures, they rarely talk to other men about deep feelings. A man may rely almost entirely on his wife for emotional support. He regards her as his best friend. Indeed she may be his only friend.

Corporate friendships are often shallow, based on a mutual interest in computers or sports. Executives don't talk intimately to their colleagues or their tennis partners. To reveal personal pain is not in the tradition of "tough." A real man keeps a stiff upper lip and hides expressions of tenderness and affection between men which are unmanly.

The woman who succeeds more easily in Stage Three is often the one who considers her husband's point of view. She learns the trick of translating the rhetoric.

"Her passion is for her job, not me," a corporate chief complained. "Even when she asks my advice, she contradicts me and doesn't follow it. All she talks about is money. Making it, investing it, her cash flow, her tax shelters. She's in love with success."

Translation: She's getting so damn smart. It scares me. What if she doesn't need me anymore?

Another corporate executive confronted his feelings when his wife sold her first novel. Although his style of speech was orotund and his manner patronizing, his wife Ellen read the subtext.

"When I see other wives taking shirts to the cleaners, when I see your papers all over the kitchen table, when I see the dishes piled up in the sink because you're too busy to load the dishwasher, I know this isn't going to be an easy proccess for us."

Translation: I wonder if I'm letting myself be pushed around. Is she turning me into a wimp?

Darlene erupted into Stage Three like a volcano. Each time she changed jobs, she was grabbing a chance to advance. When she told Cal she was joining his company, he issued a warning. "The Company runs at a near-frenetic pace."

Translation: Don't step on my turf. Don't compete with me. I have to stay here. You're free to move anywhere. Don't show me up, damn it!

In Stage One, wives give their greatest performance as mothers and nurturers, dispensers of comfort and support. In Stage Two and Stage Three, they assign that role to its proper place to become full adult partners. Husbands of good will, oafs, boors, and bastards all feel those shock waves.

Enlisting a husband's aid in Stage Three is not easy.

Nor is establishing a partnership based on mutual respect.

There is a husband's point of view, and smart wives acknowledge it.

In Stage Three, husbands and wives both lose the person they were. But they can find a better one.

20

Rewards For the Winners:
Families and Corporations

═══════════════════════════════

Many people are willing to make a dangerous journey if they are convinced they will arrive at a rewarding destination. They will withstand the bumpy roads, hold tight over the potholes, and sidestep the land mines because the end promises to be very much worth it.

American women have a history of this kind of spirit. As pioneers they crossed this vast land in covered wagons, risking Indian raids, icy mountains, and thrashing rivers because they believed life would be sweeter when they reached the Western frontier. Some did not make it. Others won against the adversities and established a new and better life with their families.

Today those Indian raids come in other guises. Subtle and insidious forces are at work in our cultures that limit our dreams. Male cultures, corporate cultures, and pre-feminist cultures have imposed behaviors on us that harm family life. Women's own fears operate to hold back their personal development.

Yet many women in the 1980s have changed their lives for the better as drastically as the nineteenth-century pioneers. Although they did not take the physical journey across this land, although they did not weather mud slides and torrential storms, they took a harrowing emotional and psychological journey into new territory. Despite the hardships along the way, women who have succeeded in Stage Three tell us they are far better off than when they started out. Healthier, wiser, and stronger.

Playing for high stakes, they took the risk and won.

Who are the winners?

You can pick them out of a crowd. You hear it in their voices, you see it in their postures. You recognize it in their attitudes. Even during the shaky time while they danced between the sun and the moon—three steps up, two steps back—they were advancing toward their destination. As they peeled off layers of *reflected* status from their husbands, they uncovered their own powers. Gaining *earned* recognition, these winners, like pioneer women, tackled the conflicts of being a real woman when society handed them a false map.

Winners threw that map away and drew up their own plan. Like pioneer women, they had courage to become birds flying freely.

And even after their arrival, the pioneer spirit continued to move them toward self-development. What are the rewards for these wives?

Winners who reach their destination say they have *real power* now. They enjoy *better sex*. They achieve *adult love* based on *honest communications*. Giving up dependency, they gain *self-esteem* and *identity*. Their metamorphosis brings *personal growth*, an *excitement* that fuels them.

The wife of the controller of a Fortune 500 pharmaceutical corporation said:

"I took a lot of shit for a lot of years and I can't figure out why. Maybe I was afraid of him, he was a God to me. I wanted to please him. I *still* want to please him. But now . . ." She chuckled. "I want to please me, too. If that's selfish, I can only tell you it feels wonderful."

Risk

Why don't the others make it to the end of the journey?

Perhaps dependency versus *risk* is the largest issue that separates women. To hang on to the status quo or sally forth into unexplored terrain?

Some people are natural risk takers. They require stimulation, and it's fun for them to take a chance. They enjoy the excitement of a new adventure and the thrill of action. They have a natural affinity for Stage Three. They are drawn to adventure. Change fulfills them. Therefore, they act.

Others avoid risk. They worry about every possible trouble that can come up along the way. They want peace, not stimulation. Calm, not excitement. They have a natural aversion to Stage Three. Therefore, they stay in place, fenced into a familiar square called a woman's place.

Stage Three is a prescription for happiness, not a guarantee. It is a map of options. In Stage Two women study the map and figure out their chances. In Stage Three they start out.

The winners, like mountain climbers who reach the top, feel a glorious sense of achievement. Their journey has changed them. They are richer in ways they hardly imagined.

"It's like falling in love. The sky is bluer and the air is sweeter. You wonder, has the world flipped over? No, nothing has changed, except I'm in control. In control of me!"

Like the mountain climbers at the summit, winners lick their finger and scribble a graffiti message to the sky: I did it!

The alternative to change is stagnation. A decline of spirit and dissipation of energy. Perhaps traditional husbands looked for traditional wives, but younger men are singing another tune, saying they prefer spirit to compliance. Many men want a real life partner, a full person who brings her own excitement to his life.

The leap toward personal fulfillment in Stage Three is rooted in a particularly American brand of optimism. An attitude that includes risk. It was established in the Emersonian concept of transcendentalism which stresses self-reliance and independence. It instructed us to go beyond, to extend ourselves by transcending imposed boundaries and limitations. Wives who hear that message reach beyond their cultural limitations and invite a sense of well-being into their souls.

The dividends of women's individual growth enrich the lives of their husbands and their families. Marriages grow stronger, relationships become tighter. Women's growth eventually seeps down into the soil of our American culture. Women in Stage Three are changing the face of America.

Conflict

The journey to self-growth requires many acts of courage for wives in dealing with all the *conflicts*. There are internal conflicts that go on in their heads. Should I do this or that? There are real conflicts that end up as screaming-yelling fights with their husbands about whose opinion will prevail.

"When I visited my mother in Ohio last May and when I invested in my company's pension plan, both times Frank saw red. See, I didn't ask for his permission, I just made up my mind and did it. He acted like I commited a crime. What fights we had! But I didn't back down. I have a right to take a trip to my mother's. I have a right to invest my own money. I told him that and how it felt good to do things on my own. I guess that's power."

The winners face conflict. The others dodge it.

As wives take action to transcend their traditional boundaries, their new strengths inevitably set up conflicts. It is no easy job to deal with a powerful husband who growls stern disapproval. But like Escher's drawings in which each line slowly changes the species until it becomes another, each conflict redefines the wife. Each small victory in Stage Three brings her a sharper definition of herself. Small steps, slow changes. But they add up.

Conflicts produce winners. Needlepoints don't.

Yet most women are not educated for conflict. They are educated to avoid confrontations, to be nice. Therefore, many kinds of conflict unnerve them. Conflicts with their husband and children. Conflicts with parents or friends. Conflicts between corporate rules and household plans. Conflicts of career and love. Conflicts over sex and money. Every step of the way Stage Three turns up another confrontation.

Traditional wives hold that women in Stage Three are fouling their own nest. They claim defiance ruins a marriage, that it is unseemly for a woman to talk back to her husband. They warn that successful women turn hard as nails and lose their femininity.

Stage Three women don't buy it. Not one word.

Perhaps success without love can prove hollow. And women, like men, can be suckered by success. Yet women have too long been trained to get satisfaction only from nurturing others, not from achievement. They have been brainwashed to believe that serving others' needs is the highest form of femininity.

This myth produced conflict and apprehension in women who were trying to advance. On the one hand, they were afraid to fail; on the other they were afraid to win. If success could lead to a loss of love and a loss of femininity, it scared them. So they hung back, dutifully taking care of their husbands. They even took on a second job: protecting his position. This served the husband and his corporation very well. Corporations got two employees for the price of one. But it violated women and instructed them to eschew achievement.

For women in Stage Three who knew better, it produced emotional and psychological conflicts. They wanted more than to be Simone de Beauvoir's *Second Sex*. But they were told it was wrong to feel that way, and they were made to feel guilty.

"Leave three kids with a baby-sitter at dinner time? For a graduate course in Hopi textile design? Are you crazy? What do you need it for?" Just a few words from an angry husband could do it. Choke them up as they drove off to class.

"What good is a career without a man?" the wife's mother admonishes her married daughter. "Start fighting with Jack and you'll wind up without a husband. Better make peace because Jack's not going to stand for it." There are two messages here. One is that choosing a career over a man's objections is a risky move that could cost you a marriage. Two is that only a man can validate a woman, so don't lose him.

To avoid conflict, some women caved in.

Internal arguments brought many women into conflict with themselves. Can I really have an equal relationship with my husband?

The burdens of freedom stretched the maturity of the couples' contract with each other. The winners saw the conflicts through, facing up to the confrontations by skillfully negotiating them. The others backed down and retreated. Cowed by threats, some wives lacked the spirit to seize what was rightfully theirs.

"He always handled our money and property. So I was afraid to ask questions. He'd get mad and it would lead to another fight." Avoiding conflict became a way of life, informing their sex life, financial life, and emotional well-being.

Yet feistiness can serve a wife well. Winners in Stage Three who had achieved a spirited self-interest stressed it as a giant step forward.

"I wasn't doing the things I wanted because I'd always wait for his approval. Until I figured I had two options. To sit around another fifteen years and spend a lot of energy waiting and complaining. Or to go out and build a life for myself. I hated to fight, and it took me a long time to stand up for myself. But I learned I counted as a person. One bleak February day, I took my money and bought a little summer cottage. He was furious! Now, eight years later, he admits it was a smart move. Of course it was! It's worth double and I own it."

The message of winners in Stage Three is always the same. "I'm an adult. I can risk. I can handle conflict. I'm not going to let life pass me by."

Control

It is unnatural to remain childlike into adulthood. Children are dependent and undeveloped human beings. They have little power. Their choices are monitored and their decisions are subject to approval. To remain in that state as an adult is to have no *control*.

It is unnatural to be controlled by a powerful husband or wife or by a powerful corporation. It is corroding to control another adult's choices. It is unwholesome and dangerous to play the tyrant and to squelch growth in another human being.

Men who encourage their wives to remain dependent bear a heavy burden of supplying financial and emotional support, and they invite, should they falter in their overlordship, a steel-gray contempt.

Young brides who go directly from the authority of their parents' house to the authority of their husband have the most difficult time. The schools, the churches, the government are all built on authority to control human behavior and they are ruled largely by men. Women are trained to obey men. Men become a revered institution instead of human beings.

In Stage Three wives say they are in control of themselves and will make decisions about what governs their lives. Daddy-husband becomes de-institutionalized.

In Stage Two, women see a vision of their souls stretching toward a better form of themselves. However, at this point only their attitudes change. In Stage Three, women reach for that enlargement of themselves and act. Now their behavior changes. In moving out of past references, they establish their own authority. They reject control by established authorities.

"The church says no birth control. Well I believe in those things. I don't want to leave the church, but as a feminist I can't obey the church."

It is the task of Stage Three women to face those conflicts. To modify their pasts to harmonize with their own authority over their minds and bodies.

The winners find that more than money or power, more than their connection to a powerful man, the establishment of their own adult authority sets them free. Divesting themselves of conflicts from outside controls, they can stand up to conflict and resolve their differences.

Amazingly, supportive husbands say their wives' growth has created new, healthful bonds between them. By stressing what is human between them, they avoid the male-female stereotypical power wars. By creating the broadest possibilities for her to become more human, husbands reap the rewards of a realized woman. Powerlessness causes emotional depression and physical symptoms of illness. As winners gain power in Stage Three, they say they feel healthier.

An agoraphobic corporate wife who didn't leave her home for two years won the battle in Stage Three. "I have fewer migraines and my depression lifted. I can make decisions more easily now because

I'm treated with respect. I no longer feel everyone is ruining my life and I worry less. Maybe people like me have the ability to cure themselves once they get some control."

Winners move forward in waves of self-growth we can clearly see. Watch the action. It's not a waltz. Not a tango. Not a jitterbug. It's her own dance, but she gets there and that's what counts.

First Step.

In Stage Two, wives change their expectations and reestablish their goals.

In Stage Three, they implement new behavior that earns them confidence and self-esteem. Change their hair color, take a trip.

Another Step.

In Stage Two, wives find out a husband's wealth and power are not nourishing. The limos, the trips abroad, and the corporate trappings are hollow rewards and do not confer happiness because the husband and his corporation are in control.

In Stage Three, women take control through personal achievement. They make decisions that earn them respect and power. Take a course. Start a project. Return to college.

Another Step.

In Stage Two, wives reexamine patriarchy and the ways in which our cultures establish men above women. They detach themselves from men as the centers of their universe and the arbiters of their moral and social choices.

In Stage Three, women create a new center for themselves and move out of the shadow of their husbands. They shake themselves loose from their limitations and establish their own authority. Start a career. Earn and invest money.

Another Step.

In Stage Two, wives get rid of the old limiting myths about how they must behave and they begin to reinvent themselves.

In Stage Three, they take steps to become fully adult, healthy and emotionally fit. They take risks; they wrest control; they face conflict. This requires bravery, that ineffable quality that must be defined by action. Explore a more satisfying sex life. Go after what makes them happy.

The winners in Stage Three establish a richer, better life for themselves which, in turn, brings dividends to their husbands and their families. They have earned their rewards. Whatever dance gets them there, they learn the steps.

Corporate Changes

Corporations are responding to the struggle, too. Once the notorious bad boys of business, some corporations are bending to accommodate women as corporate wives and corporate executives. They have to. The power of the women's movement cannot be reversed. Corporations must respond.

Make no mistake about it, corporations are still acquisitive and powerful organizations designed to make money and ensure growth. They are not centers of humanistic good works. Nevertheless, they spend millions on good deeds. The publicity is their reward. But their deeds are real.

They endow hospitals, fund symphonies, and underwrite the arts. They encourage their executives to sit on boards of trustees of dance companies, museums, and theaters.

Some companies have already taken steps to become more humanistic. They have introduced new programs to demonstrate their altruistic turnaround. They now encourage employees to take time off for community activity, to participate in the jury system, to support charities. To put to rest their image as bland conformists, they are giving employees scheduled time to be "intrapreneurs," encouraging them to develop fresh ideas without snapping the whip for bottom-line results. They are learning to listen to suggestions and to accept off-beat, non-traditional leadership.

The distrust, rivalry, and anxiety fostered by corporate politics are still very much in existence—the bottleneck gets tighter as achievers approach the top.

Nevertheless, corporations *are* changing. Their growing responsibilities to the health and welfare of families is to their credit. They, too, are reaping rewards.

21
Playing for High Stakes

Like corporations, husbands are learning that there are rewards for them, too, when their wife arrives safely and successfully in Stage Three. Sure, they grumble and balk along the way; they are human, reluctant to give up the power and control they thought was theirs. But many husbands, especially those under forty, are willing participants in their wife's growth. They find it stimulates their own growth and enhances their pleasures. Educated by tireless wives to discard their corporate and male cultures, many husbands are turning feminist.

Men have their own strengths, and one is their power to help women achieve their goals. In Stage Three, wives need every boost they can get, and many husbands are stepping forward and becoming their wife's Number One Booster.

Husbands are learning to love their wives in different ways that have less to do with money and power. Tenderness has become sexy. So have honest and open communications, divested of coyness on her part and power manipulations on his. Husbands are displaying a great deal of sympathy for their wives' causes and this establishes a real intimacy between them. They are becoming partners in both their evolutions.

The rewards are a human connection and special caring that have little to do with who makes what amount of money or who controls whom.

There is considerably less jealousy among these enlightened husbands. They encourage their wives to have friendships with other women and even with men. They are less proprietary. They treat their wives with respect and they understand their wives' non-sexual friendships at work, attachments based on a job interest, a sport, or a hobby. Women themselves have changed their views about friendships with each other. They treat other women with the admiration they once reserved for men.

"I used to navigate straight toward the men at a party because their conversations were always more interesting," the wife of a corporate vice president admitted. "Now I rush toward the women because I'm eager to hear what they're saying. I've picked up a lot of good tips and a few new friendships. I think we like each other more because we've become more."

There is a new style to manhood, too.

New daddies, once jailed in hospital waiting rooms, now coach their wives through Lamaze and talk them through "our" delivery. As soon as their child is born, they spend time together for "bonding." There is a sense of shared parenting. Couples are "partners." They participate in furniture buying (once her domain), financial investments (once his domain), and most decisions about jobs and children.

Husbands are doing "women's work" without embarrassment.

"I hate the shit work. So does she. But since we both work, we both do it." Sharing the pleasure and sharing the pain, these couples grow tighter because they are less bound by the sex roles that limited their parents. Their view of manhood has expanded. They see marriage as a shared adventure.

Of course young husbands just entering corporate life are still ambitious to move up the ladder. But they weigh the sacrifices and put a high priority on family relationships. If their corporation is too restrictive or demanding, they move on to another corporation. Corporate loyalty and job security strike them as "depression-mentality." Headhunters keep track of their movements. They see a growing number of managers who are willing to swap a $5,000 raise for a better family situation in another corporation.

Men are listening better. They are finally hearing the voices of their women. Their daughters and sisters have changed them, too. They are growing more comfortable with emotional release, more flexible, more caring. They are showing their wives that they are more than their jobs. They are redrawing a new style to manhood.

A few—a very few—have switched the rules about moving for the breadwinner. They are relocating for their wife's job. Not easy to do. A husband's advocacy in the abstract, when tested may crumble. Relocate to promote her career? Put her career first? Most men are worried about losing their self-respect and masculinity, fearful that following a wife's career will turn them into a wimp. The few who do move, however, see it as an act of courage. And given the admonitions of the male and corporate cultures, it is!

Husbands have learned from their successful Stage Three wives that her dependency can stunt his growth.

For all ages, company loyalty is giving way to more egalitarian marriages. As more middle-aged wives go back to the workforce, more 50-50 marriages take wing.

"A sizable part of me still expects her to cook and do the domestic and social business of running our family. But I can see it's grossly unfair, so we're improvising new rules."

Husbands are starting to realize that equality is liberating for them, too. Wives who share the financial burden reduce the pressures on themselves. Wives who have busy active lives don't easily wind up depressed, angry, and emotionally ill. Studies reveal that men need marriage more than women. Husbands want their marriages to work.

The smart and flexible husbands are transferring and sharing power. Couples make decisions together and work out the logistics. Where once they fought with each other, now they fight for each other. In Stage Three life becomes unthinkable without the other's growth.

Many men are applauding their wives, speaking in emotional

terms and expressing their feelings without embarrassment. You don't hear expressions like "dumb broad" much these days. The new manhood prohibits it. Men are gaining prestige and status from their wife's success.

"I feel very lucky that my wife is talented and successful. That she can bounce efficiently between her career as a decorator and our home and kids. So I'd feel guilty if I didn't share the work," a young executive said. "I also help her make contacts. I'm always on the lookout to tout her on to some big commissions in commercial buildings. No, I'm not a superior moral being. I'm not a martyr or a wimp either. I just know what's fair."

From Boasters To Boosters

There are many ways men can help their women: wives, sisters, mothers, and daughters. And they are doing it by changing the ways they interact with women. They are getting rid of recurrent patterns that limited women's potential.

"You really want to do that?" can be a sneaky directive to a wife not to.

"Alone in Toronto? My little girl?" may sound like concern, but it smacks of a put-down, meaning, "I don't think you can handle it."

A more helpful response would be, "How would you accomplish that?" It's a more open-ended question and it invites the wife to bounce her fears and ideas off her husband. An experienced, successful man can be a valuable sounding board for his wife. He can become the best booster in the world.

Picture this scene.

A dinner party. Three couples in their late thirties in a well-appointed California condo. The husbands all successful executives in Silicon Valley corporations. The wives, equally successful, are vivacious, strong-minded, and self-assured.

Janice, a film actress who's landed her first important role in a Hollywood movie, is being congratulated and toasted with champagne. Her husband Rod is beaming, his arm around her stroking her bare shoulder.

"The next thing," he says, hugging her, "she'll be Jane Fonda and I'll have to see her agent for an appointment."

Everyone's attention is focused on Janice, a strange feeling for Rod. He's used to being the center of attraction. Now every eye is on Janice, her role, her film, her co-stars.

"Poor baby," he says patronizing her behind a guise of adoration. "She never even flew without me. Who's gonna hold your hand when the plane to Athens takes off?"

No one is listening to him. They are eagerly shooting questions at her: How did her agent push her for the part? When do rehearsals start? When does she meet the famous stars? All of which is burning a hole in Rod's belly. Sure he's liberated. He's also confused by his own reaction.

A common reaction, even among young, fair-minded husbands.

On the one hand, men like Rod in egalitarian marriages are surrounded by strong women. Their friends' wives are strong achievers, and they brush up against women in their corporations who are equally strong executive types. They have come to admire women's confidence and the willingness of women to speak their minds. They have a picture of themselves as genuinely liking strong women. They do. Sort of.

It certainly makes sex better, Rod muses. He greeted Janice's sexual freedom with delight. She is playful as a kitten and eager to initiate sex and to experiment. He missed his Sunday tennis match because she felt kooky and crazy.

"I feel horny. Horny, horny, horny." She was all over him. He loved the attention she lavished on him.

But tonight, nagging doubts were surfacing.

A strong woman—he'd be the first to concede—is attractive as hell. He hated the coy types who whisper and whimper thinking they were seductive. But if Janice hits the jackpot, she might be less likely to be impressed with him and maybe she wouldn't look up to him anymore.

Maybe she won't need me anymore.

If Janice became the mover and shaker in the family, his male pride would hurt. If she outdistanced him, she'd show him up.

Maybe she'll figure out she can easily survive without me.

If Janice outearns him, she could run all over him. Make the big decisions and he could turn out to be the weak one.

Maybe I'll lose control of our relationship.

Three fears even the most liberated husbands face.

He admires his wife's keen mind—she reads everything, he brags. He boasts of her wit, her beauty, her strength. But there is a great underpinning of anger he can't face up to.

Does she want to take something away from me?

Will her strength rob me of my maleness? Diminish me?

Of course Rod supports her career, adjusts to her moods, respects her as an equal partner. That's the easy part. But right now he's having trouble.

Will Janice's success make me less strong or less attractive?

Rod is an enlightened husband. He doesn't try to get away with those old games his father played on his mother. But a part of him ungallantly hopes she won't get too strong. She might stop loving him.

Like many successful wives in Stage Three, Janice needs Rod's support more than ever. She needs his caring, his encouragement, and his commitment to her. She needs him in different ways now. Not to open doors or carry her luggage. To be there.

"I'm scared," she snuggles close as he drives home. "I know I can do it, but I need you to be my best friend. My ally. The one who fights for me."

"I'm scared, too," Rod admits. "I don't want to lose you."

He takes her hand and they start to talk.

He listens like a sympathetic friend. He feels himself shifting gears, letting go of the controlling part and feeling more secure. Her strength doesn't zap anything away from him. It's not a competition.

"Janice? What can I do to make it easier for you?"

Rod is about to make the transition *from a boaster to a booster.*

In Stage Three, husbands and wives work out a new relationship balanced between autonomy and mutuality. It's a trading off, a shifting of gears, a speeding up and slowing down in the search for equilibrium. Sometimes there comes a season as bleak as a dark afternoon in February, when they are distant and immersed in their own independent struggles, and the other partner has to stay out of the way. Then that season passes, giving way to a needy season as palpable as a torrid August afternoon, and they need to cling to each other. A season can last a day, a week, a month, and swing back and forth. In between, they may feel flashes of impatience and become cross with each other. But they balance the seasons out.

Strong men and strong women handle the shifts and establish a personalized balance. They reduce tension when they get out of sync by reestablishing their commitment, restating their shared goals, and holding tight. They don't boss each other. When the crunch comes, they don't retreat into old roles. They reassure each other and keep on redesigning the rules. The other person's accomplishments energize them. They both feel like winners.

Each one gains power, self-esteem, and respect. That's the autonomy part. But the marriage as a source of strength is deeply important to them and they are ingenious in honoring the nourishment it supplies. That's the mutuality part.

A successful wife may phone her husband at the office and say, "Don't expect dinner tonight, I'm running late. So have a big lunch on your expense account."

He accepts it as a practical suggestion. He doesn't feel put out, and she doesn't feel guilty. They've trained each other. If anyone refers to her as a corporate wife, she has to think twice. "A what?" For her the term seems as inaccurate as describing Mary Tyler Moore as a doctor's wife.

Real life goes on on many levels: corporate, marital, and personal. In Stage Three, marriage—with all its duties and responsibilities—can function as an anchor and a safety valve to corporate and career stress. Although detractors claim strong women pay a tremendous price for their success, the wives who are the winners report that the rewards are delicious. They also say that having a husband for a booster is icing on the cake. Competition between spouses can tear a family apart. But cooperation is a real boost.

In Stage Three, husbands change from boasters—"Isn't she wonderful"—to boosters—"I'll phone and arrange an introduction for you." They find concrete ways to give their spouse real help. In doing so, they reaffirm their commitment to her welfare.

Boasters talk big. Boosters do something to help the one they love.

Stage Three is an exciting adventure.

In time, the relationship between wife and husband-mentor changes again. As her self-esteem moves up to another plateau, she gives up the mentor relationship. In doing so, she acknowledges her indebtedness to her husband as booster; she is grateful. But now it is appropriate to shift power again and to redefine the relationship.

Husbands who are caring mentors do not encourage continuing the mentor-dependency. As boosters they have lighted the way, but now she has to take flight herself. Her new territory will include adventures, dangers, and rewards, but now she must handle it on her own. Strong women let go because they believe in themselves.

What about the corporate wives who don't succeed in Stage Three?

Wives who deliberately gave up an artistic life or a career to take a back seat to their executive husband are often remorseful. If they gave up their gifts to buy peace in the household, they turn angry.

"I was a dope. Stupid. I did it to build up my husband's ego. What for? Look at me now, a nothing to him. I could have been a damn good painter, had my own studio, had shows." Many admit it was a destructive and foolish strategy.

"I've tasted the anger and the terror behind dependency. The price of being taken care of is too high."

Younger wives, raised with the mindset of the women's movement, are less likely to explode into rage or curl up into depression. They do whatever they have to to establish their personhood.

Attaching oneself to an ambitious or powerful man once meant success. No more. Today corporate wives say no, that's prison. A real woman, like a real man, has her own power. She feeds her talent. She earns respect. She achieves her own success. Earning money doesn't hurt either. Money means recognition.

A strong woman values her body and her mind. That she chooses to share a life as a wife is a high compliment to the man who is her husband.

Sex

Sex between equals generates a feeling of transcendence.

When two adults make love, a set of inner meanings resonates because the lovers discover their truest and deepest selves. They are not locked into power struggles, they are not using sex to control each other. They become one with the loved one, but they still retain a powerful sense of themselves as individuals. In Stage Three, sexual passion between wife and husband can be reawakened and recharged. A ho-hum relationship can heat up.

Good sex between equals provides a couple with an opportunity to renegotiate their conflicts and handle negative feelings. Reducing tensions, it creates a sunny climate where loving spouses move into positive cycles that repair hurt feelings. Making love well deescalates quarrels and reestablishes good feelings. It unites the partners physically and emotionally.

Wives and husbands who make love well have that extra edge that combines sexual excitement, tenderness, passion, commitment, and romance. It sets them apart from others, and often you can tell who they are. They touch, they preen, they glow.

Among fearful, compliant wives, rarely do you see this. There is palpable tension. The plastic smile, weak as a fifteen-watt bulb, gives them away.

When Masters and Johnson, in 1968, came out with *Human Sexual Response*, it undermined the Freudian concept that women should assume a passive sexual role because they were anatomically inferior to men. The report unleashed a torrent of reaction among women who began reexamining their attitudes about sex. A period of history followed in which women tumbled about, uncertain and confused, combative and angry, as they changed their attitudes and their behavior.

Those that freed themselves moved on to Stage Three. They felt that the women's movement made sense. It touched them in a profound way and they would never be the same again.

The corporate wives I interviewed provided us with details of their passionate journey. To find their most authentic selves, they took stock of their sexual needs. They talked openly about sex with their husbands and, in some cases, with their lovers. They reported that sexual freedom enhanced their souls. Many wanted more than they were getting from their partner and they came to acknowledge it. They demanded to be taken seriously as an adult woman with sexual appetites, fantasies, and specific tastes.

"I have a sexual side too, and I'm not going to hide it."

New Partnerships

American women are changing the face of America. Exerting pressure on corporations to support family life. Restructuring their families toward new goals. Emphasizing the human connection they share with their husbands. Changing the meaning of marriage. Honestly facing their sexual selves.

Rich and privileged corporate women now admit that their pedestal was a prison. They reveal shocking accounts of their secret humiliations. They warn us by showing us the dangerous detours to look out for. They instruct us by telling us how to negotiate better as women. The most hazardous and exciting part of their journey came in Stage Three, when they transformed themselves from fish to birds, integrating their sexual, emotional, and intellectual parts into a whole and healthy new adult woman. These wives provide practical guide maps for any woman who is considering taking that journey.

The growing number of winners in Stage Three continues to attract women of all ages, wives in their twenties starting out, mid-life women who want to make a change, and older women who want something richer for their sixties and seventies. The promise of personal growth is tantalizing at every age.

If women are the primary movers in their own personal growth, there is evidence that alongside them a new kind of male executive is emerging, too. More flamboyant than his colorless predecessors, he is no longer a faceless manager who submerges his personality in a safety net of corporate politics. This new executive sidesteps the hierarchy and dances around the pecking order. He, too, is changing.

Corporate wives used to keep their mouths shut and smile. Not anymore. Once they were doomed to keep a low profile. Not anymore. Once they knew their place: to be nice, to entertain, to relocate on command, and to push their man up the ladder. Not anymore.

These new spirited women have added richness to American family life, and the forces of change are everywhere. All the signs tell us so. More than 200 women bared their souls in this book to reveal their intimate secrets, buried dreams, and private longings. They spoke out freely about what they want from marriage, what they need from men, and how family life must change. They provided us with the details about their journey to self-esteem. They gave answers to hard questions.

Is corporate life as good or as bad as people say? Are their husbands good lovers? Is it fun at the top, or hell? What does it cost to get there? Do their husbands cheat while they travel? Do their children suffer from the constant relocations? How do wives keep their sanity? What erotic longings do they play out in secret affairs? How do they gain their own money, power, and prestige?

Some of these women lost their husband, their health, and their confidence. Others battled the three stages of personal development to emerge successfully as Strong Women—women with their own power.

Entering the homes of the executive powerhouses you hear the heartbreak and the joy as they recount, in riveting scenes, how they risked playing for high stakes. How they analyzed what's behind the trappings of corporate life, behind the diamonds and minks. We hear the cries of their loneliness, the failures of their children dragged from one school to another, and their private suffering numbed by drugs, drinking, and love affairs.

The public image is one thing, as they call for the limo, charter the company plane, scoop up the best tickets in town. The private image is another, as they hide their pain and climb into an empty double bed.

Whether you're married to a corporate executive, a professional, or a businessman, you recognize pieces of your own marriage. Hear your own words. Observe the common thread of truth behind marriage to a powerful husband. Perhaps you even check off where you are in the journey from compliant mouse to *complete* person.

The goal persists. To establish a rich personal life—with husband, children, and marriage thriving—is still the American dream. Corporate wives, privileged on one hand, imprisoned on the other, have shown us how to sidestep the minefields, negotiate the twists, and scoop up the rewards. That success is attainable and exciting.

American women are playing for high stakes.

The trip through Stage One, Stage Two, and Stage Three is an exciting adventure. It beckons women, corporate wives or not, to take the journey. To fly free.

Index